How Courts & Judges Work

HALT's Guide to America's Civil Justice System

© 2005

Also by HALT:

Using a Lawyer

Do-It-Yourself Law

The Legal Resource Directory

If You Want to Sue a Lawyer

Using the Law Library

The Easy Way to Probate

Living Trusts & Other Trusts

Wills

Small Claims Court

Legal Rights for Seniors

The Smart Consumer

Everyday Contracts

A CITIZENS LEGAL MANUAL

How Courts & Judges Work

*HALT's Guide
to America's
Civil Justice System*

Updated by HALT

and Charles Marcus, Susan Nevelow Mart,
Vincent Moyer & Julie Horst of the University of
California Hastings College of the Law Library

HALT

AN ORGANIZATION OF
AMERICANS FOR LEGAL REFORM

Authors (Second Edition): Charles Marcus, Susan Nevelow Mart, Vincent Moyer and Julie Horst
Editors: Theresa Meehan Rudy and James C. Turner
Design & Production: Barking Dog Design/Chris McGee
Substantial Assistance Provided By: Nick Chapman-Hushek, Todd Chatman, Amy Dieterich, Geoffrey Goodnow, Tom Gordon, Daniel Kahane, Megha Parekh and Kristin Weber

The original edition of this book was authored by Katherine J. Lee and edited by Richard Hébert.

Print History:

First Edition: 1987
Second Edition: 2005

ISBN 0-910073-28-7

Contents

ACKNOWLEDGMENTS

We would like to gratefully express our appreciation to the following individuals and organizations for their support in making this book possible:

Ruth Eleanor Bamberger & John Ernest Bamberger Memorial Foundation

Michael Baxter Charitable Trust

R. Gordon & Agnes K. Black Family Foundation

Danielle Brian

Katherine S. Broderick

Charles Family Foundation

Civil Justice Fund

Louis A. Clark

Compton Foundation

Community Foundation of Tampa Bay

The Dreammaker Foundation

Catherine Elias-Jermany

Everett Philanthropic Fund

The Ferro 1986 Revocable Trust

Wallace Alexander Gerbode Foundation

Ethan Grossman Family Charitable Gift Fund

Lenora Harth Family Foundation

Hasse Family Foundation

The Hendricks Foundation

T. James Kavanagh Foundation

Kimmell Family Foundation

Conrad Martin

McMillion Foundation

George A. Miller Family Fund

The Modzelewski Charitable Trust

Bea Moulton

Stewart R. Mott Charitable Trust

William C. & Gloria A. Newton Donor Advised Fund of the Community Foundation of Jackson Hole

The Onodera Family Trust

Esper A. Petersen Foundation

David & Marian Rocker Philanthropic Fund of the Jewish Community Foundation of MetroWest

Phillip & Helen Sills Foundation

Suzanne Sloat & Ray Okonski Foundation

Stern Family Fund

Jack Taylor Family Foundation, Inc.

S.J. Ungar – J. Shapiro Family Foundation

Ullmann Family Foundation

Evelyn West Civil Justice Fund

HALT, Inc.
May 2005

Foreword

All Americans should understand how our civil justice system works, because at some point each of us will need to deal with a legal matter that involves a court and a judge. Whether it's probating an estate, serving on a jury, contesting a parking ticket or resolving a dispute with your landlord, you need to know your rights and be familiar with how our court system works. That's where this *Citizens Legal Manual* comes in.

This expanded Second Edition of **How Courts & Judges Work: HALT's Guide to America's Civil Justice System** has been updated by HALT with the assistance of Charles Marcus, Susan Nevelow Mart, Vincent Moyer and Julie Horst of the University of California Hastings College of the Law Library. This new edition not only provides the basic nuts and bolts of our state and federal court systems, it also guides you to other resources that can help you understand your rights and obligations when you must deal with a legal matter.

Because the high cost of hiring a lawyer is beyond their reach, tens of millions working Americans are increasingly forced to handle their own legal affairs without the help of an attorney, including going to court alone (in legalese, going *pro se* or *pro per*). In California and Florida, for example, more that half of the people seeking uncontested divorces are not represented by a lawyer. That is why we have added a new chapter, *Going Pro Se,* and a comprehensive Appendix of *Pro Se* Resources in this book.

For a quarter century, HALT has worked to help ordinary Americans take charge of their own legal affairs, and the book you hold in your hands is an integral part of this education and reform effort. Together with two other HALT *Citizens Legal Manuals,* **Using the Law Library** and **The Legal Resource Directory: Your Guide to Help, Hotlines & Hot Websites**, this book can help you understand how our court system works and how to find the answers to your legal questions.

These *Citizens Legal Manuals* are also designed to be used in concert with the regularly updated Legal Information Clearinghouse pages of HALT's Internet site, *www.halt.org*. There, visitors can find HALT's *Everyday Law Series* and other self-help materials, up-to-date links to legal resources on the Internet and a wealth of other consumer information.

Whether you use this book to help you deal with a court case, to understand a specific legal proceeding or to learn more about the resources available to help you deal with legal decisions, remember the most important job is still up to you—you are the one person who can take charge of your own legal affairs. We hope that the information in this book and our efforts at HALT will help you do so.

James C. Turner

Executive Director
HALT – An Organization
of Americans for Legal Reform
Washington, DC

May 2005

Introduction

The judiciary is probably the least known of the three branches of government. The work of our legislatures is regularly reported in daily newspapers and magazines and on television and the Internet, as are the actions and opinions of legislative candidates and their campaigns for election. The same is true for the presidency, governorships and many federal, state and local executive agencies.

Our contact with the courts is, however, less frequent and predictable. We read about the increasing number of lawsuits being filed and the consequent backlog of cases, but most of us don't know much about how our courts are organized or how they work. Our trips to the courthouse are probably sporadic, and when we do go, we are likely to be bewildered: Is my case in Municipal Court or Superior Court? Is Small Claims Court part of another court or is it its own separate court? Is there some place I'm supposed to check in?

We know even less about judges. We often hear about controversial judges and judicial nominees and judges who preside over well-publicized cases, yet there are thousands of judges about whom we don't hear anything in news media. So, how do people get to be judges? What can we do about the bad ones? What powers do other judicial officials have—magistrates and justices of the peace, for example?

This *Citizens Legal Manual* answers those questions. When first published in 1987, **How Courts & Judges Work** was one of the few publications that contained detailed court and judicial information for all states. Since that time there has been a tremendous growth in the amount of information available about courts (for example, the 24-hour cable channel "Court TV" or judicial Internet sites providing access to forms and decisions).

How Courts & Judges Work explains the organization and hierarchy of our state and federal courts and the relationships between them. It describes the different ways state and federal judges are selected and how you can challenge their decisions or conduct. Whether you are merely curious about the courts and their personnel or expect to be involved in a lawsuit or other court proceeding and whether or not you have an attorney represent you, this information will help you understand how the American judicial system works.

Our aim is to demystify that system. Consistent with HALT's legal reform agenda, this manual focuses on the *civil* system, not the criminal justice system. Above all, it is written with you, the consumer, in mind.

While general guidance is given to the *pro se* litigant in Chapter 6, this manual does *not* teach you how to file your own lawsuit, nor discuss other specifics of legal procedure. What **How Courts & Judges Work** will do in a concise and informed way, is tell you in what court you can or should bring your case and why. Its aim is to explain how the courts are organized, how they work and the roles of the various officials you will encounter.

Appendices at the back contain charts and specific information on court structure and judicial selection for each state, the District of Columbia, Puerto Rico and the Virgin Islands. Also included in the appendices are Internet links to court and court reform Web sites.

Appendix II traces the path of a typical civil lawsuit.

A WORD ABOUT TERMS

How Courts & Judges Work uses common, everyday language. Where familiarity with a legal term is helpful, the legal word or phrase is included, followed by a plain-language definition or explanation. This will help you become familiar with the words and phrases you will find on forms and hear from lawyers, court clerks and judges if you are involved in a lawsuit.

Appendix VII includes a glossary of legal terms found in this manual.

HOW TO USE THIS MANUAL

You probably don't need to read the entire manual to find answers to specific questions, but you should at least skim each chapter for a general understanding of how the system operates. This will help you better comprehend how the smaller pieces fit within it.

Casual readers can select from the Table of Contents whatever subjects interest them, but those who are already dealing with a court and those who are preparing to should begin by reading Chapter 1 and then either Chapter 2 or 3, depending on which court system they are in, then refer to the chapters or sections that address their concerns.

To answer specific legal questions or to do legal research, you should also consult HALT's *Citizens Legal Manual,* **Using the Law Library** and self-help books appropriate to your case.

OTHER INFORMATION

As mentioned earlier, this manual is not a guide to filing your own lawsuit. In that sense it is different from some of HALT's other manuals. **Small Claims Court,** for example, is that kind of "how-to" guide for those initiating or defending against a small claim. Similarly, the manual **The Easy Way To Probate**, written for the personal representative of a deceased person's estate, instructs about probate court proceedings.

Because the number of *pro se* litigants (people who represent themselves in court) has risen steadily over the years, we have included a new chapter in the book on "Going *Pro Se*" (Chapter 6). For more detailed information on representing yourself in court without legal help, consult the publications listed in Appendix V.

ALTERNATIVES TO THE COURTS

HALT works to assure that citizens can dispose of their legal affairs in a simple, affordable and equitable manner and within a reasonable length of time. Because proceeding through our present court system is usually complicated, expensive and slow, HALT encourages the development and use of alternatives to traditional litigation.

We hope this manual is instructive if you are contemplating going to court but urge you to seek other means of settling your dispute before resorting to a lawsuit. Many private organizations offer arbitration, mediation or conciliation services. In some states and at the federal level, courts themselves have started programs to divert cases from the traditional path to the courtroom or, once a lawsuit has been filed, to avoid a trial. Some of the more common court-sponsored alternatives are discussed in Chapter 4.

How Courts & Judges Work

HALT's Guide to America's Civil Justice System

CHAPTER 1

Court Structure

To the casual observer, we seem to have a bewildering array of courts in the United States, hardly susceptible to serving as an organized "system." New Jersey, for instance, has a Tax Court. It's easy to determine what kind of case is heard in that court, but residents of nearby Delaware are faced with Justice of the Peace Courts and Courts of Common Pleas. How do they know what cases are heard in each of them? Equally puzzling is distinguishing which cases should go to federal court instead of a state court.

A DUAL SYSTEM

We must start by understanding that we have two "systems" of courts. That is, each state has its own court system, which operates alongside the federal court system. This results from our federal system of government.

The U.S. Constitution reflects the efforts of its framers to balance the competing interests of autonomy for individual states and a strong central government. Accordingly, the power of the federal courts, like federal legislative and executive authority, is limited to those powers listed in the Constitution and specified in legislation passed by Congress. Typical of cases that can be brought in federal court are lawsuits against the U.S. government and cases involving the application of federal law.

The powers of state governments extend to all matters that the U.S. Constitution does not reserve to the federal government. Thus, state courts have the power to hear all cases that are not exclusively federal concerns. Typical state cases are accident injury claims, domestic disputes and traffic and criminal cases.

JURISDICTION

Central to understanding why a case ends up in the court it does is the concept of *jurisdiction*. Each court has its own specific jurisdiction—the geographic and subject-matter boundaries that identify what cases the court may or may not hear. For instance, New Jersey's Tax Court has no jurisdiction over the probate of a will because the laws that specify the authority of the New Jersey Courts state that the Tax Court hears only appeals from the state's Department of the Treasury. If a tax court judge did rule on a probate case, the ruling would have no effect because the tax court judge had no jurisdiction over the matter. (The jurisdiction of the *court* and the jurisdiction of a *judge* in that court are one and the same.)

Subject-matter jurisdiction describes the substantive category of disputes that a court may hear. By spelling out what cases the federal courts may hear, the U.S. Constitution defines the subject-matter jurisdiction of those courts.

Usually, subject-matter jurisdiction is related to the substance of the legal problem—for instance, a divorce, an eviction, a traffic ticket or a will contest. Sometimes, it refers to how much is at stake—for instance, small claims courts have subject-matter jurisdiction over a variety of disputes, but claims handled in those courts must be for less than a specified amount of money—a limit usually set by state law or local ordinance.

Occasionally, subject-matter jurisdiction depends not on what issue is being disputed but on who is disputing the issue. For example, a federal court has subject-matter jurisdiction over lawsuits between U.S. citizens and ambassadors or other emissaries from foreign nations.

As the name implies, *geographic jurisdiction* limits courts to those cases that arise within a certain geographic area. For instance, a landlord-tenant dispute over an apartment in New York can be heard only in a New York court, not in another state's courts.

LAW AND EQUITY

Courts make their decisions based on principles either of law or of equity. In this context, "law" refers to an established body of legal principles and "equity" refers to principles of fairness and justice. Principles of equity are used when the law provides no guidance or when applying the law leads to an unjust result or offers inadequate redress.

These concepts are vestiges of English common law, a system of rigid rules about the grounds for filing lawsuits and remedies for wrongdoing. Because strict adherence to common law sometimes produces unjust outcomes or inadequate remedies, a separate forum was established to apply the principle of *equity* when *law* did not provide just results.

For instance, one could not use the English common law courts to stop another person from committing an anticipated wrong. However, in equity courts, a judge can grant an *injunction*—an order that such a person refrain from doing the wrong.

In some states, separate courts are established for questions of equity and law, but most states apply both principles in all trial courts. If, in a judge's opinion, the letter of the law does not do justice, the judge may use the principle of equity in fashioning a remedy that will.

As an example of an equitable remedy, consider a situation where Mr. Seller sells a one-of-a-kind hand-blown Italian glass chandelier to Mr. Buyer. Mr. B makes several payments on it but still owes a balance, when Mr. S changes his mind and decides to take back the chandelier. In this case a judge might grant an injunction entitling Mr. B to that specific chandelier (equity), although he'd probably have to continue making the payments. It would not be an equitable result for the judge to rule that Mr. S can keep the chandelier he took back but must return the payments made to Mr. B, because Mr. B, acting in good faith, bargained for the unique chandelier.

The letter of the law doesn't do justice because what Mr. B really wanted was that one-of-a-kind chandelier; money itself (a cash award) will not make him whole. To reverse the situation, if Mr. B were to change his mind and decide not to return the chandelier after not making full payment, the judge may find that Mr. S would be entitled to a cash judgment.

Be warned, however, that judges will use equity to override established principles of law only in very narrow circumstances.

CHAPTER 2

State Courts

Your contacts are much more likely to be with state courts than with federal courts. It is estimated that in 2001, more than 35 million cases were filed in the trial courts of the 50 states, the District of Columbia and Puerto Rico. In contrast, only about 320,000 were filed in federal trial courts that year.

COURT ORGANIZATION

Each state decides for itself how to organize its court system. Generally this is established in the state's constitution. To illustrate state court-system structures, we'll use as examples the New Mexico and Michigan courts *(see charts)*. As you read this chapter, you may also want to refer to the chart for your state in Appendix I to familiarize yourself with its structure.

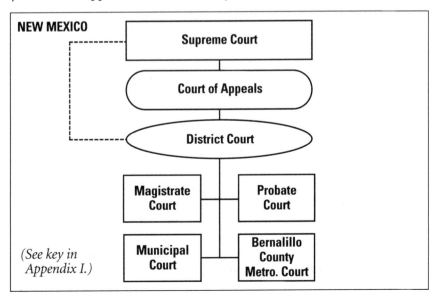

NEW MEXICO

Supreme Court

Court of Appeals

District Court

Magistrate Court

Probate Court

(See key in Appendix I.)

Municipal Court

Bernalillo County Metro. Court

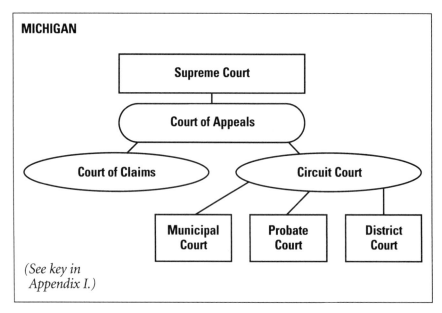

MICHIGAN

Supreme Court

Court of Appeals

Court of Claims

Circuit Court

Municipal Court

Probate Court

District Court

(See key in Appendix I.)

To read these charts, you need only know that all court systems are arranged in what can be thought of as a series of steps. Within this hierarchy, a case enters the system at one of the lower court "steps." If it is appealed, it proceeds upward to the next step and so on. References to a "lower" or "upper" court, or to the "court above" or the "court below," describe the relative position of each court within the hierarchy.

New Mexico's court system begins with four courts on the lowest step—Municipal Court, Probate Court, Magistrate Court and Bernalillo County Metropolitan Court. Above these are three levels—the District Court first, the Court of Appeals next and the New Mexico Supreme Court at the top step. Michigan, by comparison, has three courts on its first level—Probate Court, District Court and Municipal Court. Second-level courts come next—the Court of Claims, Circuit Court and its Family Division—followed by a Court of Appeals and, finally, the Michigan Supreme Court.

TRIAL COURTS

Each state's court hierarchy is divided into two categories. The lower levels are *trial courts* and the higher levels are *appellate courts*. Although most states' court systems are similarly arranged, some have only one level of trial courts and others have only one appellate court.

Trial courts are where you enter the court system. It is at this level that you file your lawsuit or defend yourself against one. New Mexico and Michigan are typical in that their two levels of trial courts consist of *courts of limited jurisdiction* at the very bottom and *courts of general jurisdiction* one step up.

LIMITED JURISDICTION

Courts of limited jurisdiction were established to provide easier access and faster resolution of disputes than did courts of general jurisdiction. Often, they were created to ease an existing court's caseload by assuming specified high-volume matters.

It is these courts, which rarely attract media attention, that have the most direct influence on our daily lives. They are where divorces are granted, wills probated, landlord-tenant disputes argued, small claims tried, traffic offenses heard, bail set and initial hearings held in criminal cases.

As their name implies, courts of limited jurisdiction are restricted in the kinds of cases they are allowed to hear, either by subject matter or by the amount of money involved. For example, Michigan's District Court hears cases ranging from contract disputes to personal-injury lawsuits, but it can only do so if the cases involve less than $25,000 or a prison sentence of less than a year.

Michigan's Probate Court, on the other hand, is an example of a court whose jurisdiction is limited by subject matter. It can hear only a narrow scope of cases—matters involving estates, trusts, guardianships and the mentally ill (which in many states are handled by the same courts that handle probate matters).

Two of New Mexico's limited-jurisdiction courts—Magistrate Courts and Bernalillo County Metropolitan Court—hear misdemeanors and civil cases that involve less than $10,000. The major difference between the two is that Magistrate Courts were established in counties that have less than 200,000 residents and Bernalillo County Metropolitan Court is for that county specifically. (Any county in New Mexico with a population of over 200,000 may establish a separate Metropolitan Court.)

Courts typically limited in subject matter in most states are probate courts, juvenile courts, traffic courts, landlord-tenant courts, and domestic or family courts. Courts that hear a variety of cases but are limited in the dollar amounts involved typically include small claims courts, justice-of-the-peace courts and magistrate courts.

In some states, the proceedings in these limited-jurisdiction courts are not *of record*. This means only that no official record, by tape recording or court reporter, is made of the hearing; the court clerk usually records only the date the case was heard and its final outcome.

GENERAL JURISDICTION

On the next tier of most court systems are courts of general jurisdiction. In a few states, this is the lowest tier. For example, in a state like Illinois, *whatever* your case involves, you must begin in a general-jurisdiction court—the first and only level of trial courts.

Typical names for courts of general jurisdiction are circuit court, superior court, district court, county court and the court of common pleas.

In states that have both limited and general-jurisdiction trial courts, courts of general jurisdiction hear all cases not specifically assigned to the limited-jurisdiction courts. In New Mexico, for instance, felony cases and civil suits that involve more than $10,000 must be filed in the court of general jurisdiction—District Court—while in Michigan, cases that cannot be handled in a limited-jurisdiction court are brought in one of three general-jurisdiction courts—Circuit Court, Court of Claims or the Family Division of Circuit Court.

In some states, these courts are truly "general," with authority to hear all civil and criminal matters. Other states have separate trial courts for civil and criminal matters and in more populated areas, courts may be further separated into divisions.

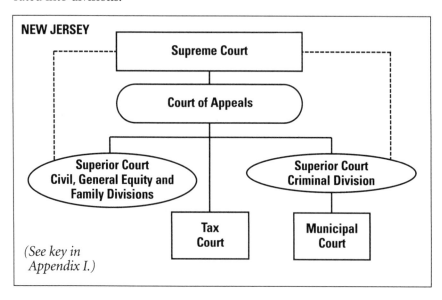

For instance, the Superior Court of New Jersey is divided into a Civil Division, which hears cases involving automobile accidents, breaches of contract and landlord-tenant disputes, a Criminal Division, which has jurisdiction over all serious criminal cases in New Jersey, a Family Division for family-related cases, and a General Equity Division for non-monetary cases.

A division of a general-jurisdiction court may look much like a court of limited jurisdiction. For example, users would probably see little difference between Michigan's Probate Court and the probate division of a general-jurisdiction court. The distinction lies mainly in how the courts are funded and managed. All divisions of a general-jurisdiction court are likely to be funded and managed as a single administrative entity. On the other hand, limited-jurisdiction courts may be funded and administered independently, as separate entities.

ORIGINAL AND APPELLATE JURISDICTION

Another way of distinguishing between courts is whether they have *original* or *appellate* jurisdiction. These terms relate to the function of the court with respect to a particular case and define where among the "steps" of a court system a case is currently pending.

Both limited and general-jurisdiction trial courts are said to have *original* jurisdiction. This means they are the first to "hear" a case, usually at a trial. The purpose of a trial is to determine what the facts are and to apply the law to those facts. Both sides are given an opportunity to present evidence and make their arguments before a judge or jury.

If the losing side in the trial court wants to appeal the outcome, the appeal must be made to the court that has *appellate* jurisdiction—a court that has authority to hear appeals of cases initially filed in "lower" courts.

Some trial courts have both original and appellate jurisdiction.

Montana's District Court, for example, not only has original jurisdiction over cases involving more than $7,000, it has appellate jurisdiction over cases originally heard in Municipal Court, City Court or Justice of the Peace Court. In other words, if you are a Montana resident who loses a case in Municipal Court and want to appeal it, you have to do so in District Court.

Similarly, a case lost in New Jersey's Municipal Court, a limited-jurisdiction court, can be appealed only to the Superior Court, a court of general jurisdiction. In this case, the Superior Court is said to have appellate jurisdiction. The route of your appeal will depend, however, on the nature of your case and in which court you started. To appeal a decision of New Jersey's Tax Court, for example, you must bypass the general-jurisdiction court and go directly to New Jersey's Appellate Division of Superior Court.

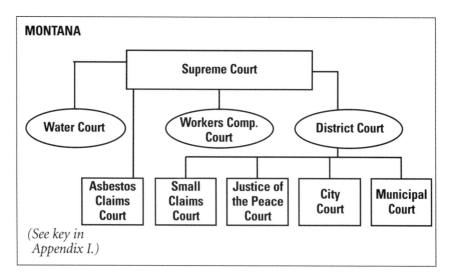

MONTANA

Supreme Court

Water Court

Workers Comp. Court

District Court

Asbestos Claims Court

Small Claims Court

Justice of the Peace Court

City Court

Municipal Court

(See key in Appendix I.)

REVIEW OR A NEW TRIAL

In considering an appeal, a court is usually limited to reviewing only the record of the lower court. That is, neither side is allowed to present new facts or evidence; the appeals court studies the transcripts of the court proceedings to see if the trial was fair and the law was applied correctly, not to question the lower court's interpretation of the facts. As part of its review, the appeals court will also read written "briefs," or arguments, by both sides and may listen to oral arguments at a hearing.

In some cases, the appellate court will hold a completely new trial, called a trial *de novo*. This provides for a new consideration of the case, as if the previous trial had not occurred. Each side is given a fresh opportunity to introduce evidence and argue its case.

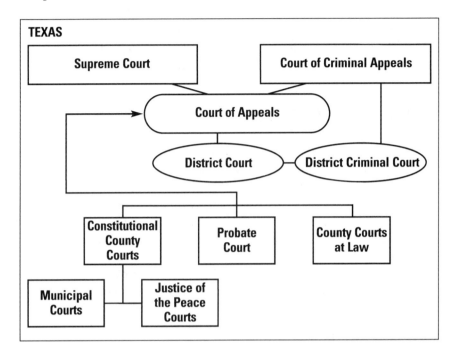

In Texas, if you appeal a municipal ordinance case from Municipal Court, the County Court at Law reviews only the record of the trial in Municipal Court. This is the same review your case would receive if you appealed from a County Court at Law to the Court of Appeals. Basically, your case is reviewed on paper only. However, if you appeal a small claims case from Justice of the Peace Court, the County Court at Law will hold a trial *de novo*. You get to appear before the judge, present evidence and so on.

APPELLATE COURTS

Each state has at least one court to which a case can be appealed. Some states have more. These are known as *appellate courts*. The main function of these courts is to review cases appealed from trial courts. Appellate courts also have original jurisdiction in some matters, but these are relatively few. That is, rarely are lawsuits first filed or trials held in an appellate court.

Of the two kinds of appellate courts, every state has at least a *court of last resort*. This is the top step of the state's court-system hierarchy and is usually named the Supreme Court, as in Michigan and New Jersey. (Be aware, however, that New York State is an exception. It names one of its lower, general-jurisdiction courts the "Supreme Court.") Michigan, New Jersey and 37 other states also have at least one *intermediate appellate court* directly below the court of last resort, generally called the Court of Appeals.

INTERMEDIATE COURTS

Most often, intermediate appellate courts consider appeals from courts of general jurisdiction, although in some instances they also hear appeals from limited-jurisdiction courts.

A person usually initiates an appeal by filing the necessary papers directly with this intermediate appellate court. If you are appealing a civil case from California's Superior Court, for instance, you must file with the clerk of the Court of Appeals.

In a few states, you appeal directly to the state's court of last resort, which then decides whether it will review the case or refer it to the intermediate appellate court. For example, if you appeal a case from Idaho's District Court, you take it directly to the Idaho Supreme Court—the court of last resort. That court may hear your case, dismiss it or refer it for review by the Court of Appeals, an intermediate appellate court. In other words, Idaho's Court of Appeals has no power to review cases unless told to do so by the Supreme Court. In that regard, Idaho is an exception; most appeals courts handle appeals directly, without need for referral from the court of last resort.

In many states, intermediate appellate courts hear appeals in cases that involve less than a specified dollar amount or less serious criminal offenses. In these states, lawsuits in which large amounts of money are at stake and cases in which the crime or potential sentence is severe are appealed directly to the court of last resort.

Most states with intermediate appellate courts have only one such court, but Alabama, New York, Pennsylvania and Tennessee have two.

In some cases, the court's review is *discretionary:* it is up to the court to decide whether to grant a request that it consider an appeal and the court may well decide it will not hear your case. In other matters, review by the court is *mandatory,* or *as of right:* the court *must* rule on the question raised in the appeal of a case.

In reviewing cases, intermediate appellate courts seek to "do justice" to all sides, looking for errors in trial procedure or in the application of the law. They also have a significant policy role. Unlike trial courts, they look beyond the facts of a case to the broader application of the law and its implications. They may harmonize conflicting past decisions or set a new "precedent" with a binding pronouncement of how the law is to be interpreted and applied in the future.

Finally, appellate courts may also prepare cases for review by courts of last resort. This is usually done by ferreting out a single issue of broad significance for the highest court to decide.

THE LAST RESORT

The court of last resort has the final say in each state's court system. Most are known as the state's "Supreme Court." In the District of Columbia, Maryland and New York, they are called "Court of Appeals" and in Maine and Massachusetts, the "Supreme Judicial Court."

Oklahoma and Texas are exceptions: each has two courts of last resort, a Court of Criminal Appeals for criminal cases and a Supreme Court for all others.

Depending upon the state, these courts hear appeals from intermediate courts of appeal, from trial courts or from both. If the court of last resort rejects a case or rules against the side that appealed it, the loser rarely has any further avenue of appeal. The only exceptions are cases that raise a "substantial federal question"; these can be appealed to the United States Supreme Court.

Courts of last resort also have original jurisdiction, but only in rare instances. Wisconsin's Supreme Court, for example, has original jurisdiction in cases of statewide concern, such as elections and bond issues.

Be warned: chances for review of your case by a court of last resort are slim. These courts are more likely than intermediate appellate courts to have broad discretion in deciding what cases they will hear. Although an appeal to a court of last resort is a logical extension of litigating one's case, as a practical matter, it is rarely worthwhile.

Even if you succeed in getting a court of last resort to hear your case, the expense of taking a case this far is often prohibitive. Before appealing to either an intermediate or last-resort appeals court, you should first consider the expense of the appeal and whether your chances for success and the amount to be gained justify the cost.

It is this cost that most often means the court of first resort is also the court of last resort. Of the more than 35 million cases filed in state courts of first resort in 2001, only about 189,000 (slightly more than half of one percent) were appealed to intermediate appellate courts and almost 89,000 (a fourth of one percent) were appealed to state courts of last resort.

CHAPTER 3

Federal Courts

The federal courts have only those powers specified in the U.S. Constitution. They can only hear:

- cases in which the United States itself is a party;

- cases involving federal law or the U.S. Constitution—known as *federal question jurisdiction;* and

- cases between citizens of different states *(diversity jurisdiction),* in which the amount in dispute exceeds $50,000.

The U.S. Congress further defines these powers in legislation that assigns specific types of cases.

Of the civil cases heard in federal court, about half are based on federal statutes such as those regulating Social Security, antitrust, civil rights and labor relations. Petitions from state and federal prisoners account for the largest group of cases brought under these statutes. Most of these challenge the prisoners' sentences, prison conditions or the constitutionality of state or federal criminal procedures. The remaining civil cases in federal courts seek to collect payment for personal injury or property damage, to enforce contracts, to collect debts or to settle property-ownership disputes.

Violations of federal criminal laws account for about one-fifth of the federal courts' workload. Some of the most common crimes prosecuted in federal courts involve immigration, narcotics and theft. The federal government is a frequent user of the federal courts. In 2002, the United States brought 29 percent of all federal cases and was a defendant in another 14 percent. State governments are also regular users of the federal courts.

The federal and state courts have *concurrent jurisdiction* over some kinds of cases. Concurrent jurisdiction means that some matters may be considered by either federal or state courts. In other words, if you have such a case, you can choose which court system to use.

This is true for federal *diversity jurisdiction* lawsuits, those between residents of two states that involve more than $50,000. For example, after an auto collision that involves residents of both Pennsylvania and Ohio, if the driver from one state, the Ohio driver for instance, wants to sue the other, the suit can be brought either in a Pennsylvania state court or in a federal court located in Pennsylvania.

Federal jurisdiction is *exclusive*—that is, the dispute may be heard only by a federal court—in matters Congress specifically assigns only to federal courts. Bankruptcy, patent and copyright disputes are typical examples. Congress gave the federal courts exclusive authority over these matters because it wanted to establish nationwide uniformity and interstate evenhandedness.

COURT ORGANIZATION

The federal courts are organized on three levels—District Courts, Courts of Appeals and the Supreme Court.

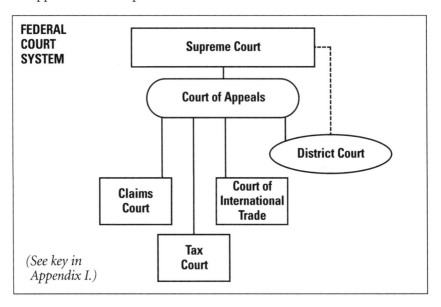

FEDERAL COURT SYSTEM

Supreme Court

Court of Appeals

District Court

Claims Court

Court of International Trade

Tax Court

(See key in Appendix I.)

DISTRICT COURTS

Almost all federal lawsuits begin in one of the nation's 94 U.S. District Courts. If you are the Ohio motorist who wants to sue the Pennsylvania driver in federal court, you must file your suit in a district court.

District courts have general jurisdiction. They hear a variety of civil and criminal cases (some federal limited-jurisdiction courts will be described later). Of the 94 district courts, 89 are located in the 50 states and one each is located in the District of Columbia, Guam, Puerto Rico, the Virgin Islands, and the Northern Mariana Islands.

Each state has at least one federal district court. Heavily populated states have more. For example, California, New York and Texas each have four. Thus, you may hear about the U.S. District Court in Wyoming, that state's sole district court, and about the U.S. District Court for the Southern District of New York, one of New York's four district courts. (A district court may also be further divided administratively into various *divisions.*)

Six-hundred-eighty judges staff these courts. Each district has from one to 28 judges, depending on the district's caseload and at least one bankruptcy judge and a U.S. Magistrate. *(The role of magistrates is described in Chapter 13.)*

In 2002, more than 328,000 cases were filed in federal district courts, 81 percent of them civil cases. This amounts to more than 1,300 lawsuits filed in U.S. district courts each working day. Although impressive, it is few compared to the 140,000 cases filed daily in state trial courts.

COURTS OF APPEALS

The U.S. Courts of Appeals were created by Congress in 1891 to ease the workload of the U.S. Supreme Court, which was until then the only federal appellate court. Since then, Congress has divided the nation into 12 geographic regions, called circuits and assigned each circuit a Court of Appeals. *(See map, pages 20-21.)* Thus, when lawyers refer to a U.S. "circuit court," for example "the Fourth Circuit Court," what they mean is the U.S. Court of Appeals for that circuit. In 1982, Congress created a thirteenth federal appeals court, the U.S. Court of Appeals for the Federal Circuit, to hear appeals from federal limited-jurisdiction courts, described later.

Each circuit includes three or more states, except the twelfth, the D.C. Circuit, which covers only the District of Columbia. These courts handle appeals of cases originally brought in the federal district courts within the circuit. Such appeals are a matter of right. For instance, if you lose your lawsuit against the Pennsylvania driver in a federal district court there and wish to appeal, you do so to the Court of Appeals for the Third Circuit. That court hears *all* appeals from the district courts in Pennsylvania, Delaware, New Jersey and the Virgin Islands. It *must* hear your appeal. Unlike state appellate courts, it cannot refuse to consider it.

In 2003, 60,847 cases were appealed to the U.S. Courts of Appeals. This

Geographical Limits of the U.S. Courts of Appeals

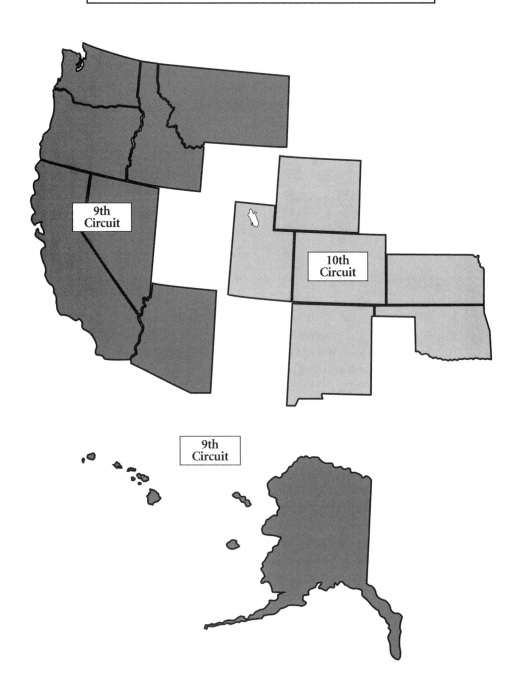

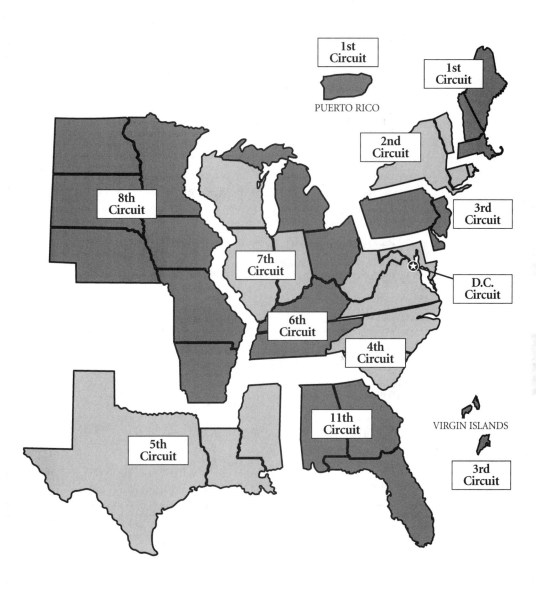

continued a steady increase in the number of appeals filed annually during the past eight years.

One-hundred-seventy-nine judges serve on the courts of appeals, ranging between six and 25 judges in each circuit. Typically, a panel of three judges listens to oral arguments and studies the written briefs submitted by the parties, then renders its decision in a written opinion. As in appeals in state courts, no new factual evidence or witnesses can be introduced; the appeals court must base its decision solely on the facts found in the lower courts.

In some cases, the Court of Appeals sits *en banc*. That is, all the judges of the circuit will hear the case. This happens when either one or both sides in a lawsuit or a judge of the circuit asks for it, usually when different three-judge panels have rendered conflicting opinions on similar cases or when the case poses what the court considers an important policy question.

Each circuit has its own rules for requesting an *en banc* hearing and the standards for judging whether a case merits one. *En banc* hearings are rarely granted, however.

THE SUPREME COURT

The court of last resort in the federal system is the U.S. Supreme Court—the court with the greatest public visibility. It is also the ultimate appellate court of the state court systems. It consists of a chief justice and eight associate justices. This number is determined by Congress and has remained at nine since 1869.

JURISDICTION

The court's powers are defined by Congress under the authority of the U.S. Constitution. Almost all of the Supreme Court's work consists of reviewing appeals from lower courts. A few are appeals directly from U.S. District Courts and others are from state courts of last resort, but most are from the U.S. Courts of Appeals.

The Constitution grants the Supreme Court original jurisdiction only in disputes that involve ambassadors or ministers of foreign countries, disputes between states or between one or more states and the U.S. government and suits filed by a state against citizens of another state or against aliens. Such cases arise only rarely. For example, during its 2003-2004 term, the Supreme Court handled only two cases in which it had original jurisdiction.

THE COURT'S DISCRETION

What is true about appeals in the state courts—that few cases are appealed to intermediate courts and still fewer of those to courts of last resort—is also true in the federal system. Although "taking your case all the way to the Supreme Court" may be an enticing idea, the reality is that the U.S. Supreme Court hears only a tiny percentage of the cases vying for its attention. In 2001-2002, for example, 8,255 cases were appealed to the court; it agreed to consider only 84 of them.

This is because in all but a few instances, the Supreme Court can choose which cases it wants to hear and need not even explain why it refuses to consider a given case. Typically, it chooses those cases that allow it to decide and explain court policy. Unless a case presents such an opportunity, the court is not likely to review it. This is a vastly different role from that of the Courts of Appeals, which can and do engage in policy-making but also spend much time correcting trial-court errors.

The Supreme Court also tends to review cases that involve questions over which Courts of Appeals are in conflict or cases in which a lower court has strayed from Supreme Court precedent. The court also concerns itself with issues that have major economic, political or social implications, such as freedom of the press, abortion, the death penalty and rules governing searches and seizures.

A *writ of certiorari,* commonly referred to by lawyers as *"cert"* (pronounced "sert") is the usual method of seeking Supreme Court review of a case. Literally, *certiorari* is Latin for "to be informed." Officially, the *writ* asks the Supreme Court to inform itself—to ask the lower court for the record of the case so the high court may review it. The court receives such requests in styles and formats that range from handwritten petitions by prisoners to 50-page typeset and bound documents. It is wholly within the Supreme Court's discretion to grant or deny such requests, and it grants them only if at least four of the nine justices vote to do so.

Although rare, an appeal *as of right* is another method of asking for Supreme Court review. This can be used only if a federal court judge has invalidated a state statute because it conflicts with the U.S. Constitution or federal laws. In such cases, federal law states that the losing party has an avenue of appeal to the U.S. Supreme Court. Although in theory the court "must" review the case, it can dismiss it summarily on jurisdictional grounds. In other words, the court may say that it has no subject-matter jurisdiction over the case because it fails to present a "substantial federal question." What is considered a federal question "substantial" enough for the Supreme Court's attention is not easily defined; the justices themselves make that determination case by case.

Remember that the policy implications of a case are the most important factor in granting review. For example, in the landmark case of Clarence Gideon, an indigent prisoner in Florida, the Supreme Court established the right of felony defendants in state courts to be represented by a lawyer. It began "unimportantly"—with Gideon's *pro se* handwritten petition to the Supreme Court for a *writ of certiorari*.

SPECIAL COURTS

Several limited-jurisdiction courts in the federal system handle specific types of cases. Following are descriptions of those you are most likely to encounter.

U.S. Court of Federal Claims. If you want to sue the federal government, you can do so in the U.S. Court of Federal Claims. Most citizens who sue in this court do so for monetary compensation from the federal government in its capacity as contractor, purchaser or employer. These are mostly non-tort cases. (A tort is a harm done to another person or property that is not based on an obligation under contract. Running over someone with your car is a tort; violating an employment agreement is not. Tort suits against the federal government are usually brought in U.S. District Courts.)

Recent examples of cases decided in U.S. Court of Federal Claims include a former federal employee who sued to recover back pay, a raisin supplier who was suspended from bidding in government school lunch contracts and California farmers who lost water rights when the government imposed restrictions to protect endangered fish.

U.S. Court of International Trade. Formerly named the U.S. Customs Court, this court has jurisdiction over disputes that involve application of federal trade laws. Most such disputes are over decisions by U.S. Customs officers regarding the duty imposed on imports, the value of the goods being taxed or the exclusion of merchandise from this country.

U.S. Court of Appeals for the Federal Circuit. This is the 13th Circuit Court of Appeals mentioned earlier. It hears appeals from the U.S. Claims Court and the U.S. Court of International Trade. It also hears cases appealed from several administrative tribunals: the Patent and Trademark Office, the International Trade Commission, the Merit Systems Protection Board and the boards of contract appeals of several federal executive agencies.

The U.S. Court of Appeals for the Federal Circuit began operating in 1982 as part of a reorganization of federal limited-jurisdiction courts. It reviews cases previously handled by two abolished courts: the U.S. Court of Customs and Patent Appeals and the appellate division of the U.S. Court of Claims.

The court regularly sits in Washington, DC, but may hold hearings in any of the cities in which the 12 other circuit courts are located. As with the other federal circuit courts, the decisions of the Federal Circuit Court can be appealed to the U.S. Supreme Court.

U.S. Tax Court. If you have a tax dispute with the Internal Revenue Service, you must first appeal to the I.R.S. Appeals Division. If you lose, still want to appeal and don't pay the disputed amount, you can take your case to the U.S. Tax Court. If you lose in U.S. Tax Court, you can seek judicial review by a U.S. Court of Appeals.

Be aware, however, that the procedure is different if you pay the disputed amount. First, you must file for a refund. If you are denied, appeal the denial to the I.R.S. Appeals Division. If you aren't satisfied with the division's decision, you can take your case to the U.S. Court of Federal Claims or to a federal district court. Appeals after that go to the appropriate U.S. Court of Appeals.

CHAPTER 4

Alternatives

Whenever you have a dispute, the first thing to try and do is to work at resolving it without involving attorneys, mediators, court or judges. The emotional and monetary costs of litigation cannot be overstated. There are numerous valuable self-help books you can use to educate yourself about your legal rights *(see the bibliography in Appendix VI for a brief list)*. Once you know where you stand, you should always try to resolve your dispute person to person.

If you are not able to resolve your dispute on your own, there is still another step you should consider before filing a lawsuit. Mediation and arbitration, known together as alternative dispute resolution or ADR, are two alternatives to litigation that you can try. Many arbitration and mediation services are privately operated and have no formal relationship to the courts. However, an increasing number of mediation and arbitration forums are being established as adjuncts to state and federal courts.

COURT-SPONSORED ARBITRATION

In arbitration, an arbitrator (or panel of arbitrators) listens to each side's arguments and evidence in a fairly short and informal hearing, then makes a decision based on the law and the facts. If the decision is accepted by both sides, it has the effect of a court judgment. Either side may reject the decision, however and request a full-fledged trial, often with the risk of a penalty if the result at trial doesn't differ significantly from the arbitrator's decision.

As of 1999, 33 states and 22 federal district courts provided for court-sponsored arbitration by statute or local rule. While federal courts generally do not compel participation in court-sponsored arbitration, state courts do. Judicial arbitration is not usually binding; either party may request a trial after reviewing the arbitrator's decision. However, courts may make it difficult to request a trial after arbitration by imposing fees or fines on litigants who request a trial and then do not obtain as favorable a result as the arbitrator's decision. The programs have different names, but some names being used are *Judicial Arbitration* (in California and Minnesota, for example), *Compulsory Arbitration* (in Delaware) or *Alternative Method of Dispute Resolution by Arbitration* (in New York). In the 22 federal district courts that have established court-sponsored arbitration programs, it is called *Court-Annexed Arbitration.*

HOW IT WORKS

Let's say you own a small print shop in California and you sue a customer in Superior Court for the $30,000 he owes you.

Case limits. Your case will be referred to arbitration if it meets certain requirements. One is the dollar-limit requirement. Cases are referred to arbitration only if the damages being requested don't exceed a ceiling, usually between $10,000 and $50,000 in state courts. In California, the amount is $50,000. In Arizona, each court sets its own ceiling up to $50,000. In the federal court system, the 1998 Alternative Dispute Resolution Act requires every federal district court to set up its own alternative dispute resolution program. In those district courts requiring arbitration, monetary limits range from $100,000 to $150,000. A few district courts require all civil actions to be arbitrated.

Most states limit the subject matter of cases that are arbitrated. They usually arbitrate only lawsuits over money, such as contract disputes, debt-collection, property disputes in divorce proceedings and personal-injury or property-damage claims. Some courts do allow the parties to choose arbitration of child custody disputes. Examples of cases usually not referred to arbitration are professional malpractice matters, disputes over title to real estate and lawsuits seeking an *injunction* that orders someone else to stop doing something. Exceptions include screening panels that handle medical malpractice claims by arbitration.

Mandatory or optional. Some states *require* you to arbitrate your case if it meets the subject-matter and dollar-amount requirements. Others make it optional and require only that both sides agree to the arbitration. In other words, in such a state you can't *force* the other side to submit to arbitration, nor can the other side force you. In California, arbitration for cases that meet the subject matter and amount in controversy limits is mandatory. In Arizona, although arbitration is mandatory, it can be waived if both sides agree and get the court's approval. Arizona differs from most states in that disputing parties can request court-sponsored arbitration even *before* a lawsuit is filed.

Arbitrators. Most arbitration panels in state and federal court use between one and three arbitrators. The arbitrators are usually lawyers or retired judges. Some states use nonlawyers, if both sides approve. Arbitrators can be paid a fee for each case or by the day. In California, they are paid $150 per day or $150 per case, whichever is greater. In a few states, arbitrators are salaried employees of the court, like judges and clerks. Many states allow parties to select their arbitrators or have input in the selection process.

Informal procedures. Fewer formal rules apply both before and during the arbitration hearing than in courtroom litigation. Before the hearing, instead of legal briefs, each side submits a statement of its position and arguments. At the hearing, each side presents its case using relaxed rules of procedure and evidence. The hearings are short, usually one to three hours, and the arbitrator announces a decision immediately or soon afterward. North Carolina has limited the time for the hearing to one hour, by statute. If both sides accept the decision, it is entered as a judgment of the court. If either side rejects the decision, a court trial *de novo* can be requested.

Costs of appealing. California and many other states build in incentives to discourage rejecting an arbitrator's decision and going to trial. These incentives help assure that arbitration will be quicker than a trial. Were arbitration awards appealed routinely and without thought to consequences, arbitration would merely add another hurdle—and therefore more time and expense—to the traditional trial and appeal process.

To assure that both sides think before appealing an arbitrator's decision, some states require that the one who appeals the decision pays the arbitrator's fees and other costs of arbitration. The costs of the subsequent trial may also be imposed. In federal court-sponsored arbitration, the one who demands a trial must pay the costs or the arbitrator's fees unless the trial verdict is for more than the arbitrator recommended.

In the California example, if you appeal the arbitrator's decision and the judgment in the trial *de novo* is not more favorable in either the amount of damages awarded or the type of relief granted, the court will order you to pay the arbitrators the amount of any county compensation, statutory costs, expert witness fees incurred by the other side, and any arbitrator fees paid by the other side. Estimating your legal expenses, the amount at stake and the likelihood of winning—important assessments whenever deciding whether to sue—are just as important when you have gone through arbitration.

COURT-SPONSORED MEDIATION

Mediation is another popular dispute resolution strategy that seeks to resolve conflicts before they reach trial. Many states' courts sponsor such programs, in which a mediator tries to help the disputing parties negotiate their own settlement. Under the Alternative Dispute Resolution Act, federal district courts can choose mediation as an alternative dispute resolution mechanism. Mediation is routinely used in commercial cases as well as cases that involve personal disputes—for instance, between neighbors or family members.

Non-adversary process. Mediation is considered better than suing, especially in personal disputes, because the two sides themselves are encouraged to create a solution rather than allowing a courtroom battle to put even more distance between them. The key to successful mediation, unlike both traditional litigation and arbitration, is that the mediator remains neutral and does not impose an agreement on the two sides. Whatever decision is reached comes from the parties themselves, not the mediator.

Court-sponsored mediation is almost always voluntary, but because of its benefits, courts try to persuade people to use it. Besides encouraging peaceful settlement instead of increased antagonism, mediation is quicker and less expensive than traditional litigation and can calm emotional fires that litigation often fans. Thus, people who mediate a dispute are more likely to be satisfied with the process and more likely to adhere to the final agreement than if they had gone through a trial and allowed a judge or jury to impose a solution on them.

Generally, the parties must pay the mediator's fees. In California, for example, the mediator's fee is set by statute at $150 a day or $150 per case, whichever is greater. In most cases, the court appoints a qualified mediator; however, many states allow the parties to select a mediator subject to court approval. The mediation process is generally confidential; however, there are a few exceptions in certain states for child abuse and neglect and juvenile proceedings. Most agreements reached through mediation are not binding until approved by the court. If mediation is unsuccessful, the cases proceed to trial.

The scope of mandatory issues to be mediated varies from state to state. As of 2001, for example, 12 states *required* mediation of family issues, including child custody, support, division of marital property or visitation disputes. There are now 38 states that have legislation that regulates family mediation. In states that have mediation statutes, most often mediation is used at the courts' discretion. Most states will not refer cases to mediation in which there are allegations of domestic abuse.

Mediation is being used in criminal courts, where victim-offender mediation is an alternative to a trial. Twenty-nine states have passed statutes implementing victim-offender mediation. Mediation is used both for juvenile offenders and for adult offenders and for crimes of property as well as crimes of violence. Restitution from the criminal to the victim is frequently part of the process. Those who have participated in victim-offender mediation have reported satisfaction with the results.

PRIVATE CONTRACTUAL ARBITRATION

If a court-sponsored program is not available and both sides agree to arbitration, you can contact a private alternative dispute resolution program to resolve your dispute. You can even look up "Mediation Services" in your local *Yellow Pages* and there will most likely be a number of listings.

Often, when you enter into a written agreement with someone, the agreement requires you to arbitrate or mediate. Increasingly, business contracts provide for arbitration or a combination of mediation and arbitration as mandatory methods of resolving contract disputes. Whole sectors of the business world have chosen contractual arbitration as the dispute resolution mechanism of choice. Examples include the real estate industry, the construction industry, the insurance industry and the health-care industry. Once the contracts are signed by both parties, each side has given up its right to go to court. The courts have usually upheld these private dispute resolution agreements.

Generally, the decision of the arbitrator or arbitrators is final and any review by a court of appeal is limited to questions regarding the bias of the arbitrator or fraud in the making of the agreement. Generally, an arbitration award will not be overturned by a court of appeal because you believe the arbitrator was mistaken about the law or the facts.

Several major private providers offer arbitration and mediation services. When you use these providers, the parties usually split the fees for the arbitrator or mediator. One of the most well known providers is called JAMS. JAMS relies heavily on retired judges to provide mediation, arbitration, private judging, mini-trials and neutral fact-finding training services. JAMS has a Web site at *www.jamsadr.com*. Another place to get information is the Association for Conflict Resolution, a 6,000-plus member organization of mediators, arbitrators, facilitators and educators. Their Web site is at *www.acrnet.org*. For a listing of mediation centers in the U.S., consult HALT's *Citizens Legal Manual,* **The Legal Resource Directory.**

COLLABORATIVE LAW

Collaborative law is an out-of-court legal process that allows both parties to retain separate, specially-trained lawyers whose job is to help them settle their dispute without court involvement. Collaborative law is a real success story. Like mediation, parties try to resolve their disputes without going to court. In collaborative law, however, the parties resolve their disputes not with the help of a mediator or facilitator, but with the help of trained collaborative law attorneys. Each party works with an attorney who acts as a counselor to that person alone. Collaborative attorneys are specially trained in this unique team approach to dispute resolution. While most attorneys are trained to resolve conflicts through litigation, attorneys trained in the collaborative process are taught to reach compromises. Bolstering collaborative law's commitment to compromise is its central premise: that neither side may go to court or even threaten to do so.

If such an action or threat occurs, the process terminates and both lawyers are disqualified from any further involvement in the case. Without litigation as an option, the parties and their attorneys have a strong incentive to work toward compromise. In fact, the knowledge that an agreement must be reached outside of court may also help the parties psychologically by decreasing the degree of confrontation between them. Finally, because the attorneys do not have to prepare for trial, they avoid the cost of litigation. Thus a case resolved through the collaborative process costs a fraction of one resolved the traditional way.

Collaborative law originated in Minnesota in 1990 and has since spread to more than a dozen other states, including California, Texas, Florida, Ohio, Pennsylvania, North Carolina, New Jersey, Massachusetts, Wisconsin and Georgia, with hundreds of practitioners. While it is used primarily as a tool in divorce cases, collaborative law is also being applied to other areas of law, including employment, probate and personal injury. For a referral to a collaborative law provider, visit HALT's Web site at *www.halt.org.*

THE MULTI-DOOR COURTHOUSE

This program also seeks means other than lawsuits to resolve disputes. Strictly speaking, the Multi-Door Courthouse is not an alternative, but an intake and referral system that matches people and their problems with the most appropriate dispute-settlement mechanism. The program started as a three-year experiment in 1984 and is still in use in several federal district courts and state courts in Georgia, Colorado, New Jersey, Texas, Massachusetts and the District of Columbia. This is how it works. You and a neighbor feud over her barking dog. She claims it is just a "stage" her puppy is going through, but you think 10 months is too long to be a "stage." You and she have had countless heated arguments. One day, you call the police in anger. The police department's citizen complaint division refers you to the multi-door program.

Among other agencies that might refer you to the multi-door program are the courts, legal services programs, social service agencies, public defender offices and community groups.

The multi-door intake centers are likely to be housed in small claims courts, media "action lines," local officials' offices, lawyer-referral services and district attorneys' offices. At the multi-door program's intake desk, a staff member listens to your complaint and suggests what mechanism (or "door") would be the best for resolving the matter. For your problem with your neighbor's barking dog, the staff might suggest a neighborhood justice center. These centers' mediation programs are particularly suited to settling problems between neighbors.

Other kinds of cases will be better suited for arbitration, a consumer protection agency, a private conciliation service or other settlement strategy. And occasionally, a dispute is so complex or irreconcilable that a lawsuit is the only reasonable route to resolution. The important element in the multi-door courthouse experiment is that disputes be matched to the most appropriate mechanism for settlement.

EARLY NEUTRAL EVALUATION

Early Neutral Evaluation is a court-sponsored, non-binding process that takes place soon after a complaint is filed. If Early Neutral Evaluation is available when you file a lawsuit, the court clerk should be able to give you information about the procedure. A neutral evaluator, who is generally an attorney with expertise in the type of lawsuit that has been filed, provides both sides with an advisory evaluation of the likely court outcome. The neutral evaluator may also offer case planning and settlement advice. The neutral evaluator will meet with each party and help him or her identify the strengths and weaknesses in his or her case. The information given to each party by the neutral evaluator is confidential.

RENT-A-JUDGE STATUTES

Some states, including Ohio, California, New York and Texas allow parties who have filed lawsuits in the trial court to bypass appointed judges and agree to submit their dispute to a paid referee. In California, for example, the parties may file a request for the court to refer the matter to a private judge. The parties agree on the issues to be decided by the private judge. These referees are usually retired judges, who are frequently allowed to use vacant courtrooms for the trials. The parties agree to pay the rent-a-judge's fees. The parties usually have some say over the procedure, but may be limited by local statute. The decision is appealable to the court of appeal, bypassing the trial court process completely.

SUMMARY JURY TRIAL

Uncertainty about a jury's view of the case and unrealistic expectations of what a jury would award are among the major hurdles that prevent pre-trial settlement of cases. "Summary jury trials" were developed in the early 1980s by U.S. District Court Judge Thomas Lambros of Cleveland, Ohio. The summary jury trial is one of the alternative dispute resolution mechanisms courts may offer under the Alternative Dispute Resolution Act. Because a summary jury trial involves a considerable amount of attorney, court and litigant time and money, the summary jury trial is only occasionally used in federal court, most often for protracted cases or routine civil litigation where the litigants differ significantly about the likely jury outcome. It is unique among alternative dispute resolution techniques because it employs the concept of trial by jury without holding a formal trial. It has been found most useful for those parties who want to settle out of court but have reached an impasse. During a summary jury trial, each side presents its case during an abbreviated half-day session before a mock jury, usually six persons. Instead of calling witnesses, the lawyers summarize their witnesses' expected testimony and present evidence they could use in a full trial, but they are discouraged from raising objections. The session occurs before a judge or magistrate, but usually in private. The "jury" then returns a verdict with comments, either as a group or individually.

If the two sides agree beforehand, the verdict may be entered as a judgment of the court. If not, both sides have gained valuable insight about what a real jury would conclude about who is liable and for what amount of damages. Armed with such information, the two sides are often better able to settle the case and avoid the costs of a full-scale trial.

LAWYERS AND ALTERNATIVES

Certain alternative dispute settlement strategies assume that each side has a lawyer. For instance, in cases referred to arbitration or summary jury trial, the amount of money at stake and the fact that a lawsuit has already been filed usually mean attorneys are involved. This is especially true for cases referred to summary jury trials. In arbitration, lawyers are not essential but, as in any lawsuit, one side going *pro se* generally has an uphill battle against an opponent represented by a lawyer.

Mediation is not designed for attorney involvement, however, because the objective of mediation is for the parties themselves to communicate directly in their search for agreement. In fact, HALT and other legal reformers believe that attorneys, trained to be advocates and adversaries, can do more harm than good in a mediation setting. Even in court-ordered mediation and in cases sent to contractual mediation, where both sides are represented by attorneys, mediators limit attorney involvement. Parties are encouraged to present the facts of the cases themselves and mediators meet with parties without counsel present.

CHAPTER 5

Not-Quite Courts

Many disputes are resolved not in the courts, but in administrative forums that sometimes look and act like courts. Two examples: injured California employees challenging denial of workers' compensation and persons denied Social Security disability benefits. Both present their cases to non-judges—the first to a state workers' compensation board administrative law judge, the second to a Social Security administrative law judge. After hearing testimony and reviewing documents or other evidence, the administrative law judge decides whether to grant the denied benefits.

Such administrative tribunals have names like "board," "commission" or "board of appeals." The person presiding over the hearing may be called an administrative law judge, a referee, an arbitrator, a commissioner or a hearing officer. Sometimes a committee or panel presides. In these and other administrative tribunals, the officer or administrative law judge is engaged in *adjudication.* That is, just like a judge, the presiding officer listens to both sides, studies the evidence and decides the legal rights and obligations of each side. The adjudication is carried out in the executive, not the judiciary branch of government: the Social Security Administration is part of the U.S. Department of Health and Human Services, an executive agency; the California administrative law judge is employed by the Workers' Compensation Appeals Board, a California state government agency charged with administering workers' compensation laws.

A SHORT HISTORY

Administrative tribunals are creatures of government. Their development has been part of the expansion of government's reach. The greater the number of public programs, the more possibility of dispute and the greater the need for grievance mechanisms to keep such disputes out of the courts.

Administrative tribunals do not share the centuries-long history that shaped our judicial system, rooted in English common law. Most of them were established during the past 50 years—each one separately, as needed. This results in even more variation in their structure and operation than is the case with our courts.

Critics charge that the executive branch, by wielding court-like powers with these administrative tribunals, is usurping power from the judiciary. However, administrative tribunals have probably contributed more than they have taken away. They have helped keep disputes out of the courts and, compared to the courts, resolving disagreements administratively is generally less formal, less expensive, less time-consuming and less hostile to the *pro se* litigant. Also, both sides in an administrative process almost always can appeal to the courts if they feel justice has not been done.

TYPES OF CASES

Many administrative tribunals have been established by local, state and federal governments to handle their disputes with individuals or businesses. If you have a dispute with a government agency and want to know what administrative grievance procedure to use, ask if the agency has an in-house complaint resolution procedure and what is required.

Sometimes, administrative forums are created for disputes between private parties in areas the government regulates. For instance, if you are accusing your employer of firing you because you were trying to organize a union, you do so not in the courts, but with the National Labor Relations Board (NLRB), a federal agency, because Congress, in enacting laws that prohibit employers from interfering with union-organizing, also provided a mechanism within the NLRB to handle these grievances.

Social Security cases are typical of the largest category of disputes resolved in administrative tribunals: usually complaints over benefits programs. Other matters commonly heard in administrative tribunals include public and many private employer-employee disagreements; income-tax and property-tax assessment disputes; real estate zoning and eminent-domain disputes and all types of business-license disagreements, from permits to sell alcohol to barbers' certificates.

RELATIONSHIP TO THE COURTS

If an agency has established an administrative procedure for handling disputes, it must be used before you can go to court. Suppose you're applying for Social Security disability benefits and your application is denied. You cannot sue; you must first go through the administrative channels within the Social Security Administration. You can take your case to court only if you are still dissatisfied after using all levels of appeal within the agency. It is at this point that administrative tribunals and courts intersect: when you seek a court's review of an administrative agency's decision. Think of court review as an "appeal" of the agency's decision.

HOW THEY WORK

Getting ready for and taking part in an administrative hearing is much less technical than preparing for a courtroom trial. In an administrative hearing, the two sides usually sit across a table from each other with the decision-maker seated at the head. Few rules govern testimony or the submission of evidence. You may represent yourself or, if you want to be represented by someone else, it does not always have to be an attorney.

The rules used by all federal agencies are spelled out in the Federal Administrative Procedure Act. Similarly, most states have adopted some version of the model State Administrative Procedure Act for their agencies, but their use varies among the agencies, even within one state. You can find both the federal act and your state's act by asking at a local law library.

Though the setting is less formal and the procedures less rigid, what's at stake—say, the granting of a business license or withholding of unemployment benefits—can be just as significant as many things being decided in traditional courts. Therefore, at a minimum, administrative tribunals use rules of "procedural due process" to assure fairness. They require, for example, that each side receives adequate notice about when and where the hearing is to take place and that both have an equal opportunity to present their case.

Administrative agencies have appellate levels similar to the courts. For instance, after receiving notice that you have been denied Social Security benefits, your first recourse is to request a reconsideration. If that is denied, you must then request an administrative hearing. If you are dissatisfied with the hearing's outcome, you can appeal to the Social Security Appeals Council. Only after exhausting all of these recourses can you appeal to the courts.

You can see that the Social Security Administration has two tribunals, the initial hearing panel and an Appeals Council. Many other agencies have similarly structured systems. For example, if you are dissatisfied with the administrative law judge's decision regarding your workers' compensation benefits in California, your next step is a petition to the state's Workers'

Compensation Appeals Board, another administrative tribunal.

This is not so everywhere, however. If you have a driver's license revocation dispute in Hawaii, for example, the Administrative Driver's License Revocation Office is the only administrative tribunal you will encounter. To challenge the Office's decision, you must take your case to a Hawaiian court, most likely the District Court.

GROUPS THAT WORK WITH ADMINISTRATIVE TRIBUNALS

There may be an agency or non-profit group that provides assistance with appearances before administrative tribunals. For example, if you need help with obtaining appropriate special education services for a child with disabilities, an organization like the Parent Information Center can provide advocacy assistance in due process hearings under the Individual Disabilities Education Act. The Center operates in several states. An example is New Hampshire's Parent Information Center, which hosts a Web site at *www.parentinformationcenter.org*.

COURT REVIEW

The process a court uses to judge the legality or propriety of administrative agency decisions varies widely, not only from one state to another but also within a state, depending on the agency involved.

For instance, a court may conduct a trial *de novo*—an entirely new trial—or it may limit itself to a review of the written record of the administrative hearing. This review may be done by a trial court, by an appellate court or, sometimes, by the court of last resort. The right to review may be based on the state's constitution or on state law. And your chances of getting court review can range from "almost never" to "almost always."

Your "right" to review. Frequently, court review is allowed by statute. This is true, for example, in Social Security cases. A federal law—the Social Security Act—specifically states that you can request court review of final decisions to the Appeals Council. A decision by the Appeals Council is a prerequisite to filing a complaint for review in the Federal District Court.

If no statute authorizes court review, you can try basing a lawsuit on state or federal constitutional grounds—by claiming, for instance, that your right to due process (say, your right to proper notice or to a fair hearing) was denied. The success of your argument depends on many things, such as what agency you're appealing from, what you want reviewed and whether you're appealing a local, state or federal agency decision.

In a few cases, Congress and state legislatures have prohibited court review of administrative decisions. There is a presumption that if you are aggrieved by an administrative decision, you can get judicial review, but that presumption may be overcome by explicit statutory language. For instance, a prisoner who made an agreement regarding transfer to a halfway house with the Bureau of Prisons was not entitled to judicial review when he wanted to challenge the agreement, as a statute precluded judicial review of the transfer agreement.

Requirements. These requirements must be met before a court will review an administrative decision:

Agencies must have the first opportunity to resolve the controversy. In disputes over Social Security benefits, for example, you must first ask the Social Security Administration for a "reconsideration."

Exhaust all administrative remedies. Only when you have received a final decision from the Social Security Appeals Council may you go to the courts.

You must have "standing." That is, you must be the one who suffered an injury to your legally protected right.

You must meet requirements that any lawsuit must meet before a court will hear your case. The court must have jurisdiction and the review must be requested in the proper form.

The proper court. The statutes that provide for court review usually also state what court you should ask to review your case and in what form. In the case of Social Security, the law says you must file your case in federal district court—the federal trial court for the judicial district in which you reside or have your place of business.

In many cases, however, court review of agency decisions is done by appellate courts. For example, U.S. Courts of Appeals review decisions of administrative agencies such as the National Labor Relations Board and the Environmental Protection Agency.

At the state level, review of administrative decisions is also typically done by intermediate appellate courts, but here again, court review is sometimes done by general-jurisdiction courts, as in workers' compensation cases in Texas and driver's license revocation hearings in Hawaii.

Asking for review. As with everything else in this chapter, the form in which you must ask for court review depends on your case. Asking for review of a Social Security decision must take the form of a "civil action," meaning, in effect, that you are filing a lawsuit. In other cases, the request for court review is made as an appeal, as though the administrative case had been originally heard in a trial court.

If no laws provide for review, you usually can request it by means of a *prerogative writ*. This is a request that a court exercise its discretionary powers, much like a request to the U.S. Supreme Court to hear your case by a *writ of certiorari*.

The court's review. Usually, the reviewing court will act like an appellate court. Even though a district court undertakes the review, it does not conduct a trial. Instead, just as an appeals court would, it studies the written record of the administrative hearing to see if the correct legal standards were applied and whether "substantial evidence" supported the decision.

The "substantial evidence" rule is commonly used by courts in reviewing decisions of administrative agencies where a more formal, trial type hearing was required. What is meant by "substantial evidence" is elusive. Under this rule the court tries to determine whether reasonable people, given the same evidence, could come to the same conclusion the agency did. In reviewing your Social Security case, the federal district court examines whether the decision was reasonably supported by the facts of your case. The court does not formulate an independent judgment about whether or not you are entitled to disability benefits.

If an agency's findings of fact are subject to *de novo* review, which is a fresh look at the evidence and the law, then the agency's decision can be overturned only if it was "unwarranted by all the facts." For example, under the Freedom of Information Act, the district court reviews the agency decision *de novo*.

FURTHER APPEALS

Once you are in the courts, you may be able to appeal your case from the first review court to a higher court. For instance, if you are still unsuccessful with your Social Security case at the district court level, you may appeal it to the appropriate U.S. Court of Appeals. The Court of Appeals would undertake its review much as the district court did—not forming its own opinion about your case, but making sure no incorrect legal standards were used and that the decision was supported by "substantial evidence." At this stage, though, it is less likely that the court will agree to hear your case, since the court will know you have already gone through an entire administrative appeals process and review by one court.

In some kinds of cases, you are allowed only one chance for court review. The law may prohibit you from appealing that first review court's decision.

CHAPTER 6

Going *Pro Se*

If you have to go to court to resolve a legal matter and are thinking of going it alone (that is representing yourself *pro se*), we need to be frank. Representing yourself in a legal proceeding is not for the faint of heart. Our courts are filled with black-robed judges, intimidating lawyers and court personnel who are skeptical about helping do-it-yourselfers. As daunting as that may sound, a growing number of people still represent themselves, often because they have no real alternative.

According to a study by the National Center on State Courts of 16 large urban trial courts, 71 percent of domestic relations cases had at least one unrepresented party. Similarly, a 1998 study done by the Boston Bar Association found that 66 percent of cases in probate and family law were handled by at least one *pro se* party.

The reason is money. Lawyers are costly and hiring them to represent you in a legal proceeding—especially if it becomes protracted—can be extremely expensive.

If you need to handle a legal proceeding without hiring a lawyer, you need to know what you're getting into. Teaching you how to represent yourself in a legal proceeding is beyond the scope of this chapter. We cannot take you, step-by-step, through the process of handling a legal case because state laws vary and because every case is different. What we can do is offer you a general overview of what it's like to go *pro se*.

The good news is that not all legal matters end up in protracted litigation before a judge and jury. Most people can handle the vast majority of legal matters (probating an estate, getting a divorce, filing for bankruptcy, various real estate transactions) with little or no help from lawyers and through fairly painless interaction with judges and the court system. That's because a growing number of courts (especially those that handle family law, landlord-tenant and housing issues) are streamlining their processes to make it easier for people to represent themselves.

The next bit of good news is that nearly every state offers a small claims court specifically designed for *pro se* litigants. These courts allow people to represent themselves in a variety of small money disputes (dry cleaning errors, fender benders, small business disputes) without the expense of hiring a lawyer. In fact, some states ban lawyers from small claims court to ensure a consumer-friendly atmosphere. To learn more about the kinds of cases accepted in small claims court and the steps involved in representing yourself, read HALT's book, **Small Claims Court: Making Your Way Through the System** or get that information from our Web site at *www.halt.org*.

If you have to settle a legal matter in court, you must start in trial court. Trial courts probate wills, grant divorces, hear traffic violations and handle countless other civil matters. If you lose in trial court and are thinking about appellate court, you should definitely seek legal assistance.

Some of the more common legal matters brought to court by *pro se*-ers are briefly described below.

KINDS OF CASES

Many routine legal matters can bring you into a courtroom. Routine matters, however, can easily become "not so routine." A straightforward probate case can turn into a nightmare if one or more of the beneficiaries contest the will. A routine "eviction" will become dicey if a tenant barricades herself in and starts destroying your property.

For the purposes of this discussion, we assume your legal matter is typical and straightforward. If serious problems develop, you should seek legal advice before proceeding on your own.

IS GOING *PRO SE* RIGHT FOR YOUR CASE?

In general, the more complicated a case is, the more money that's involved, or the more a person's personal freedom is at stake, the more likely you are to need expert legal help. Despite that, there are times when full blown litigation is the only answer and being represented by a lawyer is not an option.

In good conscience, we cannot recommend litigation. It is expensive and risky and should always be used as a last resort. We strongly urge you to exhaust all of your non-court remedies (suggest a compromise, offer to mediate or arbitrate, split the difference—whatever it takes) before you file a lawsuit. If all your efforts in that regard fail and you're forced into court

alone, take heart. There are additional books and resources that can help you
(*see Appendix V*).

Even if you feel that you are well-suited for *pro se* litigation and that you
have a valid claim, you may decide against litigating a case on your own when
you consider these factors:

Time. In order to litigate a case *pro se*, you need be willing to put in the
necessary time. Depending on the complexities involved, it could take
months or even years to settle your case.

Cost. You may save a bundle in legal fees by representing yourself, but
there are still other expenses involved, including filing fees and court costs. If
you have any doubts about the validity of your claim or just want someone
available to answer legal questions, you might consider hiring a lawyer on an
hourly basis. While a lot less expensive than hiring a lawyer outright, at $150
to $200 an hour, your costs can quickly mount.

Delay. You have a right to a speedy trial, but that doesn't mean you'll get
one. Scheduling delays and case backlogs are big problems in many court
systems and can force you to wait months, even years, to get a decision on
your case.

Energy. Most people have little idea of what it takes to pursue a legal
claim. Preparing for a trial is time-consuming. Court conferences and trials
are often in the middle of the workday, and to prepare for litigation you will
often have to give up weekends and stay up late at night. You will need to
spend time, for example, filling out interrogatories, attending depositions,
collecting evidence and so on.

Unlevel playing field. The court is the lawyer's home field. The lawyer
knows all of the rules and might even know the judge. By appearing *pro se*, you
are placing yourself at a distinct disadvantage. Lawyers and judges also use
"legalese" and throw around terms like *prima facie* and *de minimis*. Even if you
were required to take Latin in school, you may need to invest in a good law dictionary to know what lawyers and judges are talking about. You may also be
able to find many, if not all definitions for legal terms online through a web
search engine or an online legal dictionary, such as *dictionary.findlaw.com*.

WHO ARE THE PLAYERS?

When you litigate a case, you are just one of many people on the stage.
Visiting a courthouse in session before you actually try your own case will let
you see who some of these players are. It will also help familiarize you with
the process involved, show the demands the judge places on the litigant and
teach you different ways litigants present their cases.

The *parties* are the people involved in the lawsuit. The person suing is called the *plaintiff* and the person being sued is called the *defendant*. Sometimes there are a number of plaintiffs or defendants on each side. For example, if you're suing a married couple, both would be named as defendants.

The *judge* directs the pre-trial hearings and the trial. She makes decisions on motions (a request that the judge take specific action—for example, a "motion to dismiss" asks a judge to throw a case out) or objections brought by the parties, based on rules of evidence and procedure. The judge also holds conferences with the parties to resolve problems that might have come up along the way and to encourage settlements. When addressing a judge, refer to her as "Your Honor."

The *judge's clerk* takes care of the judge's calendar (the "docket"), which lists the dates for trials. During trial, the clerk is responsible for keeping track of exhibits, taking oaths from witnesses, jurors and interpreters, and helping the judge move cases along. (This person has a different job from the *clerk of court*, who accepts documents that you file with the court, such as complaints and motions.)

Attorneys present the evidence to make the conclusions needed to prove their party's claim and disprove the claims of the other party. They also object to any evidence or arguments from the other party that violates court rules. Furthermore, attorneys conduct legal research and take care of any legal documentation necessary for trial. They also help their client negotiate a settlement.

Ordinary witnesses testify to what they have "personally seen, heard, smelled, tasted or touched."

Expert witnesses are allowed to offer conclusions based on their technical knowledge, and they are almost always paid for their time.

Spectators, such as members of the family, friends and even strangers may watch hearings and trials.

PROVING YOUR CASE

If you decide you do have a valid case and want to proceed on your own, you need to become familiar with the elements needed to prove your case. Most lawsuits handled by *pro se* litigants involve some variation of a breach of contract or a statutory claim. This section lays out the basic elements of each of them.

Breach of contract. Courts try to uphold most contracts, sometimes even going as far as filling in terms that are left vague. Nonetheless, there still must be at least a basic agreement over who is making the contract and what property, time, place and price (or any other pertinent detail) is involved. In general, you will have a valid contract if you have an offer, an acceptance and consideration.

An *offer* is valid when no further action is required on the part of the person making the offer. An offer might be someone stopping you on the street and saying, "For only $10, you can be the owner of this genuine, cut-glass, fake ruby ring." Or it can be a newspaper advertisement promising a television set at the sale price of $400 to the first 10 buyers.

You can tell when an offer is made because all that's needed to clinch the agreement is your *acceptance,* signaled by your agreeing to the deal on the terms offered. This can be done by oral acceptance, signing on the proverbial "dotted line" or, in the example of the ruby ring, handing over $10 to the fellow on the street.

Both sides in the contract must be able to say what they are giving up (this is known as *consideration*) and what they are getting out of the deal. A counteroffer is not an acceptance. If you say, "Sure, I'll take that ring, but I'll give you $7 for it." You've made a *counteroffer,* not an acceptance. And, unless the fellow agrees to your counteroffer, no valid agreement exists.

So to prove a breach of a contract, you have to show: 1) Formation: there was a legally binding contract. 2) Performance: the plaintiff performed his or her part of the contract. 3) Breach: the defendant failed to perform his or her part of the contract. 4) Damage: the breach caused the plaintiff actual economic losses.

Statutory claims. When bringing a statutory claim, the elements of your particular claim will be listed in the statute itself. Suppose you are suing a car dealer under your state's "lemon law." You can look in the state's code of laws and search the index for terms such as "consumer," "consumer protection," "automobile" and "lemon law" to find the statute.

The text of the statute will tell you who the law applies to and what those people are required to do. You need to check whether the statute applies to your situation. In the lemon law example, you'll want to be sure that your dealer is not somehow exempted from the law and that the type of purchase you made is covered by the statute. For example, the law may only apply to dealers of a certain size, or you may want to sue over your purchase of a boat when the statute only covers cars.

Some of the language in the statute might not be clear. For instance, some terms may not be well defined. In our lemon law case, the statute might say that it applies to "cars" but not whether that includes light trucks. Often, other courts will have made decisions about what those terms are supposed to mean. You can find these cases in what are known as "annotated" versions of the code. In an annotated code, cases interpreting the statute are listed after the statute's language, usually with a short description of what the court decided. These cases are often as relevant to the meaning of the statute as the text itself, so it is important to check these annotations.

When you are suing under a statutory claim, you will have to prove that your situation meets every requirement of the statute. If there is just one part of your case that doesn't meet a statutory requirement, then you will lose your case.

BURDEN OF PROOF

The plaintiff's burden of proof in civil cases is lower than it is in criminal cases where she must provide proof "beyond a reasonable doubt." In a civil case, the plaintiff must only prove her claim by a preponderance of the evidence; if the evidence supporting your claim is stronger than the evidence supporting your opponent's claim, you win.

RULES OF EVIDENCE

This is the area that trips up most *pro se* litigants. If you are going to try your own case, you certainly need to have a basic understanding of these rules. If you do not, the judge may exclude some of your best evidence because of the other side's objections. You may also fail to raise an objection when the other side brings evidence that should be kept out. Although there are many exceptions, the general principle to use in planning your case is that will only be able to use verifiable evidence.

You should ask a lawyer about potential evidence problems before the trial. We suggest that before trial, you try to show your evidence to the judge in chambers (the judge's office). Also, before trial, either party can make a "motion *in limine*," which is a request for the court to exclude irrelevant or damaging evidence.

The rules govern the introduction of physical evidence (for example, a picture of a skid mark), clerical evidence (an office ledger or receipts) and statements by witnesses. The rules are specific and are intended to ensure that only authentic evidence is given to a jury. The judge rules on all objections.

A rule that comes up in nearly every case is the *hearsay* rule. Although there are many exceptions, the rule generally forbids you to ask a witness what someone else said. This is because the other side has no opportunity to cross-examine the person who actually made the statement—for example, to ask whether that person was joking, mistaken or lying. Under this rule, the judge will not permit a jury to hear the driver of a car quoting a passenger. If what the passenger said was important, you should call the passenger into court to repeat the statement to the jury.

DEFENDING YOURSELF

If you are being sued, you prepare for trial in almost the same way as the person suing you. The usual defenses are:

(1) denying the claim ("I didn't do it");
(2) arguing that the claim is exaggerated ("maybe I did something, but not like that or to that extent");
(3) asserting an *affirmative defense* ("whether I did it or not is irrelevant; you can't sue me for that"); and
(4) serving a counterclaim or a cross-claim (any combination of the above, plus your own claims against the person suing you or against someone else).

These four approaches are in no way mutually exclusive.

If you choose to deny the claim, unlike the plaintiff, you only have to disprove one of the elements of the claim. Try to find out beforehand, either by informally asking the other party or formally through *interrogatories* (written questions the opposing party must answer in writing under oath), what issues the plaintiff is likely to raise.

If you only argue that the amount of money being demanded by the plaintiff is exaggerated, you are essentially admitting partial responsibility. Therefore, you will be spending most of your efforts trying to show that the plaintiff is also partially responsible for the damages. You will also try to get an objective assessment of how much the damages actually cost.

If you assert an *affirmative defense* you are stating that there is a legal reason that the plaintiff cannot bring her claim—even if she can prove her allegations are true. For example, the statute of limitations for this particular kind of claim may require the plaintiff to bring the claim within a particular amount of time. If a contract is involved, it may require arbitration or mediation to settle disputes. If the claim involves a sale of a product or service, state or federal consumer protection statutes might protect you completely. Bear in mind, however, that you might need legal advice to unearth such defense strategies.

In addition to the type of defense you choose to assert, you may also need to assert claims of your own, either against the person suing you, against a co-defendant, or against someone else altogether. If you have been harmed by the person who has brought suit against you, you may assert a counter-claim against the plaintiff. Filing a *counterclaim* is just like filing an ordinary suit against the plaintiff: you are trying to prove that you are entitled to receive damages from the plaintiff because of her bad actions. If the plaintiff has filed a claim against both you and another party, and you also have a claim against that other party, you may assert a *cross-claim*. In other words, a cross-claim allows you to assert a claim against someone who is already a co-defendant. If there is a third party you believe is responsible for the harm to the plaintiff (for example, if you want to say, "I didn't do it; *she* did," or if you want to say, "I didn't do *all* of it; *she* did some of it"), you can bring that third party in to the case by *moving to join* her as a defendant. Finally, if you are the third party (you haven't brought suit or been sued) who has an inter-est in a case already filed, you may be able to *intervene* in the case if you can show that you have some interest in its outcome that you will lose if you are not a party to the case. Most jurisdictions have liberal rules for counter-claims, cross-claims and joinder of issues and parties. Generally, the idea behind these rules is that, whenever possible, parties who decide to go to court should be able to resolve all their disputes at one time. However, adding parties and claims to a lawsuit can become complex; if you become involved in a case with a large number of parties or claims, it might be time for you to seek expert legal advice.

STAGES OF A LAWSUIT

In Appendix II you'll find a graphic that outlines the stages of a civil lawsuit. (The stages of a criminal lawsuit have different procedures.) Four separate dia-grams illustrate the distinct stages: Pleading, Discovery, Pre-Trial and Trial.

SERVING PLEADINGS

Plaintiffs initiate lawsuits through court documents known as *pleadings*. Like small claims court, a lawsuit begins when someone files a *complaint*—a legal document that alleges the facts and legal basis for the suit. The com-plaint is the pleading that starts a civil case. The plaintiff files the complaint against the defendant with the court clerk.

As a plaintiff, you must state the *cause of action*, which is the legal and fac-tual basis for your suit, and request compensation for your *damages*, which is the monetary or other losses that resulted from the defendant's conduct.

Specific requirements for filing complaints, such as the number of copies, the paper size and filing fees, vary from court to court. Ask your court clerk about them.

Also ask the clerk for a *summons* form. The summons informs the other party that she is being sued, and requests that she provide an answer within a given timeframe. Fill out the summons form and bring it with you when you return to the clerk's office to file your complaint. The clerk will stamp the summons and the complaint, staple the summons on top of the complaint and give you a copy to present to the person you are suing.

You must now *serve* the complaint and summons on the defendant. This means informing the person you are suing about the lawsuit by making sure she receives a copy of the complaint and has a chance to respond. The complaint can be served by mail or by any person who is at least 18 years old and is not a party to the lawsuit. The defendant cannot reject service. Check your court rules, but courts usually require a sworn statement (*affidavit*) or a signed registered-mail receipt to show that the person you are suing has been served the complaint.

The answer. The defendant usually has 20 to 60 days in which to answer your complaint. The defendant answers by filing an *answer* or *response*. The response can be as simple as admitting or denying the statements in the complaint. Or, if appropriate, the defendant can raise an affirmative defense, stating a legal reason that you cannot collect damages from her, even if your claims were proven true.

The answer begins with the same case caption and civil action number as the complaint and should address, paragraph by paragraph, each of the allegations in the complaint. In some cases, if the defendant doesn't deny the allegations in your complaint, the court will consider them uncontested and therefore true. The answer must be mailed by the defendant to the plaintiff or to her attorney.

Besides answering your allegations, the defendant can also file one or more motions that challenge your suit without addressing the facts of the case. For example, a defendant might file a motion to dismiss by challenging the court's jurisdiction to hear the case, or by challenging the way the complaint and summons were served. The defendant can also file *counterclaim(s)* in the answer.

If something was mistakenly left out of a complaint or answer, you may be able to amend it. Do this by filing a new pleading (usually called an Amended Complaint) with the change in it. The plaintiff can usually amend the complaint once for any reason within a certain number of days (usually 15 to 20) and before the defendant answers. You *must* amend your complaint if something you said has changed since the time you filed the pleading. After the defendant answers or the deadline passes, you may still be able to amend your pleading, but you must either get the other side to agree to it or ask for an amendment in a motion to the court.

DISCOVERY STAGE

After the initial complaint, answer, and motions have been exchanged and filed with the court clerk, *discovery* begins. This is the process of exchanging information. The purpose is to bring out the facts and evidence so each side can evaluate its case. After both sides have each other's information, many issues or possibly the entire case might be settled without a trial.

Before discovery begins, the judge will have both sides meet with her to set deadlines for discovery. Discovery can last anywhere from a few weeks to many years, depending on court rules and the complexity of the issues in the case. The discovery period can also be extended, but only by filing a motion asking the court for an extension.

Of the many forms discovery can take, three are most common. The first, *interrogatories*, are written questions that must be answered in writing under oath. The answers must be given to the court within a specified number of days. Because interrogatories have sometimes been used to harass opponents, many courts now limit the number of questions a party can ask or the number of times a party can submit interrogatories. Ask the clerk or look at your local court rules in a law library.

A second common type of discovery is a *document request*. Each side has the opportunity to get materials from the other that may reveal important facts about the case. Generally, the rules place few limitations on what documents you can request, as long as they are related to the case. Unless the other side objects, the court will not interfere with document requests or, indeed, any other type of discovery.

A third type of discovery is the *deposition*. This is a transcript of face-to-face questioning under oath in front of a stenographer or tape recorder. The person being questioned can be the plaintiff, the defendant or a witness who has pertinent information.

To get someone to attend a deposition or to come to trial and testify, you can use the court's *subpoena* power. A *subpoena* (Latin for "under penalty") is a court form that orders someone to appear in court. The clerk can give you the necessary form. Fill it out and serve it on the person you want to appear. You must show proof of service to the court, which you can often do by filling out a short affidavit on the subpoena form itself. Ask the clerk whether you must pay a witness fee and, if so, how much and whether it must be included with the subpoena.

If the other side is not responding to your discovery requests, you can file a motion asking the court to compel cooperation after the time for response expires. This is merely a pleading that informs the court that your requests were within the period allotted for discovery, were reasonable, violated none of the court's rules and are being ignored for no good reason.

Continuances. Throughout the process, you will encounter deadlines that you simply cannot ignore. Time limits are set for answering a complaint, for answering interrogatories, for answering summary judgment motions, etc. These deadlines can be 10, 20, 40 or more days. As a result of these time limits, it is common to ask for *continuances,* also called an *enlargements of time.* (Beware: in some states, these names mean different things.)

To get more time, ask the other side to agree to a continuance, and then file notice of your agreement with the court. If the other side doesn't consent, you can file a formal request with the court. It will probably be granted, especially if it is the first time you've asked for an extension, if the extension you want isn't too long and if you have a good reason.

Continuances are a major reason cases take so long. That's because they are so common. As a matter of professional courtesy, lawyers almost never refuse to consent to each other's requests for more time. They realize that they, too, may someday need extra time. Be prepared for such requests and know that you have this option as well, if you need it. Unfortunately, there is a chance that *pro se* litigators might not receive the same kind of courtesy as lawyers do.

PRE-TRIAL STAGE

There are two types of *motions* that ask the judge to decide a case before trial: a *motion to dismiss* and a *motion for summary judgment.* You have already read about motions to dismiss in the "Pleadings" section above. A motion for summary judgment asks the judge to review all pleadings and additional affidavits (sworn statements of the facts of the case) and to rule in your favor. To grant a motion for summary judgment, the court must decide that, even if the facts are what the other side says they are, this still would not be enough to support a legal claim. Sometimes a court will hold a hearing on the summary judgment motion, but usually this is brief and no witnesses are questioned.

In order to file a motion you need to give a *notice of motion* to the other party—usually a copy of the motion itself along with additional information, including when the motion will be heard, what the grounds are for such a motion and what supporting documents you will be referring to. Every motion should have a short description of the rule of law applicable to this state. If the issue is more complex, then a lengthier explanation citing different legal authorities would be appropriate. The notice should also reference supporting documents, copies of relevant documents or statement of the facts. At the end of the motion, you should include a proposed order that the judge can sign if she grants your motion. A party must have a valid legal basis for filing a motion, otherwise sanctions might be handed out to the party and his attorney.

When motions are not opposed, they are usually granted by the judge without a hearing. If a motion is opposed, then the judge might decide based on papers alone without a hearing, or he will call a short hearing, sometimes giving each side just a few minutes to argue their reasons for favoring or objecting to the motion. The judge usually makes the decision shortly after the hearing.

The party filing the motion must schedule a court hearing. In order to schedule a court hearing for a pre-trial motion, you should call the court clerk. The court clerk will tell you how to proceed. Typically, the clerk will ask you for your case number as well as the exact date in which you would like to have the hearing. Motions will probably only be heard on certain days of the week. After setting up the hearing, you should check again to confirm the date one day before.

During the hearing, the clerk will state the name of the case, and then you and the other party will approach the counsel table. The moving party (the party making the motion) will argue first—make sure that when arguing you are not simply repeating what the judge has already read on paper. After hearing the arguments of both sides, the judge will either make an immediate ruling or announce that she will rule at a later date. If the judge grants a motion for summary judgment, then the side making the motion wins the case. If the judge denies the motion, then the case will go to trial.

Before the trial begins, the judge will hold a pre-trial conference. At a pre-trial conference, the parties will try to clarify what matters remain unresolved and what evidence will be presented at trial. Each side will present a "pre-trial memorandum" that will list the contested as well as the uncontested facts, the exhibits it plans on showing at trial and who will testify. There also might be some information on jury instructions.

You can also expect other pre-trial activities such as settlement discussions and conferences in the judge's office. During these conferences, the judge might ask you to negotiate with the other party regarding the established facts to which both sides agree. These are recorded as stipulations. You should also take good notes of the stipulations, since they are likely to come up during trial, and you want to make sure that the other party does not deny them later.

If you are trying a case *pro se*, it is not a good idea to request a jury trial. Even veteran lawyers find that jury trials are expensive, protracted and difficult. As a nonlawyer, your difficulties will be even greater. In a trial without a jury (also known as a bench trial), some judges may be willing to guide you through the court's rules and procedures. In a jury trial, however, the judge will adhere to the rules much more strictly and the judge will not cut you any slack, lest he or she appear to be playing favorites. Do not request a jury trial yourself. If your adversary requests a jury trial, it's time to look for legal help.

A trial is divided into several parts. First, each side will present its opening statement. Next, the plaintiff presents his case, during which he presents his evidence through the testimony of witnesses. The defendant may cross-examine these witnesses. After the plaintiff is finished presenting his case, the defendant presents his case, during which the plaintiff may cross-examine the defendant's witnesses. Next, the plaintiff may call rebuttal witnesses to try to disprove what the defendant's witnesses said. Finally, each side presents its closing argument.

TRIAL STAGE

Opening statement. Right after your case is called, trial begins. First, each side gets to make an opening statement—introductory remarks about the facts, your theory of the case and an outline of how you plan to proceed. This is your chance to describe the documents or other evidence you expect to get from your witnesses, and then explain why it supports your interpretation of the facts. Finally, tell the judge exactly what you would like the outcome to be. It is important to remember that this is not the time to argue with the other side.

Do not be surprised if the judge cuts you off right away. If you feel like you have something important to say, ask the judge for time to make a specific point. The opening statement should be no longer than a few minutes. The defendant can choose to make his opening statement either after the plaintiff's statement or after the plaintiff's witnesses (this is called "reserving" your opening statement).

During your opening statement, make sure you only refer to evidence that is sure to come up at trial. This would include information that either you received through personal knowledge, in a letter or some kind of record (government or business), in discovery (in a deposition or in an interrogatory) or in statements from a witness you have interviewed many times.

Direct examination. Each witness is questioned first by the party who called him to testify. This is called direct examination. As a *pro se* litigator, you are likely to be testifying as well. You should probably be the first or the last to testify. If you testify first, you have the opportunity to immediately place the case in the right context. If you testify last, you may be able to leave a lasting final impression.

When you testify, you will sit in the witness stand, and present your testimony. You are allowed to return to the counsel table to review your notes, as long as you ask the judge for permission to do so.

As each witness approaches the stand, he or she takes an oath. As you examine each of your witnesses, make sure that an "easy-to-follow" story is coming across. To get the most out of your witnesses, you need to prepare carefully and ask short, clear questions. This will be easier if your questions follow a chronological order. Focus the judge's attention on the most relevant facts. It is also a good idea to let witnesses testify in their own words – this lends more credibility to their account, and it does not look like you are putting words into their mouths.

However, there is a limit as to how open direct examination questions can be. Narrative questions, such as "Tell us your story," are generally restricted since witnesses might divulge evidence that was ruled inadmissible or might waste the courts time with unnecessary information. However, open questions, which are slightly more specific and in the context of previous answers, are permitted, such as "After event X took place, what happened?" Closed questions, such as "What time was it when event X happened?" are always accepted. The most problematic questions are leading questions, such as "You were drunk that night, weren't you?" This suggests an answer to the witness and violates the basic principles behind direct examination.

It is also important to establish a witness' personal knowledge. This means that you must show that your witness personally observed what he or she is now telling the court. When the testimony is regarding a conversation, you should have the witness establish when the conversation took place, who was present, and any other important details that might be relevant. If a witness says that he does not remember, you can ask if giving him a particular document would help refresh his memory. Then, show him the document and mark it as an exhibit. After the witness has seen the document, take it back, and go back to your place and ask the witness again. If the witness is really not cooperating, you can ask the judge to treat him as a hostile witness, and then you are allowed to ask leading questions mentioned above. After you finish your examination, say, "No further questions."

Cross-examination. After one side questions a witness, the other side has a chance to ask questions. This is called cross-examination. Cross-examination is limited to matters testified about on direct examination. If the opposing side wants to ask the witness questions on other topics, she or he needs to call the witness as his or her own witness. When the judge says, "You may now cross-examine," feel free to ask the judge for a few minutes to put your questions together. When you cross-examine, you can read all of your questions directly from your notes. And unlike direct examination, you can ask leading questions during cross examination, such as: "And then you saw the green sedan hit the red Volvo, didn't you?"

One of the main functions of cross-examination is the impeachment of witnesses—showing why their testimony is not credible. This can be done primarily in three different ways:

Bias. The witness would benefit either emotionally or financially from a particular outcome of the case. For example, the witness is the plaintiff's wife.

Impaired Ability to Observe. For example, if at the time of the car accident the witness was in a spot where she couldn't possibly have seen if the traffic light was red or green.

Prior Inconsistent Statement. For example, the witness who now says that he saw exactly what happened, only a week before said that he couldn't see clearly what happened.

Remember to be respectful toward your witnesses. Usually cross-examination consists of no more than a few questions. Realize also that in real life cross-examinations are much less dramatic than on TV. Do not be surprised if you are unable to change much of a witness' testimony during this short time.

If after your opponent's cross examination, you feel that you have to answer the points he raised, you can ask the judge for a re-direct examination. After the redirect there might be a brief re-cross, but no other rounds of questioning.

Objections. During both direct and cross-examination, objections can be raised if the opposing party is not following the procedural rules or is inquiring into something not permitted by the rules of evidence. The judge often has a good deal of discretion regarding objections. What one judge might find to be an appropriate objection, another might disagree with completely. If you get an objection that you do not understand, you can approach the bench and ask for more specific directions.

To make objections, stand up, speak only to the judge and state your objection quickly and succinctly, before the witness gets a chance to answer. Be polite. Also, don't argue your objection until the judge agrees to hear you.

Try not to raise too many objections. Object only when you believe the evidence to be important. As a *pro se* litigant, if you get into an objections war with the other party, you are very likely to lose.

Closing Argument. After all of one side's witnesses have been questioned, it is time for the party's closing arguments (a plaintiff may ask the judge to reserve a small amount of time for a rebuttal, usually five minutes, after the defendant's closing argument). The closing argument is your chance to take the evidence you presented and make all the necessary connections and conclusions to show how you proved your case.

First, specify which issues still need to be addressed in light of the elements of your case, any rulings the judge might have made during trial, or any stipulations that were agreed to by both parties. Then, if you are the plaintiff, simply go through each element of your case that still needs to be proven, highlighting the best evidence you have to prove each one. Make sure also to show why the evidence the other party presented does not disprove your elements, and if any of the other party's evidence is incorrect, tell the judge why. You will also want to discuss the credibility of the other party's witnesses, but try not to accuse the other party of outright lying. Conclude by telling the judge what you want and why you believe this would be fair.

THE VERDICT

After both sides have made their closing arguments, the judge will reach a decision, often after calling for a recess.

APPEALS

If you lose, you probably have the right to appeal to a higher court. To preserve that right, you must file a notice of appeal within a specified time after the decision is rendered, usually 30 or 60 days. Filing an appeal is beyond the scope of this guide, which deals with trial procedure. Also, appellate litigation is much more complicated and technical than trial litigation and requires a great deal of legal knowledge and training. For this reason, HALT strongly recommends that you hire a lawyer if you wish to appeal your case.

EXECUTING (OR COLLECTING) A JUDGMENT

Taking your case to court and winning doesn't necessarily put the money in your pocket. The court actually does surprisingly little to help you retrieve the money they have ruled as rightfully yours. So before you decide to sue in court, the question you should be asking yourself is, "Can I collect if I win?"

Once you have a court judgment, there are legal methods available to you, as a creditor, for collecting the amount owed. Although some of the processes can be long, detailed and involved, the up side is that your patience is often rewarded because most judgments are binding for at least 10 years and can easily be renewed.

Informal collection. Your first approach should be to write a letter to the person who owes you money and politely demand payment (don't forget to include a copy of the judgment order). Remember to wait until the allotted time for an appeal has expired before you send the letter. If you're lucky, she will respond with a letter and a check. If she fails to respond, however, you must adopt a more aggressive policy.

Oral examination. To begin with, you must know what her assets are so that you know what sources can be tapped for your payment. Unless she has a job, money in the bank or real property, it will be incredibly hard, if not impossible, to collect on your judgment.

If you do not know the extent or location of her assets, you can compel her appearance in court to get that information through a series of questions. This step is known as an oral examination, and the forms for this procedure can be picked up at the court clerk's office.

She must answer all your questions, or risk being held in contempt of court. Should she fail to appear for the oral examination, then the court has the power—upon your request—to issue a warrant for her arrest. Once in court, if she is uncooperative and refuses to answer questions straightforwardly, ask her to take out her keys and go through them one-by-one to learn about possible houses, cars, etc.

Attachment or garnishment. If you already know where her assets are, then ask your court clerk for a *writ of execution*. This is a court order that can be obtained for a nominal fee. It allows you to put a levy on her wages (garnishment) or other property (attachment). You need to complete the writ, make copies and send it (along with a copy of the judgment) to the sheriff or marshal of the county in which the assets are located. Most states have a time limit that ranges between 60 and 80 days, so be sure to get the writ out as soon as you realize the payment is being delayed.

You can help the sheriff or marshal do their job by giving them all the information you've collected about her assets (e.g., the make, model, year and color of her car, or the name and address of her employer or the address and account number of her bank), as well as several copies of the writ so that the sheriff can keep one and give the other to her.

Keep in mind that most states exempt a certain amount of property from levying. For example, on average, state and federal law permits you to garnish only 25 percent of her wages—or even less—depending on the amount of money she makes. You cannot garnish from Social Security, unemployment, pension or disability checks.

Because your court order is formally filed against her employer, the employer has an incentive to give you the money before paying it to her. Similarly, money may be gained from the sale of her car, but a portion of the car's equity will remain exempt; thus, if she hasn't paid for most of the car, there may be little money left above the exemption minimum. Moreover, in some states, you are unable to levy an automobile if it is the person's "tool of trade," meaning that it is used to conduct business.

If the major source of her money is real property (real estate), then you must consider placing a lien on it. A lien basically changes a court judgment into a claim against whatever property is subject to the lien. In some states this process is referred to as an "Abstract of Judgment."

You can pick up the abstract form at the court and, after it's filled out, file it with the County Recorder's office in the county where the property is located. Most states require you to file an abstract for each piece of property you wish to have a legal claim for, or a lien on. Some will allow one form to cover all possible properties.

Liens are fairly passive measures that most likely won't push your debtor into bankruptcy. But if she files for bankruptcy under Chapter 7 of the Federal Bankruptcy Act and lists you as a creditor, then most of your rights to collect a judgment disappear. Part of the bankruptcy code is "lien avoidance" which allows her to completely wipe out a lien on her property. There are some exceptions, but it is wise to make sure, before filing a lien, that the she hasn't already gone into bankruptcy. One way to do that is by searching public records.

If she tries to sell the property to a third party, your debt will remain recorded, and therefore must be paid off by the third party. There are no laws that require a lien to be paid before property is sold. However, most prospective buyers check to see if there are any outstanding debts before they purchase, so it is unlikely that your debtor will be able to sell anything until her debts have been paid.

CHAPTER 7

Judges

When we think about those responsible for the administration of justice, judges are the first to come to mind. They are the key players in the judiciary branch. The mere title of "judge" carries with it an aura of prestige and power. In the courtroom, judges sit elevated above the others. A sense of authority and infallibility surrounds them, much as the black robes they wear.

Yet, for all the impact judges' decisions have on the lives of individuals and the conduct of society, the average citizen knows little about the people wearing those robes. Who are the people who become judges? How are corrupt or incompetent judges dealt with? Where do judges get their power and what happens if it's abused? This and the next five chapters will answer these questions for both federal and state judges.

THE IDEAL AND THE REALITY

The ideal trial-court judge is an impartial, objective decision-maker, dispassionately considering a dispute between others. Personal bias and outside influence have no bearing on the ideal judge's decision. Rather, the judge is able to mute personal bias and objectively apply the law to the facts presented in court with logic, relying on precedent and a sense of what is fair and just.

In reality, it's not so simple.

Judges are, first and foremost, human beings. They bring to the bench with them their own feelings and opinions, ailments and emotions. Each has been shaped by different influences and experiences that bear subconsciously on the decisions that judge is asked to make.

Furthermore, who gets to be a judge is, more often than not, a political choice. It is a rare event that a governor or a president will appoint someone with a dramatically different viewpoint to the prestigious position of judge. As one writer has stated, "A judge is a member of the bar who once knew a governor." Thus, those who become judges may not necessarily be the most qualified candidates for the job in the ideal world. This is not to say that few judges are qualified: almost all are. However, they are not necessarily the best qualified.

Even with the "best" people, perfection on the bench should not be expected. They are still people, subject to the same limitations as other people. What should be demanded are conscientious, hardworking, temperate judges who are aware of their own personal biases and try to mute them, who are knowledgeable in the law and unyielding in their allegiance to fairness and justice.

WHAT JUDGES DO

Judges are responsible for settling disputes between individuals and conflicts between the government and its citizens. Judges get their authority from the constitutions and laws of the states and nation. The laws that confer jurisdiction upon a *court* to hear and decide cases also give *judges* in that court authority to make legally binding judgments. For example, when it is said that a small-claims court has no jurisdiction over a child-support battle, it means that a judge sitting in small-claims court has no power to order someone in that court to pay back child support.

The most visible work of trial judges is what they do in the courtroom. It's up to the judge to keep the courtroom orderly. The judge decides when the day's session will begin, end and break for recesses. The judge manages the flow of cases called for that day. During a trial, the judge oversees its conduct and pace. The judge listens to and questions attorneys, litigants and witnesses. Finally and most importantly, the judge makes rulings, gives orders and renders judgments.

In their offices, called *chambers*, judges study and decide cases they didn't rule upon in the courtroom. They are expected to read journals and cases to keep up with the latest developments in the law and judicial decisions. They also tend to administrative duties, such as supervising their support staff and meeting with other judges of the court to discuss case flow, court policies and court rules.

JUDICIAL INDEPENDENCE

Within the bounds of their authority, judges are given a great deal of discretion. They have a broad range within which the exercise of their powers is appropriate. To some, it may seem they have too much latitude, but judicial independence is a long-held and highly regarded value in our culture. Historically, we have insisted that our judges be able to act and decide freely, without fear of retribution or influence by offers of favors.

Judges must be entrusted to make fair but unpopular decisions, to protect individuals or minorities within a community from a popular, majority opinion that is unjust. At the same time, this independence must be balanced by accountability to the public they are paid to serve. To this end, judges may render decisions that do not strictly follow the letter of the law in order to reinforce public policy in accordance to the needs of the community.

JUDICIAL ACCOUNTABILITY

Because judges are given wide discretion, some mechanism must ensure that they adhere to high standards of fairness and impartiality. As part of our system of government, judges must ultimately be accountable to the public.

This judicial accountability is provided, in theory, by the way judges are selected. Some are chosen through popular election, others are appointed by executive branch officials and still others are nominated by a public commission subject to the approval of the chief executive.

However, the theory of public accountability rarely works in practice. Accountability through the selection process is remote at best. Many of us weaken it further by not participating in the selection process and, when we are involved, by not bothering to learn about the judicial candidates. In fact, most of us don't become familiar with our local judges until we are forced to face one in a courtroom. That is when we may be rudely awakened by the clash between our ideal notions about judges and the reality.

Once judges are selected, we have other options for enforcing accountability: reelections, retention elections, impeachment, resolution, recall, appeals, disqualification motions, complaints to a judicial conduct organization or lawsuits against a judge. Some options are more appropriate for widespread public involvement and others are better suited for individuals who have a specific problem with a judge. Thus, the options vary in practicality and results. They are all discussed fully in the next five chapters.

The American people deserve a legal system operated by judges who are honest and publicly accountable. HALT closely monitors the judicial system to ensure that it is operating ethically and responsibly. HALT's Judicial Integrity Project seeks to strengthen protections against judicial conflicts of interest and to educate consumers about their rights. The Judicial Integrity Project focuses on two key issues: financial disclosure and junkets for judges—the corporate practice of wining and dining judges under the guise of "judicial education."

CHAPTER 8

Selecting State Judges

Most state judges are selected in one of five ways:

- *Partisan election.* Candidates run for judicial office under a political party label.

- *Nonpartisan election.* Candidates run without official party affiliation.

- *Legislative election.* The state legislature elects the judges.

- *Gubernatorial appointment.* The governor (sometimes with the consent of another body, such as the state senate or executive council) selects the judges.

- *Merit plan.* A judicial nominating commission submits names of candidates and the governor makes a final selection from among them. This is also referred to as the commission plan, the Missouri plan (after the state that first adopted it) and the Kales plan (after Albert Kales, who developed the prototype in 1913).

Few states use identical plans and most use different methods at different levels of the court system. Also, one method might be used to choose a judge at the beginning of a term and a different method for filling the same office left vacant in the middle of a term. To learn how judges are initially selected for the various courts in your state, see Appendix I.

The most common method is merit-selection, some form of which is used in 34 states. Seventeen of the states either adopted or expanded use of the plan between 1980 and 1999. Judicial elections are the next most common form of selection. Thirty states use elections to choose some, most or all of their judges.

In only four states (California, Maine, New Hampshire and New Jersey) do governors alone appoint judges. In three states (Hawaii, Illinois and Louisiana) the judges themselves elect or appoint their colleagues. Virginia and South Carolina are the only states in which the legislature appoints all their judges.

The length of state judges' terms also varies—from three years to as long as a life term with "good behavior." Terms of from four to 10 years are most common.

PROS AND CONS

Direct election. Seventeen states hold nonpartisan elections and another 13 hold partisan elections for some or all of their judges. The main attraction of this method is public accountability: the judge is placed in office by the public and can be removed by the public. An elected judge, especially in a nonpartisan race, is presumably less likely to be subject to control or favor by another public official or politician with a personal agenda.

Although judicial elections are attractive to those who believe the general public should choose its own judges, in practice the benefits of public accountability aren't always achieved. It is a common phenomenon in states with elective systems that most elected judges are not truly elected; they are appointed by the governor to fill a vacancy. This is because departing judges frequently time their retirement to allow a governor to appoint a successor. Once appointed, these judges must run for reelection, but almost all judges win reelection, often unopposed as an "incumbent judge."

Public apathy is a factor as well. Judicial elections have an even lower voter turnout than legislative elections, due in part to lack of voter interest and in part to a lack of information about the candidates. Low voter turnout also happens because judicial races are often uncontroversial, and are of little interest to the average voter. The citizen who does vote typically chooses a judge because of name recognition, party affiliation or personality, rather than ability or judicial temperament.

One problem with direct election of judges in partisan races is that control of judgeships often passes to political party bosses or special-interest groups. On the other hand, in nonpartisan elections, although this feature is not as pronounced, the lack of a party label does erase what is often the typical voter's only way of identifying the candidate.

Yet another objection to judicial elections is that highly-qualified candidates who scorn politics and campaigning are left out and those who do campaign are likely to be asked for political favors by their supporters once they are in office.

Gubernatorial appointment. In four states the governor appoints judges without the help of a nominating commission, but the selections are subject to confirmation by the state senate. The flaw in this system is that a governor may have in mind considerations other than competency and fitness when appointing judges. It is not uncommon for a governor to use the appointive power to reward someone for past services or for future political advantage.

Legislative election. This form of election is currently used in only two states, Virginia and South Carolina. Where it is in use, legislators tend to use judgeships to reward their colleagues or former colleagues in the statehouse. South Carolina, though, modified its legislative election of judges in 1996, even though the legislature had directly elected the state's judges throughout its history. By the mid-1990s, all five Supreme Court justices and more than half the Circuit Court judges in the state had served in the General Assembly before being elected to the bench. In 1996, South Carolina voters were angered enough to approve a constitutional amendment creating a Judicial Merit Selection Commission. This commission considers the qualifications of judicial nominees and submits up to three names to the legislature.

Merit plan. Several variations of the merit plan are in use. Features common to all of them are screening by a nominating commission and appointment by the governor. South Carolina is the lone state with a nominating commission and legislative election. The accepted definition of a "true" merit plan is one in which a permanent, nonpartisan commission of nonlawyers and lawyers independently recruits and screens candidates and submits a list of their names to the governor, who makes the appointment from that list. After that, the judge is subject to periodic retention elections in which the sole question is whether that judge should remain in office.

Variations include commissions composed only of lawyers and commissions that only review the nominations of other governmental units or officials.

The merit plan was designed to assure well-qualified judicial candidates by using the nominating commission to select them and to preserve public accountability by making the selected judges subject to retention elections.

The merit-plan system is perhaps the best yet devised for selecting judges, yet it falls short of its stated goals in several respects. Ample room still exists for political influence, even under a "true" merit plan. In appointing nonlawyer commission members, the governor can choose those with the same political values. As some observers note, the commission is often made up of the same people the governor would consult about nominees if the merit plan were not in place. Others believe the organized bar is freer to wield its considerable influence under merit plans than under other methods of judicial selection because of the bar's influence over the nominating commissions.

Yet another criticism of the merit plan is that, unless commission membership is rotated frequently, commission members can themselves become an elite rather than a truly representative group. Commission membership terms range from two to eight years, with four- and six-year terms most common.

Most "experts" agree that merit plans don't remove politics from the process. However, merit-plan proponents hope at least that the worst elements of partisan politics are eliminated—for instance, distributing judgeships as patronage or as rewards for previous political activity.

RETENTION ELECTIONS

Retention elections for judges have also failed to fulfill their intention of public accountability. The drawbacks of direct initial elections—for instance, low voter turnout—are not overcome in retention elections. Compared to direct elections, retention elections are even less interesting, because they do not involve a contest between candidates. The sole question in a retention election is whether the judge should stay or go. It is rare that a judge is turned out of office in this way. According to a study of retention elections in 2000, voters retained an average of 98.7 percent of judges.

However, divisive issues such as abortion or capital punishment do spark intense public interest in judicial elections, turning a retention election into single issue referendum on a judge's ruling. For example, Tennessee Supreme Court Justice Penny T. White was ousted in a 1996 retention election by voters incensed over her vote in one death penalty case.

A SHORT HISTORY

Judicial selection has been debated and experimented with throughout American history. Most changes have resulted from dissatisfaction with the existing system's failure to produce unbiased and independent judges. For instance, colonial judges were appointed by the king. After the American Revolution, the states reacted by giving the power to appoint judges not to the chief executive but to the legislatures elected by property-owners or to the governor only with the consent of the council.

With the rising influence of Jacksonian Democracy came movement toward a judiciary chosen not by property-owners, but by all citizens in popular elections, a "reform" spearheaded in New York in 1846. By the time of the Civil War, 24 of the 34 states were electing their judges.

It soon became obvious that the partisan election of judges was, like other elected public offices, subject to the control of political "machines." This prompted a movement in favor of nonpartisan elections, led by the organized bar. These also quickly came under attack because, even in nonpartisan elections, most candidates were chosen by party leaders.

After that "reform" removed party labels from judicial candidates, most voters knew even less about the candidates than they had before. By the early 1900s, many observers were speaking out against all elective systems, partisan or not. In 1913, judicial scholar Albert Kales devised an early model of what is now known as the merit plan, but no state adopted it until Missouri did so in 1940. Although retention elections in the merit plan suffer the same shortcomings as direct elections, the merit plan does include an aspect unlike that of any other judicial selection system in this country's history: initial screening and selection by a nominating commission with nonlawyer representation.

WHO THE JUDGES ARE

Studies conducted during the past 30 years conclude that no matter what method is used, the characteristics of judges selected tend to be much the same. Not all state constitutions or statutes require judges to hold a law degree or to have a specified amount of legal training or experience. In practice, however, most successful judicial candidates have a legal education, have been practicing attorneys and have had trial-court experience, despite research that shows that nonlawyer judges "are virtually indistinguishable from lawyer-judges in how they conceive and perform the key elements of their jobs." (*Judging Credentials,* Doris Marie Provine, University of Chicago Press, 1986.)

Most state judges have more than law degrees in common. They came from middle-class backgrounds, attended Ivy League or state university law schools and held other government positions, such as those of state legislator, prosecuting attorney or local judge, before joining the state bench. The majority is also politically active and politically well-connected, a logical result of the tie between recruitment of judicial candidates and state and local politics.

Most judges are also male and white, though many more female judges have been appointed since the first edition of **How Courts & Judges Work.** In 1985 just seven percent of the justices serving on state appellate courts were women, but by 2001 that number had increased to 23 percent. The number of minority judges in U.S. federal and state courts has grown as well. A 1985 study found that there were a total of 695 minority judges in the United States. A more recent study found that number had increased to

3,281 in 2001. What should not be surprising is that most of the new women and minority judges have many of the same characteristics as the majority of their colleagues. They, too, attended law schools at prestigious institutions of higher learning, were politically active and came from middle-class families.

CHAPTER 9

Selecting Federal Judges

According to the U.S. Constitution, all federal court judges are nominated by the President with the advice and consent of the U.S. Senate. They serve lifetime terms: once appointed, they cannot be removed from office as long as they are on "good behavior."

No educational or professional requirements for federal court judges are specified in the Constitution. To be a federal judge you do not have to be a practicing attorney or a member of the bar or even hold a law degree. By custom, however, all candidates for the federal bench are lawyers. And, as we will see, they tend to come from a select group of attorneys.

The simple process written into the Constitution has evolved into a complex screening system that now includes, along with the President and the Senate, the White House staff, the Department of Justice, the American Bar Association (ABA), state political leaders, state judges, the Federal Bureau of Investigation and no shortage of political maneuvering.

DISTRICT COURT SELECTION

The custom of "senatorial courtesy" dominates the selection of district court judges. This unwritten rule gives the two U.S. senators from the state in which the district is located unparalleled influence. (If the senators are of different political parties, the senator of the same political party as the President makes the choice alone.) The senators, through "senatorial courtesy," are virtually assured of getting their nominee appointed. Although the practice is rooted in tradition, not in the Constitution or legislation, it is so strong it operates as though written into law.

Because federal-district boundaries do not cross state lines, the two U.S. senators from the state in which a district vacancy has occurred are given a virtual "veto" over judicial candidates by use of the "blue slip"—an expression to the Senate Judiciary Committee of their views. Under "senatorial courtesy," the wishes of the senators are invariably respected, even by the President, who officially makes the appointment.

If the senator or senators and the President are of the same political party, the appointment of the senators' choice is virtually assured: the President knows that the senators can block appointment of a nominee not to their liking.

If the senators are of a different political party from the President's, the President has more say, but the senators may well insist on their own nominee in exchange for support for other Presidential appointments or for their needed votes on important legislation. Alternatively, they can swap their support for the President's choice in exchange for some other Presidential concession. Whatever the deal, "senatorial courtesy" gives the home-state senators a decided upper hand.

'COURTESY' AT WORK

As soon as a federal district court vacancy is announced, the senators from that state begin gathering names of possible nominees. Suggestions come from state judges, state political leaders, personal friends and judicial candidates themselves. The Justice Department—usually the attorney general and deputy attorney general—also takes an active role in seeking potential candidates.

The Justice Department and the senators' staffs work closely in collecting information about the candidates to determine whether they are legally qualified. They look into the candidates' educational background, legal experience, political party affiliation, attitudes on major issues, leadership abilities, temperament, intellect and health.

The White House staff screens candidates to make sure that they are politically acceptable to the President and communicates the President's wishes to the Attorney General.

Until the administration of President George W. Bush, the Justice Department sent the names of candidates to the American Bar Association (ABA). The ABA was formally involved in the screening of all federal judgeships from 1945-1999. The ABA's Standing Committee on Federal Judiciary conducted its own investigations, focused on the various candidates' professional backgrounds and legal histories. It ranked each candidate in one of four categories—"exceptionally well-qualified," "well-qualified," "qualified" or "not qualified." At the beginning of his administration, President George W. Bush put an end to the ABA's formal role. Over the years, the influence of the ABA waxed and waned with various presidents, but critics have suggested that the George W. Bush administration's paradigm enables the executive branch to maintain even greater control over the selection process, since the Department of Justice need no longer disclose its findings to the ABA.

The FBI is another routine participant in the screening. It is called upon to do a security clearance and loyalty check of each candidate.

The staffs of the state's two U.S. senators, the White House staff and the Justice Department engage in further negotiation and bargaining to reach agreement on a person whose name will be forwarded to the president for nomination.

The candidate's name is then sent by the president to the Senate Committee on the Judiciary, which holds hearings and makes a formal recommendation to the full Senate for its "advice and consent." It is in this committee that the wishes of the home-state senators, as expressed in the "blue slip," are paramount.

It takes a majority vote of the full Senate to approve the nominee. Because the president's people—the Justice Department and the White House staff— have worked closely with the senators' staffs, and because the tradition of senatorial courtesy is so strong, Senate approval is all but assured if the candidate is recommended by the Committee on the Judiciary.

Two examples. The strength of political influence overriding senatorial courtesy in the federal judicial selection process was exemplified by the nomination of R. Samuel Paz by President Bill Clinton in 1994. Paz was a prominent California civil rights attorney who was recommended to Clinton by California Senator Barbara Boxer, a fellow Democrat. Paz was rated "qualified" by the ABA and passed the scrutiny of the FBI and was considered a "shoo-in" for the federal bench. But after a Republican majority assumed the Senate in 1994, police groups and conservative organizations began to criticize the nominee for having represented clients in brutality cases against police. President Clinton subsequently withdrew his name, anticipating the nominee's likely rejection.

Party politics also played a significant role in the 1996 nomination of Missouri Supreme Court Justice Ronnie L. White to sit on the federal bench in the Eastern District of Missouri. White, an African-American, was recommended to President Clinton by Democratic congressman William L. Clay and introduced to the Senate Judiciary Committee by Clay and Missouri Republican Senator Christopher "Kit" Bond. Bond called White "a man of the highest integrity and honor" and said he had the "necessary qualifications and character" for the lifetime appointment. Despite the bipartisan support, White's nomination was held up in committee by Missouri's other Republican Senator John Ashcroft. Bond was reelected in 1998 by a wide margin (including 33 percent of Missouri's African-American vote).

However, in October of 1999, the Senate rejected White on a party-line vote, with Ashcroft and Bond leading the opposition. Bond's vote in particular sparked outrage among black leaders, who said that Bond had promised them during his senate campaign that he would support White.

APPEALS COURT SELECTION

Senatorial courtesy isn't nearly as significant in the selection of judges for the U.S. Circuit Courts of Appeals. Because the boundaries of circuits embrace more than one state, no pair of senators or state political organization can dominate the process.

Instead, a different "courtesy" operates: generally, an appeals court vacancy is filled by a person from the same state as the outgoing judge. For example, a judge on the Fifth Circuit Court of Appeals whose career and political life were shaped in Texas is likely to be succeeded by a Texan. Inasmuch as states within a given circuit are already represented fairly evenly by the judges on that Court of Appeals, the custom assures that such a distribution of judgeships continues. Senators negotiate with Justice Department staff and the White House staff in the selection of appeals court judges, much as they do with district court judgeships, but they must also bargain now with their colleagues from other states within the circuit. *(The map in Chapter 3 shows the boundaries of the federal circuits.)*

Two examples. Presidents have their political concerns addressed in the selection of nominees of judges to the Federal Courts of Appeals or Circuit Courts, and they often become closely involved in the nomination's process. Since federal judges are appointed for life, a president's choices of appellate court judges have legal, social and political impact far beyond the four- or eight-year term of the president. During his administration, President Jimmy Carter, in order to diversify the judiciary, set up a controversial Circuit Court Nominating Commission, a "merit plan" for the Federal Judiciary, to reshape the judicial selection process. The Commission upset many members of the Senate because it curtailed their traditional, starring role in the selection of judges. The end result of the Commission's operation was that the Carter administration greatly increased the number of women and minorities on the federal bench. The Commission was discontinued by the subsequent Reagan and Bush administrations, which preferred to keep their nomination preferences centrally controlled within the executive branch.

President George W. Bush, during his campaign for the presidency, promised to appoint judges that followed his conservative philosophy. Though the majority of his early appointments were approved by Congress, several controversial appellate court nominees set off political battles. In one such case, Miguel Estrada, a Bush nominee to the U.S. Court of Appeals, was a young, conservative lawyer. Though he had bipartisan support, he was viewed by many Democrats as too unpredictable a nominee. Estrada was unwilling, during his Senate confirmation hearings, to express his legal views (he asserted that it would be improper to provide information as to how he might rule on cases), and refused to provide the committee with any legal memos or writings from his clerkship for Supreme Court Justice Anthony Kennedy. With 51 seats held by Republicans in the Senate, a floor vote on Estrada would have given him the seat if the vote went along party lines. Senate Democrats were able to fend off his confirmation vote procedurally, by threatening to hold an extended debate or filibuster, which could only end by a 60-vote majority on the floor. Republicans, with only 51 votes, were unable to attract the support of nine Democrats needed to break the filibuster. After a stalemate of two years, Estrada withdrew his nomination to return to his law practice.

SUPREME COURT SELECTION

The president is the dominant actor in the initial screening of nominees to the Supreme Court. The Senate plays no significant role until the name of a candidate is submitted for confirmation. The president and attorney general gather the names of prospective nominees from congressional leaders of their party, state and federal judges, major interest groups, personal friends and political supporters. After the president makes his choice, the Senate Judiciary Committee conducts hearings on the nominee. A vote is then taken on the floor of the Senate for confirmation.

Although the Department of Justice, the FBI and the ABA's Standing Committee on the Federal Judiciary (until 2000) are all involved, the process depends much less on custom and tradition and more upon ideology and the political activities of candidates. Because Supreme Court justices are by far the most visible of all judges in the United States, the process of choosing them also draws more public attention.

For example, the nomination of Judge Robert H. Bork in 1987 by President Ronald Reagan provoked a national debate over the role of the United States Supreme Court and its justices. Bork was nominated to replace the retiring Justice Lewis Powell, an overall moderate on the court but a pro-civil rights swing vote on the issue. Bork's legal credentials were indisputable, having served on the faculty at Yale Law School, as Solicitor General and as a federal appeals court judge. But he was openly critical of the court's decisions in a number of areas including the constitutional right to privacy and the First Amendment. Bork's nomination sparked unprecedented grass-roots activism in his opposition. Television commercials and advertisements attacked his record on civil rights; letters from 1,925 law professors opposing his nomination were sent to the Senate. In Bork's five days of televised testimony before the Senate Judiciary Committee, he failed to ease the fear that his harsh criticism of several landmark Supreme Court decisions reflected the attitude he would bring to the court. The Senate Judiciary Committee voted 9-5 against his confirmation, but passed the nomination to the Senate floor where, after three days of debate, it was defeated 58-42.

From the appointing president's point of view, an ideal candidate for Supreme Court Justice is one who both shares the president's political views and provides symbolic representation to major groups of voters. Thus, when President Reagan chose Sandra Day O'Connor in 1982 as the first woman to serve on the high court, not only did he choose a jurist with a similar political outlook, he provided the nation with a highly visible sign of his belief in the abilities of women.

Selection of a Supreme Court Justice is an extremely political event. Almost all of the justices selected to sit on the court have political backgrounds, and nearly 60 percent of them were close political friends or acquaintances of the appointing president at the time of their selection. Clarence Thomas, for example, was appointed by President George Bush in 1991, and the two had previously worked together in the Reagan administration.

WHO THE JUDGES ARE

District and appeals courts. One would expect from the highly political nature of the judicial selection process, that most federal judges would have been politically active. According to a statistical study of federal district and appeals court judges, since the start of the Carter administration through the first two years of the George W. Bush administration, of the 1,028 district-court judges appointed, 59 percent had been previously involved in party politics; of the 248 appeals court judges appointed during the same 26 years, 68 percent were active in party politics. Not surprisingly, presidents also appoint a very high proportion of judges who are of the same political party—almost 84 percent of the 1,028 district-court appointees and 87 percent of the appeals-court judges since 1977.

According to the same study, Federal judges tend to be male (81 percent of both district and appeals court appointees) and white (84 percent of both district and appeals court appointees).

Although the law doesn't require it, all federal court judges are lawyers. Of the district court judges appointed since 1977, 48 percent attended public law schools, 14 percent attended Ivy League law schools and 38 percent attended other private law schools. Sixty percent of the appeals-court appointees attended Ivy League or private law schools.

Most appointees also have had previous judicial experience: 43 percent of district court and 53 percent of appeals court appointees served as judges.

Supreme Court Justices. The 113 justices that have served on the high court throughout its history are an even more homogeneous group. All but two, Sandra Day O'Connor and Ruth Bader Ginsburg, have been men and all but two, Thurgood Marshall and Clarence Thomas, have been white. Although they don't necessarily have prior judicial experience, Supreme Court Justices overwhelmingly have had prior histories of political activities.

CHAPTER 10

State Discipline

If you have a complaint about the behavior of a state court judge, you can file a grievance with the state's judicial conduct organization. Keep in mind, however, that even if your complaint is found valid and the judge is disciplined, the organization will *not* compensate you for any money you lost, nor will it change the outcome of any case the judge ruled on. As their founders intended, judicial conduct organizations were established to identify and respond to the disability or misconduct of individual judges, not to redress judicial decisions.

In 1999, 12,207 complaints about judges were acted upon in the 47 states (and the District of Columbia) for which statistics are available. Of those complaints, 90.5 percent were dismissed without a formal or informal hearing. Informal sanctions against judges were imposed five percent of the time. Formal sanctions, including censure, admonition, reprimand, suspensions and fines against judges were imposed in only about 2.25 percent of the cases. Sixteen judges were removed from office and another 62 judges left office during the investigation. During the period between 1980 and 2000, a total of 278 judges were removed from office as a result of discipline proceedings.

Although the number of complaints per year rose steadily during the 1980s, the rate of increase has slowed down. Between 1996 and 1999, the number of complaints increased three percent.

JUDICIAL CONDUCT ORGANIZATIONS

Judicial conduct organizations are called "commissions" in most states (as in the Kansas Commission on Judicial Qualifications). They are also named "committees" (Maine Committee on Judicial Responsibility), "councils" (Connecticut Judicial Review Council), "boards" (Ohio Board of

Commissioners on Grievances and Discipline) or even "courts" (Delaware Court on the Judiciary).

They were established by provisions in state constitutions, by referendum, by statute or by court rule. Beginning in 1960 with California and ending in 1981 with Washington, every state in the United States and the District of Columbia has established formal procedures to address questions of judicial misconduct and physical or mental incapacity. Most organizations are composed of six to 11 members representing some combination of judges, attorneys and nonlawyers. Typically, the judge members are appointed by the state supreme court, attorneys by the state bar and public members by the governor. Appendix III lists the names, addresses and telephone numbers of judicial conduct organizations for all states. HALT's Web site also provides links to the state judicial complaint agency for each of the 40 states whose agency is online at *www.halt.org.* Anyone—members of the public, lawyers, court employees, other judges—may file a complaint. Most commissions handle complaints against any state court judge, although some complaints against the judges of some limited-jurisdiction courts are handled separately by the state's supreme court.

The commission investigates the charges. In states with "unitary" systems, the commission holds a hearing, then orders or recommends a sanction to the state's highest court. In states with "two-tier" systems, the commission refers the charges and the findings of its investigation to a separate board or court for a hearing and recommendation.

WHAT IS AND ISN'T DISCIPLINED

It cannot be over-emphasized that a complaint will be dismissed without an investigation or hearing if it relates only to the merits of your case—if your *only* complaint is that the judge made a mistake in ruling against you. Remember, judges have wide discretion when exercising their judicial powers. A judge will not be disciplined for making a particular decision or even for making an error. The most common reason given for dismissal of a complaint is that the complainant was asking the judicial conduct organization to review the merits of litigation.

Instead, you must show that the *manner* in which the judge behaved or made the decision was inappropriate. You must show that the judge had fraudulent, corrupt, immoral, illegal or dishonest motives, or that the judge was physically or mentally incapable of carrying out judicial duties.

For example, a judge erroneously instructs the jury that it should rule in your favor if it finds *you* have proven your case when, in fact, the proper legal standard places the burden on your opponent to *disprove* your case. Your usual recourse in such a situation is to appeal the case to a higher court, *not* to file a disciplinary complaint. Errors in the law and mistakes in procedure are the sorts of things appeal courts are meant to redress. In most cases, they are not proper grounds for discipline.

If it can be shown, however, that the judge ruled a certain way because of a bribe or because of prejudice—say, ruling against you solely because of race or sex—it is appropriate to file a disciplinary complaint. Also, if a judge accumulates a record of such mistakes, even without improper motives, that record may be reason enough to investigate the judge's competence. Just because most complaints are rejected, don't be deterred from filing a complaint in an appropriate case. Even if your complaint is not acted upon, it may be considered if a judge is trying to advance to a higher position in the courts.

Charges of bias or dishonesty can be difficult to prove, however, and a pattern of legal errors is not likely to be noticed by a single litigant. Rather, it is more likely that such complaints will be brought by other judges, or by lawyers who regularly practice in the court. Further, disciplinary action won't be taken unless you can show the judge lacked impartiality and objectivity or had a disability—not simply that the judge was guilty of an oversight or mistake. And remember, if you want the ruling in your case changed, you must appeal the case to a higher court. Filing a disciplinary complaint won't do it.

GROUNDS FOR DISCIPLINE

The grounds for disciplining a judge are spelled out in each state's constitution, statutes or court rules. The following violations are typical. Note that a single instance of judicial misconduct can occasion more than one cause for discipline.

Willful misconduct. Wrongful acts that judges commit intentionally, knowing they are violating a rule of law or standard of behavior, are called willful misconduct. Sometimes a distinction is made between misconduct that is related and that which is unrelated to judicial duties. Examples of the former: Matthew W. McMillan, a Florida judge, promised to favor the state and the police in his campaign attacks on his opponent. He also made unfounded attacks on his opponent, the local court system and local officials, and he presided over a case in which he had a conflict of interest. The judge was removed from office. Oliver Spurlock, an Illinois judge, was removed from office for engaging in "intimidating and sexually inappropriate behavior in the courtroom toward the state's attorneys and for having sex in chambers with a court reporter." An example of willful misconduct unrelated to judicial duties happened in New Jersey. Wolf A. Samay, a trial court judge, was charged with driving while intoxicated. The judge resigned, but the Supreme Court of New Jersey thought his conduct reflected badly on the judiciary and required a public reproval.

Habitual intemperance. Persistent intoxication is also grounds for discipline. Robert A. Bradley, a California judge, was twice convicted of drunk driving and had been arrested four times for alcohol-related probation violations. The prosecution said that no other judge had suffered so many criminal convictions, come to work intoxicated, been barred from the courtroom as a security risk and been unable to perform his judicial duties because he was in jail. The judge was publicly censured and retired from the bench. He may not practice law in California.

Conduct prejudicial to the administration of justice. This is sometimes referred to as *conduct that brings the judicial office into disrepute.* It includes violations not committed with the intent of acting improperly but which nonetheless appear to the objective observer to be improper conduct.

For instance, Robert A. Ferreri, a judge in Ohio, was suspended for making false statements about parties to a custody proceeding after a Court of Appeal had reversed the judge's decision in the custody case.

In a recent Texas case, James Barr was removed for consistently referring to the female district attorneys as "babes." The tribunal found that the judge's conduct cast public discredit on the judiciary.

An issue receiving greater press attention lately is on judges who hear cases in which they have a financial conflict of interest. HALT has appeared in both print and non-print media in news stories in Missouri, Minnesota and New York, which document numerous instances in which U.S. District Court judges held a financial interest in a party appearing before them. Not only did the judges fail to recuse (disqualify) themselves from hearing the cases in which they held a conflict of interest, but in some instances the judges entered procedural and dispositive court orders. HALT has made efforts to secure support from Congress in helping to make the financial information of federal judges more accessible to the public.

Failure to perform judicial duties. Such failure includes excessive absences and tardiness, failing to decide cases within the allotted time, letting others sign warrants and failing to keep documents safe. For example, Lawrence F. Waddick, a Wisconsin Circuit Court judge, was suspended and then resigned after the Judicial Commission found that he had continually delayed deciding cases over a seven-year period and had filed false certificates regarding the status of his calendar.

Serious disability. Serious mental or physical disability is also handled by judicial conduct organizations in almost all states. Rather than being punished, however, the disabled judge is usually removed from office or asked to retire.

Incompetence, corruption, felony conviction, violation of the lawyers' Code of Professional Responsibility and **violation of the Code of Judicial Conduct** are other common grounds for disciplining judges.

The Code of Judicial Conduct (which is currently under review and is scheduled to be updated by 2005) is a set of model standards that govern judges' behavior. The code was formulated by lawyers on the American Bar Association's Special Committee on Standards of Judicial Conduct and approved by the ABA in 1972. The Code of Judicial Conduct was last revised in 1990, and 49 states and the District of Columbia have adopted the model code, many with modifications. Only Montana uses a judicial conduct code different from the ABA's model.

Judges are required to abide by the canons of ethics in the code. For example, Canon 2 states: "A judge should avoid impropriety and the appearance of impropriety in all of the judge's activities."

By itself, the code has few "teeth." It must be enforced through disciplinary procedures. A violation of the Code of Judicial Conduct is a basis for discipline, even though such a violation might also be named by one of the above categories.

PROCESSING A COMPLAINT

The following procedures are typical of those used by most judicial conduct organizations in processing complaints against judges. For specific information, contact the commission in your state. *(See Appendix III.)*

When you file a grievance against a judge, submit a written statement describing the specific circumstances and explaining what the judge did or did not do that constitutes misconduct. Some states require you to complete a form designed for this purpose, but most do not.

Your complaint will be reviewed to determine whether it has merit and whether the commission has jurisdiction. An example of a complaint dismissed out of hand because it has no merit is one that states, "I lost my case because the judge kept interrupting my attorney." Note, too, that the commission has jurisdiction only over complaints about judges in that state's court, and that in some states it does not discipline judges in limited-jurisdiction courts. In these states, judges in limited-jurisdiction courts are subject to a separate discipline system administered by the state supreme court.

If your complaint doesn't make it through the initial screening, it will be dismissed and you will be notified. (You will be informed of a dismissal at whatever stage it occurs.) While many commissions do not provide an explanation for dismissal, some may be willing to provide a rationale if you call the commission after you receive your notice of dismissal.

Otherwise, the commission conducts an investigation. The judge is notified of the charges and given a chance to respond. Many investigations end here, once the judge has had an opportunity to explain himself or herself.

If the investigation continues, the commission may question other judges, attorneys and witnesses about the impropriety and may request more information from you. Ask if you (the complainant) are allowed to attend all proceedings. Regardless, if the commission does not find enough evidence to proceed further, the complaint is dismissed at this stage. To this point—through the filing and investigation stages—the process is confidential. You, those conducting the investigation and those contacted by investigators are warned not to disclose any information about it.

In some cases the judge's wrongdoing is not considered serious enough to warrant a formal sanction yet worthy of what is considered "informal action." This usually means the judge is warned and the investigators receive the judge's assurances that the behavior will be corrected. This occurs in almost 52 percent of the cases that aren't immediately dismissed.

If the investigation reveals the judge probably did engage in misconduct, the commission holds a formal hearing or, in states with two-tier systems, brings charges against the judge before a second adjudicating body. In 22 states, confidentiality ends at this point, when formal charges are filed.

If the commission or the second body, after reviewing the record, finds that disciplinary action or removal is warranted, it recommends this to the state's highest court. Nineteen states make the proceedings public at this point. That court may request more information or listen to arguments by each side, then decide to reject, accept or modify the commission's findings and recommended sanction. Nine states and the District of Columbia make public the fact of an investigation only if a public sanction is ordered.

SANCTIONS

In states that discipline judges who are convicted of a felony, the sanction is removal from office. In all other situations, the commission or court determines the sanction case-by-case. Almost all states use the following sanctions:

Private admonition, censure, reprimand. All of these terms mean essentially the same thing: a commission or court informs a judge in confidence that he or she has been found guilty of misconduct. The private "slap on the wrist" is intended to ask the judge to "go and sin no more." This happened in 48 percent of the cases in which sanctions were imposed in 1999. These sanctions are kept confidential and will not appear on a judge's public record.

Public censure, reprimand. This means that there is public disclosure of a judge's wrongdoing. This occurred in about 26 percent of the sanctioned cases in 1999.

Vacation of office. This happened in 15 percent of the cases in 1999.

Removal. This occurred in four percent of the 1999 cases that ended in sanctions.

A number of methods have been established to remove state judges. Most states' constitutions set forth the removal methods that are available. Most states employ some form of removal that involves the state's highest court and the state's judicial conduct organization.

Suspension. Most states also use temporary removal from judicial duties. This was used as a final sanction in more than three percent of the 1999 cases that ended in sanctions.

Costs, fines. In some states the judge may be fined or ordered to pay the costs of the investigation or witnesses. This was used in only one case of the 1999 cases that ended in sanctions.

Limitations, conditions on duties. The judge may be given a reduced caseload or may not be assigned new cases for a specified time or pending rehabilitation.

Discipline as an attorney. The judge may be suspended from the practice of law or disbarred. In some states, disbarment as an attorney is automatic cause for removal from judicial office. Other states require a separate investigation by the judicial commission before a judge can be removed.

EFFECTIVENESS OF JUDICIAL CONDUCT COMMISSIONS

Little evaluation has been done of the work of present judicial conduct organizations. What is known is that their effectiveness varies widely from state to state. In theory, the procedures are at least an improvement over *impeachment, removal* or *recall,* which, before judicial conduct organizations, were the only ways to rid the bench of unsatisfactory judges in states that did have judicial elections.

Impeachment is described in detail in Chapter 11. The constitutions of 47 states have impeachment provisions. Hawaii, North Carolina and Oregon appear to be the only states without them. The process is similar to the process for removing federal judges. The lower house of the state legislature investigates and votes on the charges (Articles of Impeachment) and the upper house holds a trial on the charges, with its members as jury.

Resolution is a way some state legislatures can remove judges without formal investigations or hearings. In some states, both houses simply vote to remove the judge. In others, both houses vote to ask the governor to do so.

Recall is also provided for in the constitutions of some states. It is similar to initiative and referendum procedures in that a specified number of voters must sign a petition to have a judge's recall placed on the ballot. The judge is then removed if enough votes are cast favoring the removal.

These methods are rarely used because they are time-consuming, cumbersome and costly. In the last 15 years, only two state court judges have been impeached. Only one was convicted under articles of impeachment. Five more judges were involved in the impeachment process. In 1997, California judge Nancy Wieben Stock was the subject of a recall attempt after she granted O.J. Simpson custody of his children, but the recall attempt was unsuccessful.

The grounds for impeachment, resolution or recall are usually severely limited. For instance, in Minnesota a judge may be impeached for "corrupt conduct in office or for crimes and misdemeanors." This means lazy, inept or arbitrary judges cannot be sanctioned by these methods, and even if they could, the only sanction usually available is the drastic one of removal from office.

Legislatures don't often consider judicial discipline a priority and recall is almost always an expensive measure. Thus, these methods provide little practical means for dealing with problem judges and are clearly not suited for handling less serious offenses.

In contrast, judicial conduct organizations are staffed independently of the legislature or judiciary, and commission members presumably are chosen for their ability and desire to do the job. As a result, judicial discipline is no longer a task begrudgingly undertaken by legislatures, although the traditional methods of impeachment and resolution are still available. A further advantage is that commissions may recommend sanctions other than removal, making it possible to deal with and correct moderately errant judges before their behavior becomes more serious.

At the least, commissions give the public a formal means of complaining about judges. Whether they provide greater public accountability remains to be seen.

Conflicting goals. According to the ABA's 1990 Model Code of Judicial Conduct, the Code "is designed to provide guidance to judges and candidates for judicial office and to provide a structure for regulating conduct through disciplinary proceedings." In the process of revising the Model Code, the delegates of the ABA considered the views of the members of the judiciary, the bar and the general public. In the 1995 ABA Model Rules for Judicial Disciplinary Enforcement, the preamble states: "The regulation of judicial conduct is critical to preserving the integrity of the judiciary and enhancing public confidence in the judicial system." However, not all those involved in judicial discipline—commission administrators, bar groups, judicial groups, scholars and observers—consider public protection or public confidence in the judiciary the paramount goal of judicial discipline. To many of them, the public's needs are secondary to the main goal of discipline: ensuring a competent judiciary. In their view, judges and lawyers know best how to assess what constitutes misconduct and should therefore be the primary users of the complaint mechanism. Also, they contend, the process should assure that judges who make mistakes are promptly corrected or removed from office if they are unable or unwilling to change their conduct. They believe the public is ill-served by using the complaint mechanism. Public complaints, they say, arise mainly from discontented litigants, who are bound to be dissatisfied when their complaints are then dismissed because they don't raise the right questions.

HALT disagrees. That position is inconsistent with the goal of instilling public confidence in the judiciary. If judicial conduct organizations insist on focusing on judicial competence, they must still educate the public about why complaints are dismissed for "lack of jurisdiction" or why investigations don't result in discipline.

What would best serve the public are judicial commissions that seek first to protect the public, not the professionals of the bench. Public-disclosure laws are needed and the public must be assured that its complaints will be investigated and judges disciplined with vigor.

Presently, formulating rules and carrying out judicial discipline are done mostly by lawyers and judges. The public needs to have more meaningful involvement in these processes. Finally, the public needs to do its part to provide accountability through the judicial selection process. Greater participation in choosing who assumes the bench will not eliminate the need for discipline, but it should reduce the frequency of complaints.

That the present secrecy clashes with the need for public accountability is exemplified by the problem caused by Nevada's "gag rule" laws mandating confidentiality for misconduct complaints filed against Nevada judges. A person who files a complaint against a Nevada judge is prohibited from disclosing to anyone that a complaint has been filed, unless and until the commission issues a formal finding indicating it is reasonable to believe there was judicial misconduct. If no such finding is made, the complainant may not disclose the existence of the complaint.

Over-reaction to criticism. Judges sometimes overreact to criticism, whether from lawyers or litigants. This requires constant monitoring. Judges will be told the name of the complainant, so retribution is always a possibility and should be taken into consideration before filing a complaint. Judges have responded to their critics by holding them in contempt of court and by fining or imprisoning them. In some cases, lawyers have been reported to the state bar.

In one case, Harvard Professor Alan Dershowitz so angered a judge with criticisms he had made of the judiciary in his book *Reversal of Fortune* that the judge banned Professor Dershowitz from appearing in his court. These kinds of abuses of judicial authority should not be tolerated.

The 1990 Model Code of Judicial Conduct does emphasize a judge's responsibility to report known judicial (and lawyer) misconduct. A judge who knows of a violation "shall" report it to the "appropriate authority." The Code, in effect, requires judges to report serious misbehavior of other judges and lawyers to disciplinary organizations. Lawyers have a unique advantage in identifying undesirable judges and bringing complaints against them: unlike clients, they can compare the behavior of different judges and watch the same judge's performance on a succession of cases. Unfortunately, lawyers are often those most reluctant to complain because they fear not only flagrant retribution but also more subtle reactions from the judges in whose courts they must practice. They know that, consciously or not, a judge is likely to hold lawyer-critics in disfavor, possibly enough to affect the way the judge rules on the next case those lawyers bring to that court.

PEREMPTORY CHALLENGES TO JUDGES

If you are involved in a lawsuit and you feel that the judge that is assigned to your case is unfair, either because you know of a reason the judge may be prejudiced against you or people like you or because you just "have a bad feeling" about the judge, 12 states permit a litigant to file what is called a peremptory challenge against a judge. Generally, this means that you don't need a reason to challenge the judge, so long as the challenge is within the time frame and in the format required by the state. The states are: Alaska, Arizona, California, Idaho, Illinois, Minnesota, Missouri, Nevada, New Mexico, Washington, Wisconsin and Wyoming.

CHAPTER 11

Federal Discipline

The procedure for disciplining federal court judges was established by Congress in 1980 with the Judicial Councils Reform and Judicial Conduct and Disabilities Act.

Anyone—litigant, attorney or judge—may file a complaint against a district court judge, a circuit court judge, a bankruptcy judge or a magistrate. (The 1980 Act contains no provision for filing a complaint against a justice of the U.S. Supreme Court, however.) You need only submit a written statement of your complaint to the clerk for the chief judge of the circuit in which the accused judge sits. For example, if you want to complain about a district court judge in Nashville, Tennessee, file a complaint with the chief judge of the Sixth Circuit Court of Appeals, as Tennessee is one of the four states in the Sixth Circuit.

Grounds. According to the 1980 Act, a complaint must state either that a judge is "unable to discharge the duties of office by reason of mental or physical disability" or that the judge is engaged in "conduct prejudicial to the effective and expeditious administration of the business of the courts." The type of conduct included in the latter category is much the same as that described for discipline of state court judges in Chapter 10.

The chief judge. The clerk is required to send your complaint immediately to the chief judge for review. If your complaint is against that chief judge, the next most senior judge in the circuit will review it. The clerk also sends a copy of your complaint to the judge you are accusing. The chief judge can dismiss your complaint only on one of three grounds:

- it does not address a standard of misconduct or disability specified in the law;
- it is directly related to the merits of a case or procedural ruling; or
- the complaint is frivolous.

The chief judge also can end the process if "appropriate corrective action" is taken. This usually means the chief judge has taken the accused judge aside, discussed the problem and received assurances that the conduct in question will be corrected or won't be repeated.

If the complaint is dismissed or concluded, the chief judge sends both you and the accused judge a copy of the order.

Special committee. If the complaint is not dismissed or concluded, the chief judge must name a special committee composed of an equal number of court and district court judges, plus the chief judge. After an investigation, the committee must submit a written report of its findings to the judicial council of the circuit.

Judicial council. Each of the nation's 13 federal court circuits has a judicial council composed of appeals court and district court judges. Each council operates under the direction of the chief judge of each circuit. These councils are responsible for seeing to it that the circuit courts operate efficiently. Judicial discipline is one part of these responsibilities. The councils also handle such chores as reassigning judges to help overloaded district courts or infirm judges and ordering judges to decide cases left languishing too long.

When it receives a disciplinary investigation report from a special committee, the circuit's judicial council may further investigate if it believes that is necessary. The council also notifies accused judges and gives them the opportunity to defend themselves. HALT's Web site provides links to the judicial council sites for each circuit, at *www.halt.org.*

Sanctions. If the council finds that discipline is warranted, it can issue a private or public reprimand, temporarily strip the judge of case assignments, certify the disability of the judge, request voluntary retirement or take "such other action as it considers appropriate under the circumstances."

A judicial council also has the power to remove a bankruptcy court judge or a magistrate, but it cannot remove a judge appointed under Article III of the U.S. Constitution—district court, circuit court and most special court judges.

Judicial Conference. If a judicial council finds grounds for removing a judge from office, it recommends impeachment to the U.S. Judicial Conference. If the council is unable or unwilling to make that decision, it can refer the complaint to the conference for it to decide. The Judicial Conference is a policy-making body composed of the Chief Justice of the U.S. Supreme Court, the chief judge of each circuit, a district court judge elected within each circuit and the chief judge of the Court of International Trade. In addition to handling judicial discipline cases referred to it by the circuit councils, the conference sets rules of procedure for the federal courts, comments on federal legislation affecting U.S. courts and makes recommendations for more efficient and uniform judicial administration among the circuits. The conference may impose on a judge any of the sanctions that the councils may, or it can recommend impeachment to the U.S. House of Representatives. Because some authorities interpret the U.S. Constitution as vesting impeachment power solely in Congress, authors of the 1980 Act did not grant this power either to the Judicial Conference or to the judicial councils.

Impeachment. The term *impeachment* does not mean removal from office. It is an accusation of a public official that may then lead to removal. The process begins in the House of Representatives, which investigates and brings charges (called articles of impeachment) against the accused judge, then serves as prosecutor in a trial-like proceeding in the U.S. Senate. The Senate acts as a jury in deciding whether the judge is guilty of the charges and should be removed. A two-thirds majority vote by the Senate is required for removal.

Very few federal judges have been impeached. Throughout the history of the United States, only 12 federal judges have been impeached. Out of the 12, four were acquitted and one resigned from office while the articles of impeachment were pending. The other seven judges were convicted and removed from office. From 1937 to 1986, there were no judges impeached. Then, in 1986, U.S. District Court Chief Judge Harry E. Claiborne of Las Vegas, Nevada, was convicted of income tax evasion and began serving a two-year prison sentence. The judge maintained his innocence throughout: he refused to resign and continued to collect his full salary while in prison. Incensed, the House of Representatives unanimously approved four articles of impeachment and the Senate then convicted him of "high crimes and misdemeanors" listed in three of the articles. In 1989, Alcee L. Hastings was removed for perjury and soliciting and accepting a bribe. Walter Nixon, who had been previously convicted in federal court of perjury and bribery in connection with cases pending in his court, was also impeached in 1989.

Appeals. If the chief judge dismisses your complaint, you may appeal the decision to the judicial council. If the judicial council refuses to review the chief judge's order, you have no further avenue of appeal. You or the accused judge may, however, appeal other decisions of the judicial council, such as the imposition of a sanction, to the Judicial Conference. Neither you nor the judge has any avenue of appeal beyond the Judicial Conference.

Confidentiality. The proceedings and complaints under the 1980 Act are confidential unless the accused judge consents to public disclosure. The only other situation in which the records become public is when a council, the Judicial Conference or the House of Representatives releases information deemed necessary for impeachment proceedings.

Limitations. As with complaints against state judges, pursuing a complaint will have no effect on court cases handled by the accused federal judge. If you want to overturn a federal judge's decision in a case, you must appeal that case to the next highest court. If the chief judge dismisses a complaint, the rules now require that the dismissal restate the allegations and give the basis for the dismissal; in 80 percent of the dismissed complaints, the basis for the dismissal was that the complaint "was directly related to the merits of the decision or procedural relief."

EFFECTIVENESS

It is difficult to evaluate the effectiveness of the 1980 Act, as most of the proceedings are confidential and statistics are not regularly gathered. However, the National Commission on Judicial Discipline and Removal did request a review of the discipline and removal process. This 1993 study does provide some statistics: from 1980 to 1991, there were 2,405 complaints filed and 2,143 of them were dismissed by chief judges because they were improperly filed, addressed the merits of a specific case, were deemed frivolous or a combination of these problems. Sixteen complaints were withdrawn. In 73 cases, corrective action was taken. In one case, the judge was impeached. One judge voluntarily retired and two more judges voluntarily retired under a certified disability. Five judges were censured. Records reveal little about what the judicial councils actually did in each case because results are reported without explanation and without revealing very much about who brought the complaints or how many persons petitioned the council to review their complaints. In the 1993 study, nonlawyers filed 79 percent of the complaints; attorney complainants filed the remaining complaints.

It's almost impossible to compare the effectiveness of these procedures with those in place before 1981, as the earlier methods of disciplining judges were informal and no records were kept.

At the least, the current mechanism represents a small inroad into the previously impervious position of these lifetime appointees in that it recognizes that the public is entitled to a formal means of complaining about judicial behavior. The reasons will probably remain unknown until more public disclosure is required.

Before 1981, chief judges or judicial councils usually "disciplined" misbehaving judges in confidential discussions with them, advising them of the improprieties and the likely consequences if they weren't corrected. In cases of mental or physical disability, the council or a fellow judge merely requested voluntary retirement.

Those actions were defended as effective and appropriate because of circuit judges' familiarity with the errant judge, the issues and local custom. To the public, however, such familiarity is itself an obstacle to proper handling of misbehavior by judges. When judges are left to discipline their brethren without public oversight, public confidence in the judicial system is bound to erode.

Also, although the informal measures sometimes worked, judges occasionally disregarded the orders and recommendations of judicial councils because their powers were not well defined. Perhaps the most celebrated challenge was that by Judge Stephen Chandler of the Western District of Oklahoma in 1965. After 22 years on the federal bench, the Tenth Circuit Judicial Council stripped him of all his cases because of concern over his large case-backlog and his failure to disqualify himself from several cases in which his impartiality had been questioned. Judge Chandler had also become obstinate and neurotic, publicly calling oil company litigants "shady characters, pirates and vultures" and accusing other judges of trying to poison him.

The judge sued the Judicial Council, claiming its actions were an unconstitutional attack on his judicial independence. The U.S. Supreme Court sided with the Council, but Judge Chandler, although all his pending cases had been taken from him and no new cases were ever assigned him, continued to keep both his title and his salary.

CHAPTER 12

Suing a Judge

If you disagree with a judge's decision or the way it was reached, you may think appealing the case and filing a disciplinary complaint against the judge don't offer you enough redress because neither is going to compensate you for the losses you suffered as a result of the "faulty" decision. You may want also to sue for damages, accusing the judge of abusing power or not following the law. However, suing a judge is probably a waste of your time and money. In fact, it could result in your being cited for contempt of court.

IT ISN'T EASY

First, you have virtually no chance of winning such a lawsuit based on the rulings, decisions or orders the judge made. Judges enjoy considerable discretionary power and are granted extremely broad immunity.

Second, you will probably have to search far and wide for a lawyer willing to sue the judge. When the case is over, win or lose, the lawyer can expect a difficult time getting a fair shake in that judge's court.

Third, you may have difficulty getting a lawyer to represent you *after* you've sued a judge. Judges have friends who are lawyers. And whether or not they are the judge's golfing partners, local lawyers may not want to risk associating with you.

Fourth, it's not wise to fight this kind of lawsuit without a lawyer, because a case against a judge is hard to win even *with a lawyer* and whenever you are a *pro se* litigant fighting someone represented by a lawyer, you can be sure that lawyer will take every advantage of your unfamiliarity with legal procedure and technicalities. A judge you sue has even bigger advantages of cronyism and "inside" information about the courts, lawyers and other judges.

JUDICIAL IMMUNITY

A basic rule of the American legal system holds that judges are not liable in civil lawsuits for their actions as judges, as long as they have jurisdiction over the matters they judge. This rule, which applies to state and federal judges alike, is known as "judicial immunity."

Take as an example a judge who upholds the opposing attorney's objection to testimony that was crucial to your case. The facts show the judge was wrong to allow the objection and as a result, you lost your case. You *still* cannot win a lawsuit against that judge for the money you would have won if the judge had ruled correctly, whether the error was made in good faith, or even if the judge had acted for purely corrupt or malicious reasons.

The judicial immunity rule is invoked to preserve judicial independence: judges must be free to act without fear of reprisals, such as the threat of a lawsuit. That is why the rule of judicial immunity operates *even if the judge has made an error out of malice toward you.* In our example, the judge made an error in law. The way to correct that kind of mistake is to appeal the case to a higher court. If the judge erred because of malice, bad faith or even drunkenness on the bench, the legal error can be addressed both by appealing to a higher court and by filing a disciplinary complaint about the judge's behavior.

JURISDICTION

In theory, judicial immunity shields judges from lawsuits only if they have jurisdiction over the matter at hand. (Remember, jurisdiction means the judge has the power to hear and decide the case.) Nevertheless, even judges who *exceed* their authority are likely to be immune. To win a lawsuit against a judge, you must prove the judge was acting with a clear absence of authority. This is most likely to occur in limited-jurisdiction courts.

However, courts bend over backwards to rationalize that a judge has jurisdiction. Such was the finding in the case of Indiana Judge Harold Stump. At the request of Linda Sparkman's mother, Stump had granted a petition for an order to have Linda sterilized when she was 15. The judge did not notify Linda, did not appoint a guardian to represent her and did not file the order in the court records. Linda was sterilized during an operation she was told was an appendectomy.

No common-law or statutory grounds provided for sterilization of minors, even at their parents' request. What law did exist applied only to the mentally disabled and they were afforded due process protections that Linda was not given.

Yet, in 1978, the U.S. Supreme Court determined that a judge would not be deprived of immunity because the action he took was in error, was done maliciously or was in excess of his authority, but rather he would be subject to liability only when he had acted in the "clear absence of all jurisdiction." The Court held in the Stump case, that there was not a "clear absence of all jurisdiction" in the circuit court to consider the sterilization petition. Because the Indiana Circuit Court was a court of general jurisdiction, neither the procedural errors Judge Stump may have committed, nor the lack of a specific statute authorizing his approval of the petition in question, rendered him liable in damages for the consequences of his actions.

A SHORT-LIVED EROSION OF IMMUNITY

In 1984, the U.S. Supreme Court relaxed the doctrine of judicial immunity, at least as it applies to state court judges in narrow circumstances.

A Virginia county magistrate, Gladys Pulliam, was sued by two defendants she had jailed improperly. Although they had been charged with minor, non-jailable offenses, she ordered them jailed when they couldn't post bond money. They filed a Civil Rights Act suit, claiming that by wrongfully jailing them, the magistrate had deprived them of their due process and equal protection rights. They won and demanded that the judge pay their lawyer's fees, too. Although the magistrate had made a mistake in a case in which her jurisdiction was undisputed, she was held liable for their attorney fees under the Civil Rights Attorney's Fees Awards Act of 1976.

Judges and other critics assailed the Pulliam decision as an erosion of judicial independence. Numerous bills have been introduced in Congress to restrict or reverse the impact of the case. In 1996, Congress passed the Federal Courts Improvement Act which legislatively reversed the Pulliam decision in some respects. The Act provides that "injunctive relief shall not be granted" in an action brought against "a judicial officer for an act or omission taken in such officer's judicial capacity," "unless a declaratory decree was violated or declaratory relief was unavailable."

CRIMINAL LIABILITY

Like any other citizen, however, judges can be prosecuted for crimes they commit, whether or not they commit them in a judicial capacity and everyone has a right to alert the appropriate prosecutor's office of a judge's criminal conduct. Authorities are likely to be pressured by the accused judge and the judge's friends and political allies, however, especially in small communities. It is not infrequent that such pressure results in a decision not to press charges or in a cover-up of the incident. Also, remember who will be asked to judge the judge who is being accused of a crime—a fellow judge.

Yet courts have repeatedly upheld the rule that judges are not immune from criminal responsibility, even when acting behind the shield of judicial office. For example, judicial immunity does not protect judges from criminal liability in cases of fraud or corruption or for soliciting bribes. And in some states, conviction of a judge on certain crimes (such as bribery, extortion, assault and other felonies) results in automatic removal from office. Such criminal cases against judges are brought by law enforcement officials, not by private citizens.

CHAPTER 13

Magistrates & Justices of the Peace

The courtroom bench is often occupied not by a judge but by a judicial officer who has lesser powers. These officers perform many of the same tasks that judges do—hearing and deciding cases—but their powers are limited: they are allowed to hear only certain kinds of cases or to make only some kinds of decisions. These officers are used both in the federal courts and in all states.

IN THE STATES

Justices of the peace. These are one of two main types of such officers. Most justices of the peace are elected to office. They are like judges in that, for cases over which they have authority, they have broad powers. Like judges, they hear cases on their own, preside over jury trials and make final decisions. What distinguishes them from other judges is that they are allowed to hear only certain kinds of cases.

Thus, you are most likely to encounter justices of the peace in limited-jurisdiction courts. They hear civil cases that involve relatively small sums of money and minor criminal cases, such as misdemeanors.

Most of them have no equity powers. That is, they can decide only cases that are rooted in common law, not relatively newer cases for which equitable remedies have been established—for instance, disputes over title to real estate or slander, libel and malicious prosecution cases; nor do they have the power to issue injunctions.

Justice of the peace courts have been criticized. It has been claimed that the low salaries paid to justices of the peace do not attract the most qualified personnel. Most justices of the peace are not lawyers and many aren't even high school graduates. A 1976 Supreme Court opinion cited a study indicating that 33 percent of the justices of the peace in Mississippi "are limited in educational background to the extent that they are not capable of learning the necessary elements of law." Some states such as Arizona have instituted training programs for justices of the peace and other nonlawyer judicial officers.

Magistrates. Other non-judge judicial officers help judges but do not themselves have authority to make final decisions. These are called, in various states, referees, commissioners, hearing officers, magistrates or masters. They are assigned cases by their supervising judge or judges. They serve in both limited- and general-jurisdiction courts but are most often employed in divorce, juvenile and traffic cases.

For example, *masters* are used to gather facts in divorce cases for the Chancery Courts of populous counties in Arkansas. Judges assign cases to the masters, who then hold hearings and take testimony from the spouses and witnesses, if necessary. The masters may also attempt reconciliation of willing couples and have authority to subpoena reluctant ones. They file reports of their findings for the judges to use in settling the divorce or preparing it for trial.

Maryland uses masters in cases that involve juveniles. They conduct hearings to investigate the facts and draw conclusions of law, then make recommendations to the judge. Either side may appeal the master's recommendation or parts of it. The judge reviews it, sometimes after another hearing, then adopts, modifies or rejects the master's recommendation.

Similarly, *probate commissioners* in Oregon can do almost everything a probate judge can do except enter the final order. After gathering information, the probate commissioner submits a recommended order to the judge, who may accept, amend or reverse it.

Unlike justices of the peace, most magistrates and similar judicial officers are appointed to office, usually by judges and sometimes by the governor. In New Hampshire, superior court and supreme court justices become judicial referees upon retirement. They are assigned to hear cases and recommend decisions or to help judges in pending cases, but they do not preside over jury trials or enter final judgments.

Nonlawyers. Most states allow nonlawyers to serve as justices of the peace or as magistrates or other judicial officers. As of 1998, 38 states allowed nonlawyers to serve in these positions. Some state laws allow nonlawyer justices to serve in sparsely populated areas or if no attorney is available. These nonlawyer judges play an important role in the American judicial system. In fact, as of 1999, 29 states allowed nonlawyer judges to adjudicate civil matters in certain limited-jurisdiction courts.

One component of a 1970s "court reform" movement for more unified, efficient and well-managed court systems was an effort to require that all judicial officers be lawyers. Although it is argued that this would improve the quality of justice, the argument is advanced with little empirical evidence. An extensive study of nonlawyer judges in New York in the 1980s concluded that nonlawyer judges in courts of limited jurisdiction were as competent as lawyer judges. Advocates of the continued participation of nonlawyer judges suggest that more training and education would address most concerns raised about nonlawyer judges.

Nonetheless, some states are beginning to eliminate nonlawyer judges. For example, the California Supreme Court ruled that the use of nonlawyer magistrates violates the state's constitution.

At the same time, a national movement promoting alternatives to courtroom litigation has embraced the notions of nonlawyer adjudicators and more informal, community-based dispute resolution programs that rely on mediation, conciliation and arbitration instead of lawyering.

IN FEDERAL COURTS

Magistrates. These are the federal district court equivalents of state court referees or masters. They preside over hearings and make rulings in civil pretrial matters and may even preside over jury and non-jury trials if all parties agree. Magistrates also conduct trials in criminal misdemeanor cases when the defendants consent.

The specific duties of magistrates vary with each district's procedures for handling cases. In some courts, magistrates act as additional judges and perform the same tasks as their supervisors. Some magistrates are specialists in such cases as Social Security appeals or prisoner petitions. Finally, some are charged with handling only pre-trial stages of litigation.

The magistrate may enter an order or merely submit a recommendation to the judge. In either case, the judge is free to accept, reject or modify the magistrate's decision.

Magistrates are appointed by district court judges and must be licensed members of the bar of the state in which the court is located. Their authority was established by Congress in 1968. In 1979, Congress expanded the authority of magistrates by authorizing them to conduct all civil trials as long as the parties consented and by allowing them to preside over misdemeanor trials as long as the defendants waived their right to a trial before a district judge. In 1990, Congress changed their title from magistrate to magistrate judge. The number of magistrate judgeships is determined by the Judicial

Conference of the United States and is subject to congressional funding of the requested positions. There are more than 500 full-time and part-time magistrate judges, serving in all but a handful of the federal district courts.

Special masters. Neutral third parties called special masters are sometimes hired to help manage the course of federal litigation. According to the Federal Rules of Civil Procedure, the term "master" includes referee, auditor, examiner or assessor and their use shall be "the exception and not the rule." For instance, in a complex case a special master may be placed in charge of all *discovery* procedures, the often long and complex process lawyers use to collect information from each other before going to trial. The master usually has authority to impose deadlines and prevent abuses and delay of the process. Special masters are also used to help with complex or technical litigation, such as the antitrust lawsuit by the U.S. government against Microsoft and the tobacco products liability cases. Their major role is managerial, but they sometimes also have limited powers to adjudicate.

A special master may also help implement court decrees after trial. This was common practice in school desegregation cases, in which special masters helped school systems develop plans that met court-imposed guidelines.

Unlike federal magistrates or their state-level counterparts, special masters are not public employees. They are appointed by judges and paid a private fee by the two sides in a lawsuit. They are usually private attorneys, law professors or retired judges, often with technical expertise in the subject matter being litigated.

CHAPTER 14

Court Clerks

One of the first courthouse officials you are likely to meet in both state and federal courts—and among the most important to you—is the court clerk. In large metropolitan areas, this may be one of several deputy clerks working under a chief clerk. Courts in less populated areas employ only one court clerk and some rural courts do not even have a full-time court clerk. Instead, a judge or justice of the peace doubles as clerk.

THE FIRST STOP

Readers of HALT's *Citizens Legal Manuals* are repeatedly advised to "ask your court clerk" for information specific to their case and their state's laws. This is for a very good reason: the court clerks have better access to such information than any other public official to which you are likely to have easy access. The clerk can and should give you general information about routine procedures of the court.

This is also your primary contact for transacting court business, whether it is to start a lawsuit or to change your name. Whatever you are doing, each step of the way you're probably going to have to stop by the clerk's office to ask a question, pick up a form or hand over an official document. To file documents with the court, for example, you give them to the clerk, who then collects any necessary fees, puts the clerk's official seal on the documents and routes them to the appropriate person or file. Although it's not required, it may prove worthwhile to bring a copy of any document you're filing and get it stamped as well, so that you have a copy for your records.

Suppose you go to the courthouse to probate your mother's will. You must first call or visit the office of the probate clerk or "registrar," as this person is called in some places. The clerk will tell you to make application to the probate court and may give you the proper form. You fill out the form and give it back to the clerk, along with the deceased person's will and other papers—such as a copy of the death certificate—required in your state. The clerk then opens a file for administration of the estate.

What to expect. The amount of information or help you can expect from a court clerk varies from state to state and from court to court. Some clerks will only refer you to written rules of procedure or suggest that you ask a lawyer. Others will tell you the basic steps you need to take, then refer you to lawyers and legal-help organizations. In our example above, for instance, the probate clerk might tell you the different types of procedures available for estates of varying sizes. In Maryland, HALT helped pass a law that requires probate clerks to give information about settling an estate to the public.

Few clerks, however, will give you specific advice on how to handle your case. For example, few probate clerks will tell you how to calculate the value of the estate's assets or which procedure is best suited to your mother's estate. Clerks may not know this information or they may not have much time to devote to individuals, but often, their reluctance stems mostly from admonitions from judges and lawyers that the clerks not engage in the "unauthorized practice of law."

In some cases, more help. In small claims courts, where all or most litigants represent themselves, clerks are generally more willing to help. Many courts publish pamphlets or brochures with general information about how to file a small-claims case. These pamphlets and other useful information are often available at the court's Web site. In the Washington, DC, clerk's office you can even view a videotape that explains how to proceed in the Small Claims and Conciliation Branch of Superior Court. Another useful hint is to make a simple phone call to the clerk's office; many offices provide useful taped information about filing lawsuits.

A number of jurisdictions have established legal information kiosks, which rely on touch screen technology to provide forms, instructions, referrals and other relevant information to self-represented litigants. Arizona, for example, has implemented a system called QuickCourt. Nearly every courthouse in Arizona contains a computerized kiosk where self-represented litigants can follow simple on-screen instructions and have divorce and other court papers completed for filing. Information about the location of these kiosks can be obtained by contacting the clerk's office.

A few states require clerks to give specified over-the-counter help to the public in completing certain basic forms. For instance, Florida Family Law Rule of Procedure 12.105 provides that clerks shall assist in the preparation of the petition for dissolution and other papers to be filed in simplified uncontested divorces meeting a few basic requirements.

In California, court clerks can give you copies of your court's local rules and forms or they can tell you where to get them if they don't have the forms you need. They can give you general information about court rules, procedures and practices. They can provide you with information about local lawyer referral services. They can provide court schedules and information on how to get a case scheduled. Frequently, they can answer questions about court deadlines and how to compute them. They can also tell you about important information, like courtroom hours, locations and filing fees. However, as in all states, court clerks in California can't give legal advice. The California courts have also set up a Self-Help Center on the Internet that provides a lot of useful practical court information.

Many more court procedures can and should be simplified and court clerks should routinely be required to provide help to the public in all such instances. To this end HALT continues its efforts to streamline and de-lawyer routine legal matters such as wills and probate, name changes, uncontested divorces, uncontested adoptions and small claims.

OTHER DUTIES

The typical clerk's most important duty to most courthouse visitors is as described above. Most clerks also have other responsibilities, however, including some or all of the following:

Custodian and record-keeper. Clerks are the custodians of court files and maintain the lists of cases and records of legal matters such as liens, adoptions and name changes. They are responsible for what is called the docket, a record for each case of the papers filed and hearings held. By checking the docket, the clerk can tell you the current status of any case you are interested in.

Court calendar. Clerks in busy, metropolitan courts also maintain the court calendar. With this, they keep track of what cases are ready for trial and notify the interested parties when the trial date is set.

Juror administration. Some court clerks are also responsible for maintaining juror rolls and supervising jurors when they report for jury duty. In larger jurisdictions, this job is done by a jury commissioner.

In court. The clerk sits beside the judge with all files of cases to be heard that day. Besides calling the case names and handing files to the judge, the clerk administers oaths to jurors and witnesses, stamps documents and exhibits, keeps minutes of court proceedings, reads verdicts and writes official entries on the case dockets.

Other duties. In some states, clerks also have duties that are unrelated to the operation of the courts. They serve as recorders of deeds for the county, as registrars of election rolls or as the keepers of vital statistics, maintaining records of births, marriages and deaths.

SELECTION AND AUTHORITY

In most states, at least some court clerks are elected by the public. In states that appoint clerks, the appointment may be by a judge or the governor. In heavily populated areas, employees of the clerk's office may be hired and fired under the county's executive branch personnel system. In the federal courts, clerks are appointed by the judges of the court for which they work.

The clerk's powers and duties are spelled out by the constitutions of some states and by state laws in others. Terms (length of service) for court clerks vary. For example, the Maryland state constitution provides in Article IV, sec. 17 that, "There shall be a Clerk of the Court of Appeals, who shall be appointed by and shall hold his office at the pleasure of said Court of Appeals." And the Massachusetts state constitution provides, "The legislature shall prescribe, by general law, for the election of sheriffs, registers of probate and clerks of the courts, by the people of the several counties." (Amend. Article XIX.)

CHAPTER 15

Jury Duty

Probably the most important way citizens participate in our system of justice is by serving as jurors. The right to a trial by a jury of one's peers is one of the basic guarantees of the U.S. Constitution. This right will be discussed briefly, as a full analysis of this constitutional issue is beyond this book's scope. This chapter is an introduction to how the jury system operates.

YOUR RIGHT TO A JURY

The right to a jury trial in civil cases heard in federal court is found in the Seventh Amendment to the U.S. Constitution. This federal guarantee has not been extended to the states, but constitutional provisions similar to it can be found in most state constitutions.

For criminal cases, the right to a jury trial is specified in Article III, Section 2 of the U.S. Constitution and in the Sixth Amendment. It is considered so fundamental a right that it was made binding on the states in the Fourteenth Amendment's "due process" clause. However, the Supreme Court has interpreted the Constitution to require trial by jury only in "serious" crimes, not in "petty" ones.

Thus, the constitutional right to a jury trial is neither automatic nor absolute. It comes into play only under certain circumstances. Predictably, what crimes should be considered serious enough for a jury trial has long been debated.

The U.S. uses two kinds of juries. *Petit* juries hear cases at trial and *grand* juries decide which cases should be tried.

PETIT JURIES

Both civil and criminal trial juries have traditionally consisted of 12 members. In recent years, however, most states have adopted smaller juries in an attempt to reduce court costs and delays. Juries of fewer than 12 jurors are used in most states for some civil cases and also for some criminal cases.

Many federal district courts use six-person juries for civil cases. In federal criminal cases that involve the right to a jury trial, the jury must consist of 12 persons unless both the defendant and the prosecutor agree to fewer in writing.

BECOMING A JUROR

To be selected for jury duty, your name will be drawn from a voter registration roll, a motor vehicle registration list, the tax rolls or some similar compilation of residents. Some states rely on only one list, others draw their juror pool from two or more lists.

Summons. Typically, if your name is drawn you will be notified of your obligation to serve as a juror by a *summons* sent through the mail. It will ask you to report to the court at a certain date and time. Your summons may have a phone number for you to call at a given time or direct you to the court's Web site to determine if or when you are required to appear at the courthouse.

Exemptions and excuses. Rules and laws that once exempted lawyers, physicians, teachers, students, mothers and specified others from jury duty are being repealed with increasing frequency. As more and more interest groups (such as bus drivers, embalmers and retired firefighters) gained exempt status, the pool of prospective jurors became alarmingly small and unrepresentative of the general population. Doing away with such exemptions thus has gained popularity with court officials in recent years.

For the same reason, it is also becoming more difficult to be excused from jury duty because of business commitments or personal plans. Most courts will allow you to change the date on which you report, but each court has its own policy about excusing persons from jury duty. Some grant such excuses liberally while others require a showing of extreme hardship or emergency.

Length of service. This also varies with the court. In some states, you may report to the courthouse only to sit for days without being called to serve on a trial jury. Other states call you in only when it is known that jurors are needed, but you may still have to serve from 10 to 30 days at a stretch or for the duration of your assigned trial.

You may not have to serve at all, simply because they always call more prospective jurors than are needed. Increasingly, courts are utilizing Web sites or automated phone services to determine when prospective jurors need to appear.

Because of the hardship such lengthy jury duty imposes, many courts utilize the "one day, one trial" rule. In the courts that have adopted this system, if you are not chosen for a jury on the first day, you are excused; if you are selected for a jury, you serve for the length of that trial only—usually two to three days.

The jury panel. When you report to the courthouse, you will be assembled with other prospective jurors, perhaps as many as a few hundred. You are all known as *veniremen* until you are selected as a juror for a case. From that larger group a panel of, say, 25 to 35 will be called and seated in the courtroom.

At this point, if not earlier, the judge will introduce you to the case to be tried, explaining whether it is a civil or criminal trial and introducing the lawyers for each side. In some courts, 12 people will be told to sit in the jury box and the rest are seated in the courtroom's general seating area.

Voir dire. Pronounced "vwar deer," this phrase is from the old French for "to speak the truth." It is the questioning process by which each potential juror's suitability for a case is determined. The intention is to select a fair and impartial jury.

In most states, the judge and attorneys all have an opportunity to question prospective jurors. Some states, however, allow either judges or attorneys, but not both, to do the questioning. Others, and all federal courts, provide for questioning by the judge or attorneys at the judge's discretion.

Challenges. Attorneys are allowed to exercise two kinds of challenges to prospective jurors. One is the *challenge for cause*. An attorney asserts this challenge if he or she feels the juror is not legally qualified to serve or cannot be fair and impartial. An example of a challenge for cause is that the prospective juror is a close friend of a key witness in the trial. The attorney must state the reason for the challenge. If the judge agrees, the juror is excused. Each attorney may exercise an unlimited number of challenges for cause.

The second type of challenge, the *peremptory challenge*, allows an attorney to have a juror excused without stating a reason and without asking the judge to rule on the juror's suitability. Each side's attorney is given an equal number of peremptory challenges, typically six or eight. Questioning and challenges continue until the required number of jurors are seated that are satisfactory to both sides and the judge. Ordinarily, the exercise of peremptory challenges cannot be contested. However, the Supreme Court has created an exception, holding that the Equal Protection Clause forbids intentional discrimination based on race and gender in the exercise of peremptory challenges.

GRAND JURIES

Grand juries function differently from trial juries. They are called "grand" because they are larger—between 16 and 23 jurors—than trial *(petit)* juries. If you are called to serve on a grand jury, one of your roles is to decide whether persons charged with a crime should be brought to trial.

According to the Fifth Amendment to the U.S. Constitution, a person cannot be tried for a serious federal crime unless the charges are first brought before a federal grand jury. Many states also use grand juries for serious state crimes. Other states use a preliminary hearing or "information" procedure to order a person tried.

During a grand jury proceeding, the prosecutor (the U.S. Attorney in federal court, a state's attorney or district attorney in state courts) presents evidence and witnesses to the jurors in an attempt to convince them that enough evidence exists to bring the accused to trial. At this stage, the prosecutor need not prove guilt, only that a crime was committed and that there is evidence to charge the accused with committing it.

Conclusion

HALT supports a program of comprehensive reforms to improve the operation and staffing of our courts. These include:

Improved efficiency. To reduce the delay and backlog of cases, many courts are experimenting with ways to speed the processing of cases without affecting the quality of justice. Among the methods: strictly enforced court deadlines, limiting the use of pre-trial discovery procedures and the length of written briefs and using telephone conferences instead of courtroom hearings. HALT also favors efforts at the federal and state level to improve efficiency through e-filing—using the Internet to file briefs, pleadings, motions and other lawyer-generated documents.

Court-clerk assistance and self-help centers. HALT advocates that court clerks be allowed to dispense basic information over the counter and help on simple, routine legal matters, especially in state courts, those most frequently used by average citizens. Court clerks should also be required to help citizens complete nonadversary legal tasks such as uncontested divorces, probate and name changes. HALT also supports self-help centers where court staff help people to represent themselves. A self-help center in San Francisco's Superior Court even hosts a professionally-staffed day care center to ease the burden on parents using the court to resolve family law issues.

Downloadable court forms. More and more state courts are posting online court forms, for handling both civil and criminal cases. HALT supports this development as it allows consumers to view, download and complete court forms from the comfort of their home or office. HALT also supports the use of computer kiosks in court houses which provide step-by-step instructions on how to fill out court forms and then generates completed court forms for immediate use.

Jury service. HALT believes that courts should continue to offer jury service methods such as "one day, one trial" to ensure representative juries with minimum disruption of citizens' work or other obligations.

Increased alternatives. Court-sponsored and private alternative dispute settlement programs have been proven to effectively decrease the adversary nature of dispute settlement, keep some cases out of court and narrow the disputed issues in cases that do go to trial. They can do this without compromising important rights. HALT supports these programs and works to ensure that they continue to be inexpensive, speedy and fair.

Judicial conduct organizations. HALT believes the activities of states' judicial conduct commissions should be made public. The complaint and investigation stages are confidential in all states and in only 12 states does the confidentiality end when formal charges are filed against a judge. In about half the states the public is not informed until the commission makes a recommendation to the state's supreme court for discipline. Worse yet, in the remaining states, the public finds out only if public discipline is ordered.

In addition, some state commissions need more funding so complaints may be thoroughly pursued. Greater citizen representation is needed on some commissions and all commissions need to be more visible and accessible to the general public.

Federal judicial discipline. HALT successfully supported reforms that established the federal court disciplinary framework, giving consumers a formal grievance system for the first time. That law can be improved, however. The process should include full public disclosure and accountability and provide for public participation in formulating procedures. Also, those procedures should be made uniform among the circuits to eliminate uncertainty and unpredictability in the processing of complaints against federal judges.

Financial conflict-of-interest disclosure rules. HALT is working to enforce financial conflict-of-interest disclosure rules which require judges to disclose any economic interests they may have to the cases over which they preside.

In sum, HALT aims to lift the veil of secrecy and misunderstanding from our courts, their staffs and their procedures, so you can be an informed user of the system and work to improve it.

Appendixes

State Court Systems

This appendix describes the structure of court systems in all 50 states, the District of Columbia, Puerto Rico and the Virgin Islands. The descriptions are accompanied by organizational charts and include information on each court's jurisdiction, how judges are chosen and how many there are. Court homepages are given for each state. The appendix incorporates changes in the laws through 2002-2003. The year of the latest amendments included in the research is noted for each state. Laws may change at any time, however, so check your state's statutes in your local law library, or ask the court clerk. An excellent online resource for current state statutes can be found at Findlaw (*www.findlaw.com/11stategov/index.html*).

The key below will help you read the charts. Cases enter the court system at or near the lowest level in each chart and, if appealed, work their way up through the court system. The following notes should help you understand the descriptions of each court.

JURISDICTION

Jurisdiction means the kinds of cases a court has authority to hear; these are listed for each court. A court can hear cases in two ways. The first is by *original* jurisdiction, meaning it is the first court to hear the case, at a trial. If one of the parties at the trial appeals the case, it is heard by a court in the second way—by *appellate* jurisdiction to review the lower court's decision.

This distinction is made in the appendix by simply listing the types of cases for which each court has original jurisdiction, and using the words "review" or "appeals of" to signify cases over which it has appellate jurisdiction. Unless the term "may" is used, it means the court *must* hear the appeal—in other words, it does not have the option to refuse to hear the case.

Many courts of last resort and appeals courts have the power to issue *extraordinary* or *necessary* writs. These are orders those courts may use to hear cases themselves or, more often, to command other courts to decide a case.

Jury trials are permitted in courts where this is indicated, but remember: even if jury trials are allowed, it does not mean they are automatically granted for all cases in that court.

The number of courts or the number of administrative divisions (such as circuits) is indicated for most courts. Their locations are listed if they exist in only a few places.

JUDGES

The number of judges and other judicial officers and how they are selected is described for each court. The method of filling a vacancy during an unexpired term, which may differ, is *not* listed.

Nominating commission refers to a panel, usually composed of judges, lawyers and nonlawyers, that screens candidates and recommends a list to the appointer (usually the governor). Nominating commissions are known variously as "Judicial Nominating Commission," "Supreme Court Nominating Council," "Judicial Selection Board" and so forth.

Law degrees are required for judicial officers unless stated otherwise.

KEY

Court of last resort:

Intermediate appellate courts:

Courts of general jurisdiction:

Courts of limited jurisdiction:

Route of appeal in most cases: ————————————

Route of appeal in some cases: -

ALABAMA

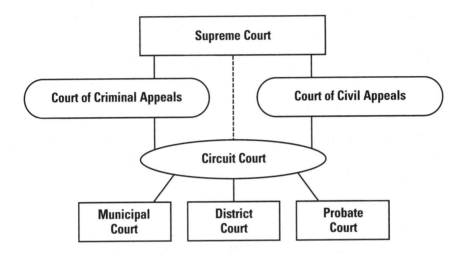

Court Homepage: www.judicial.state.al.us

Constitution: Art. 7, Am. No. 328.
Statutes: Code of Alabama (2004), Title 12 (Courts).

SUPREME COURT
Jurisdiction: Extraordinary writs. Reviews death-penalty cases, civil cases over $50,000, real estate, equity, administrative law cases. May review other cases from courts of Civil, Criminal Appeals. If the governor or legislature asks, has authority to give advisory opinions regarding important constitutional questions. *Judges:* 9; selection, retention by partisan election; 6-year terms.

COURT OF CRIMINAL APPEALS
Jurisdiction: Extraordinary writs. Appeals of all felony and misdemeanor cases, including city ordinance violations, habeas corpus and post-conviction writs. *Judges:* 5; selection, retention by partisan election.

COURT OF CIVIL APPEALS
Jurisdiction: Extraordinary writs. Original appellate jurisdiction of civil cases under $50,000. Also reviews domestic relations cases, cases from administrative agencies (except Public Service Commission). *Judges:* 5; selection, retention by partisan election.

CIRCUIT COURT
Jurisdiction: Extraordinary writs. All civil cases over $10,000; concurrent jurisdiction with the District Court for matters over $3,000 but under $10,000, equity, land-title payments. Felonies and related misdemeanors. Appeals from

all lower courts. Jury trials permitted. 41 circuits. *Judges:* 142; selection, retention by partisan election.

DISTRICT COURT
Jurisdiction: Concurrent jurisdiction with the Circuit Court on civil cases under $10,000, exclusive jurisdiction in civil cases under $3,000, evictions, cases involving minors, adoptions. Misdemeanors, preliminary felony hearings, traffic violations. In each county seat and some cities. 67 districts. No jury trials. *Judges:* 102; selection, retention same as for Supreme Court.

PROBATE COURT
Jurisdiction: Wills, probate, guardianships, adoptions and commitments. In all counties. *Judges:* 68; selection, retention by partisan election; 6-year terms. Probate judges are not constitutionally required to be admitted to the practice of law.

MUNICIPAL COURT
Jurisdiction: City violations and violations of state law which might also be considered a violation of city ordinances. In 258 cities. *Judges:* 174; city governing board appoints, retention by partisan election; 6-year terms.

ALASKA

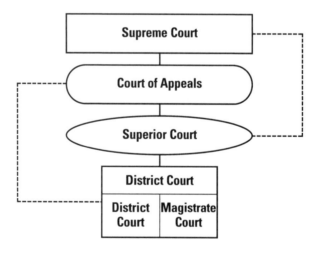

Court Homepage: www.state.ak.us/courts

Constitution: Art. IV; 6.
Statutes: Alaska Statutes (2004), Title 22 (Judiciary).

SUPREME COURT
Jurisdiction: Extraordinary writs. Reviews civil, administrative agency, juvenile

and disciplinary cases. Reviews civil cases from Superior Court. May review Court of Appeals criminal decisions. May review significant questions of constitutional law or a question of substantial public interest, if the question is certified by the Court of Appeals. *Judges:* 5; governor appoints from Alaska Judicial Council nominees, retention by nonpartisan election after at least 3 years; thereafter, elected 10-year terms.

COURT OF APPEALS

Jurisdiction: Reviews criminal cases from Superior Court; may review criminal cases from District Court. May issue writs, injunctions and other process related to its criminal jurisdiction. *Judges:* 3; selection, retention same as for Supreme Court; 8-year terms.

SUPERIOR COURT

Jurisdiction: Civil and criminal. Exclusive jurisdiction for domestic relations, children's probate, guardianship and civil commitment matters. Appellate jurisdiction of District Court cases. Jury trials permitted. 4 districts. *Judges:* 32; selection, retention is same as for Supreme Court; 6-year terms.

DISTRICT COURT

Jurisdiction: Civil cases under $50,000; small claims under $7,500. Criminal cases jurisdiction for misdemeanor, drunk driving, traffic and local ordinance violation cases. Has jurisdiction to hear emergency juvenile cases and preliminary hearings. Jury trials permitted. 4 districts; 58 locations. *Judges:* 18; selection same as for Supreme Court, retention by nonpartisan election after at least 1 year; thereafter, elected 4-year terms.

MAGISTRATE COURT

Jurisdiction: Civil and small claims cases under $7,500. Concurrent criminal jurisdiction for misdemeanors, ordinance violations and felony preliminary hearings. Jury trials permitted. *Magistrates:* 39 full and part time; appointed by Superior Court presiding judge in district; serve at judge's pleasure. Law degree not required.

ARIZONA

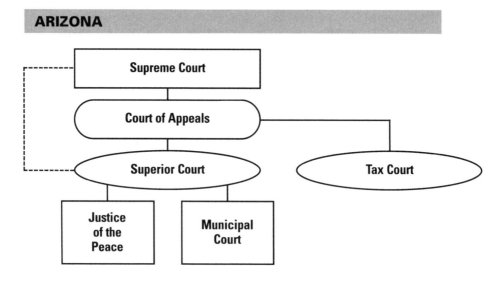

Court Homepage: www.supreme.state.az.us

Constitution: Art. VI.
Statutes: Arizona Revised Statutes (2004), Title 12 (Courts and Civil Proceedings) and Title 22 (Justice of the Peace and Other Courts Not of Record).

SUPREME COURT
Jurisdiction: Extraordinary writs. Exclusive jurisdiction of disputes between counties. Reviews death-penalty, life-imprisonment cases. Reviews cases from Court of Appeals. Reviews judicial disciplinary matters and bar admissions. *Judges:* 5; governor appoints from the Judicial Nominating Commission's list, retention by nonpartisan election within 2 years; thereafter, elected 6-year terms.

COURT OF APPEALS
Jurisdiction: Extraordinary writs. Appeals from Superior Court; criminal appeals except death penalty, life imprisonment; appeals of unemployment compensation, Industrial Commission cases. In Phoenix and Tuscon. *Judges:* 22; selection, retention same as for Supreme Court.

SUPERIOR COURT
Jurisdiction: Civil cases over $5,000, equity, domestic relations, juvenile matters, probate, land title. Legality of taxes, assessments, city ordinances. Felonies, misdemeanors. Hears appeals *de novo* and on the record in both civil and criminal cases from the lower courts. Reviews appeals from some administrative agencies. Jury trials permitted. In 15 counties. *Judges:* 159; selection, retention same as for Supreme Court; 4-year terms. In some counties with less than 250,000 population, selection, retention by nonpartisan election; 4-year terms.

TAX COURT
Jurisdiction: All disputes relating to taxes; small claims jurisdiction for matters where the taxes are less than $5,000 or the full cash value of the real and personal property is less than $300,000; small claims cases are non-appealable. In Maricopa County, the court is a department of the Superior Court. *Judges:* Superior Court judges serve; selection, retention same as for Superior Court.

JUSTICE OF THE PEACE COURT
Jurisdiction: Exclusive jurisdiction in civil cases under $5,000, small claims (under $2,500), recovery of leased or rented property if less than $1,000 value and $5,000 damages. Misdemeanors, crimes with less than $1,000 fine or 6-month sentence; felony preliminary hearings. Jury trials permitted, except for small claims. In 84 locations. *Judges:* 83; selection, retention by partisan election; 4-year terms. Law degree not required.

MUNICIPAL COURT (also called Police Court)
Jurisdiction: City, town violations, domestic violence. In 84 cities and towns. Jury trials permitted in some locations. *Judges:* 133 full-time. Usually appointed by city or town council; 4-year terms.

ARKANSAS

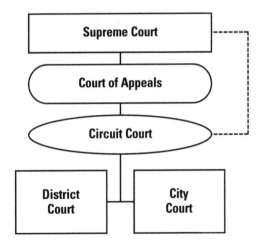

Court Homepage: www.courts.state.ar.us

Constitution: Art. VII, Am. 80.
Statutes: Arkansas Statutes Annotated (2004), Title 16 (Practice, Procedure and Courts).

SUPREME COURT
Jurisdiction: Extraordinary writs. Statewide appellate jurisdiction. Original

jurisdiction over questions of state law certified by a federal court, sufficiency of state initiative and referendum petitions. Mandatory jurisdiction in death penalty, lawyer disciplinary and some administrative agency cases. Discretionary jurisdiction over other appeals. May review cases involving oil and gas, torts, deeds and wills, and law and facts of equity cases. *Judges:* 7; selection, retention by nonpartisan election; legislature may refer issue of merit selection of judges to voters in general election; 8-year terms.

COURT OF APPEALS
Jurisdiction: Writs. Appeals from Circuit Court not reserved for Supreme Court review. *Judges:* 12; selection, retention same as for Supreme Court.

CIRCUIT COURT
Jurisdiction: Civil cases over $5,000, criminal cases. Retries appeals from lower courts. Jury trials permitted. 28 circuits. *Judges:* 28; selection, retention same as for Supreme Court; 6-year terms.

DISTRICT COURT
Jurisdiction: Civil and small claims cases under $5,000, city ordinance and traffic violations, misdemeanor criminal cases and felony preliminary hearings. No jury trial. *Judges:* 110; selection, retention by nonpartisan election.

CITY COURT
Jurisdiction: Operates in smaller communities where District Courts do not exist and exercises city-wide jurisdiction. *Judges:* 92; selection and retention by nonpartisan election. Law degree not required.

CALIFORNIA

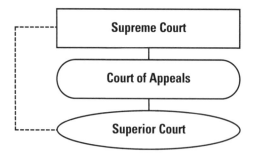

Court Homepage: *www.courtinfo.ca.gov*

Constitution: Art. VI.
Statutes: West's Annotated California Codes (2004), Code of Civil Procedure secs. 33-304.

SUPREME COURT
Jurisdiction: Extraordinary writs. Appeals of death-penalty cases; may review all other appeals. *Judges:* 7; appointment by governor, confirmation by Commission on Judicial Appointments until next gubernatorial election, retention by nonpartisan election; 12-year terms.

COURT OF APPEALS
Jurisdiction: Extraordinary writs. Reviews appeals from Superior Court except death-penalty cases. 6 districts. *Judges:* 105; selection, retention same as for Supreme Court.

SUPERIOR COURT
Jurisdiction: Trial court of general jurisdiction for all civil and criminal cases. Jury trials permitted. In each county seat. Small claims division hears cases under $5,000. Appeals from small claims cases and limited civil cases (where $25,000 or less is at issue) is in the appellate division of the Superior Court. *Judges:* 1,498; selection same as for Supreme Court or by nonpartisan election, retention by nonpartisan election; 6-year terms.

COLORADO

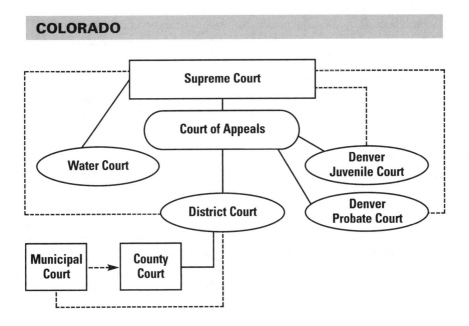

Court Homepage: www.courts.state.co.us

Constitution: Art. VI.
Statutes: Colorado Revised Statutes (2004), Title 13 (Courts and Court Procedure).

SUPREME COURT

Jurisdiction: Extraordinary writs. Appeals challenging constitutionality of state law, municipal charter provisions or ordinances; electoral cases; Public Utilities Commission decisions; some water cases; death penalty. May review other cases. *Judges:* 7 (may be increased to 9 if court requests and legislature concurs); governor appoints from nominating commission's list, retention by nonpartisan election after at least 2 years; thereafter, 10-year terms.

COURT OF APPEALS

Jurisdiction: Appeals from lower courts except those reserved for Supreme Court review. Appeals from state board and agency decisions. *Judges:* 16; selection, retention same as for Supreme Court; 8-year terms.

DISTRICT COURT

Jurisdiction: Civil cases, domestic relations, probate and juvenile cases (except Denver). Criminal cases. Reviews or retries cases of record from Municipal, County courts. Jury trials permitted. In 22 districts. *Judges:* 132; selection, retention same as for Supreme Court; 6-year terms.

DENVER PROBATE COURT

Jurisdiction: Probate, wills, guardianships. Jury trials permitted. Denver only. *Judges:* District Court judges and magistrates serve; selection, retention same as for Supreme Court; 6-year terms.

DENVER JUVENILE COURT

Jurisdiction: Cases involving minors. Denver only. Jury trials permitted. *Judges:* District Court judges and magistrates serve; selection, retention same as for Supreme Court; 6-year terms.

WATER COURT

Jurisdiction: Water rights, uses, administration. Jury trials permitted. 7 locations. *Judges:* 11; District Court judges appointed by Supreme Court.

COUNTY COURT

Jurisdiction: Civil cases under $15,000 except land title; small claims. Misdemeanors, felony preliminary hearings. Retries cases not of record from Municipal Court. Jury trials permitted except in small claims. In all counties. *Judges:* 106; selection, retention same as for Supreme Court; 4-year terms.

MUNICIPAL COURT

Jurisdiction: City, traffic violations. Jury trials permitted. In 206 cities. *Judges:* 250; municipal governing board appoints for at least 2 years, retention by reappointment for 2 or more years. Law degree not required.

CONNECTICUT

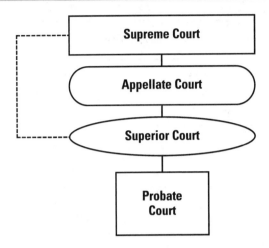

Court Homepage: *www.jud.state.ct.us*

Constitution: Art. V, XXI.
Statutes: Connecticut General Statutes Annotated (2005), Title 45a (Probate Courts and Procedure) & Title 51 (Courts).

SUPREME COURT
Jurisdiction: Exclusive jurisdiction over constitutionality of state statutes or constitutional provisions, election or primary disputes, criminal cases with more than 20-year sentence or possible death penalty, judicial misconduct, extraordinary writs. May review other appeals. ***Judges:*** 7 (who also serve in Superior Court); appointed by General Assembly from judicial selection commission's list; 8-year terms.

APPELLATE COURT
Jurisdiction: Reviews appeals except those reserved for Supreme Court review; hears administrative-agency appeals. ***Judges:*** 9; selection, retention same as for Supreme Court; 8-year terms.

SUPERIOR COURT
Jurisdiction: Civil, equity cases except probate; criminal cases, family law cases and juvenile cases. Appeals from administrative agencies. Jury trials permitted. 12 districts. ***Judges:*** 180; selection, retention same as for Supreme Court.

PROBATE COURT
Jurisdiction: Probate, adoption, commitment and conservatorships. In 133 cities and towns. ***Judges:*** 133; selection, retention by partisan election; 4-year terms. Law degree not required.

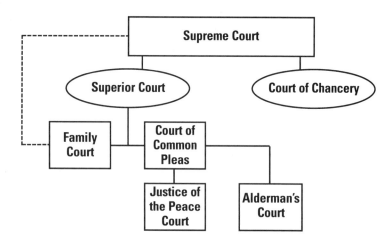

Court Homepage: *www.courts.state.de.us*

Constitution: Art. IV.
Statutes: Delaware Code Annotated (2004), Title 10 (Courts and Judicial Procedure).

SUPREME COURT
Jurisdiction: Extraordinary writs. Appellate review of Court of Chancery, Superior Court and Family Court cases. May issue advisory opinions. *Judges:* 5; governor appoints from judicial nominating commission with Senate's consent; 12-year terms.

COURT OF CHANCERY
Jurisdiction: Equity cases—land title, commercial and corporate matters, contracts, guardianships, trusts, estates. No jury trials. 3 locations.
Chancellors: 1. *Vice-Chancellors:* 4; selection, retention same as for Supreme Court; only a bare majority can be of the same political party.

SUPERIOR COURT
Jurisdiction: Civil cases, commitment of mentally ill, criminal cases. Reviews cases from administrative agencies, some cases from Court of Common Pleas. Retries some cases from Court of Common Pleas, support orders from Family Court, cases from Aldermen's, Justice of the Peace courts. Jury trials permitted. 3 locations. *Judges:* 19; selection, retention same as for Supreme Court.

COURT OF COMMON PLEAS
Jurisdiction: Civil, non-equity, cases under $50,000. Non-drug-related misdemeanors. Jury trials permitted. *Judges:* 9; selection, retention same as for Supreme Court.

FAMILY COURT
Jurisdiction: Domestic relations, adoptions, cases involving minors. Jury trials not permitted. *Judges:* 15; selection, retention same as for Supreme Court.

JUSTICE OF THE PEACE COURT
Jurisdiction: Civil cases under $15,000. Minor traffic, misdemeanor violations. Jury trials in some cases only. 19 courts. *Judges:* 58; selection, retention same as for Supreme Court, without political party diversity requirement; 4-year terms. Law degree not required.

ALDERMEN'S COURT
Jurisdiction: Varies; usually civil cases, minor misdemeanors, city and traffic violations. *Aldermen:* 8; selection, retention determined by local law. No jury trials. Law degree not required in some locations.

DISTRICT OF COLUMBIA

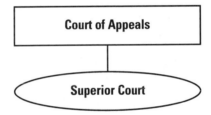

Court Homepages: www.dcappeals.gov (Court of Appeals)
www.dcsc.gov (Superior Court)

Statutes: District of Columbia Code (2004), Title 11 (Organization and Jurisdiction of the Courts).

COURT OF APPEALS
Jurisdiction: Appeals from Superior Court, city agencies; appeals of orders and decisions by mayor, city council, answers questions of law certified by the U.S. Supreme Court, a Court of Appeals, or the highest court of any state. *Judges:* 9; U.S. President appoints from Judicial Nomination Commission, U.S. Senate confirms for 15-year term; retention by reappointment; 15-year terms.

SUPERIOR COURT
Jurisdiction: Divisions: Civil—civil, equity, landlord-tenant disputes, small claims (under $5,000). Family—family disputes, divorce, marital property, commitment, juvenile cases. Probate—probate, guardianship. Criminal— violations of D.C. criminal code. Jury trials permitted. *Judges:* 59; selection, retention same as for Court of Appeals.

NOTE: Violations of D.C. criminal code may be tried in U. S. District Court for D.C. if indictment is for both D.C. and federal crimes.

FLORIDA

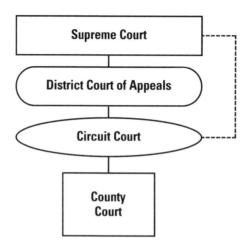

Court Homepage: *www.flcourts.org*

Constitution: Art. V.
Statutes: Florida Statutes Annotated (2004), Title 5 (Judicial Branch).

SUPREME COURT
Jurisdiction: Extraordinary writs. Mandatory review of cases involving death penalty, bond validation, utilities, state officials; interpretation or validity of state statute or constitutional provision and certain orders of the Public Service Commission. May review cases of "great public interest," appeals from some state administrative agencies. *Judges:* 7; governor appoints from nominating commission's list, retention by nonpartisan election after at least 1 year; thereafter, 6-year terms.

DISTRICT COURT OF APPEALS
Jurisdiction: Extraordinary writs. Appeals from Circuit Court, 72 state administrative agencies. 5 districts. *Judges:* 62; selection, retention same as for Supreme Court; 6-year terms.

CIRCUIT COURT
Jurisdiction: Civil cases over $15,000. Cases involving equity, land title, domestic relations, minors, probate, guardianship, commitment of mentally ill. Felonies and related misdemeanors. Reviews or retries appeals from County Court (except those reserved for Supreme Court review), local administrative agencies. Jury trials permitted. 20 circuits. *Judges:* 527; selection, retention same as for the Supreme Court; 6-year terms.

COUNTY COURT
Jurisdiction: Civil cases under $15,000; small claims. Preliminary felony hearings, misdemeanors, city and county violations, traffic violations. Jury trials permitted. In all counties. *Judges:* 269; selection, retention by nonpartisan election; 6-year terms.

GEORGIA

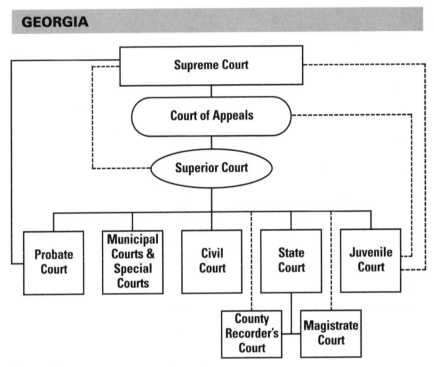

Court Homepage: *www.georgiacourts.org*

Constitution: Art. VI.
Statutes: Official Code of Georgia Annotated (2004), Title 15 (Courts).

SUPREME COURT
Jurisdiction: Extraordinary writs. Appeals involving death penalty, interpretation or constitutionality of laws, election contests, equity, land title, wills, divorce, alimony. May review cases of "great public import" from Court of Appeals or review questions of law from any state or federal appellate court. *Justices:* 7; selection, retention by nonpartisan election; 6-year terms.

COURT OF APPEALS
Jurisdiction: Extraordinary writs. May review cases not reserved for Supreme Court review, including claims for damages, child custody cases, administrative law cases and all criminal cases except capital felonies. *Judges:* 12; selection, retention same as for Supreme Court; 6-year terms.

SUPERIOR COURT

Jurisdiction: General jurisdiction trial court, including civil cases, land title, divorce, other equity cases (except probate). Felonies, including violent juvenile crimes, misdemeanors. Appeals from inferior courts. Jury trials permitted. 49 circuits. *Judges:* 188; selection, retention same as for Supreme Court; 4-year terms.

NOTE: No uniform system of lower courts. County and some city systems created by special legislation, sometimes by grand jury recommendation. Following are some typical courts, but local applications vary.

JUVENILE COURT

Jurisdiction: Exclusive jurisdiction for deprived or unruly juveniles. Concurrent jurisdiction with Superior Court in cases involving capital felonies, custody and child support cases and in proceedings to terminate parental rights. Jurisdiction over consent to marriage and cases involving the Interstate Compact on Juveniles. 159 locations. *Judges:* 80; appointed by Superior Court judge; 4-year terms.

STATE COURT

Jurisdiction: Civil cases, except those within the exclusive jurisdiction of the Superior Court. Misdemeanors, preliminary felony hearings and traffic violations. May review cases from lower courts. Jury trials permitted. 63 counties. *Judges:* 100; selection, retention same as for Supreme Court; 4-year terms.

PROBATE COURT

Jurisdiction: Probate, guardianship, commitment of mentally ill, marriage licenses. Traffic (some counties); truancy (some counties). In all counties. *Judges:* 159; selection, retention by partisan election, except in 25 counties with selection, retention by nonpartisan elections; 4-year terms.

MAGISTRATE COURT

Jurisdiction: Civil cases under $15,000. Preliminary felony hearings, county violations. In all counties. *Chief Magistrates:* 159; selection, retention same as for Probate Court. *Magistrates:* 346; appointed by chief magistrate for indefinite terms or by partisan election. Law degree not required.

MUNICIPAL COURTS AND SPECIAL COURTS

Jurisdiction: Generally city, traffic violations; preliminary felony hearings. 380 courts. *Judges:* 307; special courts and municipal courts serve incorporated municipalities under various names and with varying jurisdictions; selection, retention locally determined.

COUNTY RECORDER'S COURT

Jurisdiction: County violations, criminal case preliminaries. In Chatham, DeKalb, Gwinnett, Muscogee counties. *Judges:* 16; selection, retention locally determined.

CIVIL COURT
Jurisdiction: Civil law cases under $7,500 in Bibb County, under $25,000 in Richmond County. Misdemeanor and felony preliminary hearings. Jury trials permitted. In 2 counties. *Judges:* 4; selection, retention locally determined.

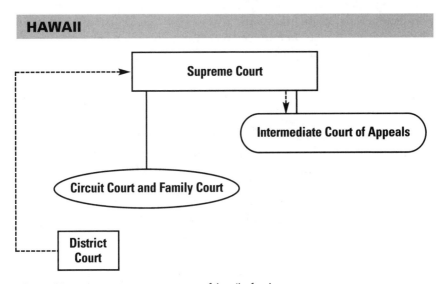

Court Homepage: www.courts.state.hi.us/index.jsp

Constitution: Art. VI.
Statutes: Hawaii Revised Statutes (2004), Titles 32-36 (Courts and Judicial Proceedings).

SUPREME COURT
Jurisdiction: Extraordinary writs. May review appeals from lower courts, administrative agencies. Original jurisdiction to answer questions of law certified to it by a federal court and entertain cases submitted on agreed statements of fact. *Judges:* 5; governor appoints from nominating commission's list with senate confirmation; 10-year terms.

INTERMEDIATE COURT OF APPEALS
Jurisdiction: Reviews cases assigned by Supreme Court. *Judges:* 3; selection, retention same as for Supreme Court.

CIRCUIT COURT AND FAMILY COURT
Jurisdiction: Civil cases over $20,000; exclusive jurisdiction in probate, guardianship and criminal felony cases. Circuit Courts have concurrent jurisdiction with District Courts in non-jury cases between $10,000 and $20,000. The First Circuit also sits as the Land Court for applications for land title and land rights and the Tax Appeal Court for tax disputes. The Family Court Division hears cases involving minors. Appeals from some

administrative agencies. Jury trials permitted. 4 circuits. *Judges:* 29 judges and 16 district family judges; selection, retention same as for Supreme Court.

DISTRICT COURT

Jurisdiction: Civil cases under $20,000 (except land title, libel, slander); exclusive small claims jurisdiction for matters under $3,500. Concurrent jurisdiction with Circuit Court non-jury cases between $10,000 and $20,000. No jury trials. 4 circuits. *Judges:* 22; appointment, retention same as for Supreme Court; 6-year terms.

IDAHO

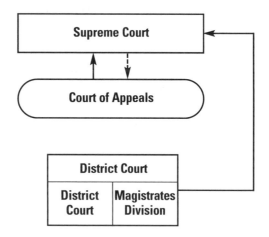

Court Homepage: www.isc.idaho.gov/judicial.html

Constitution: Art. V.
Statutes: Idaho Official Code (2004), Title 1 (Courts and Court Officials).

SUPREME COURT

Jurisdiction: Extraordinary writs. Original jurisdiction for claims against the state. Reviews appeals of death-penalty cases, cases from Public Utilities, Industrial Accident Commissions. May review cases from lower courts. *Judges:* 5; selection, retention by nonpartisan election; 6-year terms.

COURT OF APPEALS

Jurisdiction: Reviews cases assigned by Supreme Court. *Judges:* 3; selection, retention same as for Supreme Court.

DISTRICT COURT

Jurisdiction: Civil, equity, criminal cases. Appeals from Magistrates Division, state agencies and boards. Jury trials permitted. 7 districts. *Judges:* 39; selection, retention same as for Supreme Court; 4-year terms.

MAGISTRATES DIVISION OF DISTRICT COURT

Jurisdiction: Civil cases under $10,000 assigned by District Court. Probate, domestic relations, cases involving minors. Liens under $2,000. Small claims under $3,000. Criminal cases with less than $1,000 fine or 1-year sentence. Preliminary felony hearings; warrants. Jury trials permitted. 7 districts. *Magistrates:* 83; District Magistrates Commission appoints for 18 months; retention by nonpartisan election; 4-year terms.

ILLINOIS

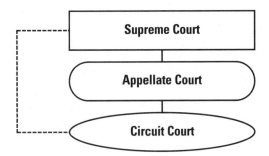

Court Homepage: www.state.il.us/court

Constitution: Art. VI.
Statutes: Illinois Compiled Statutes (2004), Chapter 705 (Courts).

SUPREME COURT

Jurisdiction: Original jurisdiction in cases relating to revenue, mandamus, prohibition or habeas corpus. Circuit Court judgments imposing a sentence of death are directly appealable to the Supreme Court. Appeals from the Appellate Court to the Supreme Court are a matter of right, if a federal or state constitutional question arises for the first time, or if a division of the Appellate Court certifies that a case decided by it involves a question of such importance that the case should be decided by the Supreme Court. Other cases are appealable from Circuit and Appellate courts to the Supreme Court as provided by Supreme Court rule. The Supreme Court also has jurisdiction to hear cases involving redistricting of the General Assembly and the ability of the governor to serve or resume office. *Judges:* 7; selection by partisan election, retention by nonpartisan election; 10-year terms.

APPELLATE COURT

Jurisdiction: Appeals from final judgments of a Circuit Court are a matter of right to the Appellate Court, except 1) in cases appealable directly to the Supreme Court, and 2) from judgments of acquittal in criminal cases. The Appellate Court also provides direct review of certain administrative actions.

5 districts. ***Judges:*** 42 (Plus additional judges may be assigned by the Supreme Court to the Appellate Court, temporarily, on a showing of need); selection, retention same as for Supreme Court.

CIRCUIT COURT

Jurisdiction: Court of original jurisdiction; hears most cases, including civil, equity, and criminal cases. Small claims actions and traffic cases. Hears cases relating to revenue, mandamus, prohibition and habeas corpus, if the Supreme Court chooses not to exercise its jurisdiction. Reviews administrative orders from certain state agencies. Jury trials permitted in most cases. 22 circuits. ***Judges:*** 509 Circuit judges and 391 associate judges. Circuit judges are elected for 6 years, may be retained by voters for additional 6-year terms and can hear any kind of case. Associate judges are appointed by Circuit judges, under Supreme Court rules; 4-year terms.

NOTE: Illinois Court of Claims, a quasi-judicial part of the legislative branch, hears civil claims against the state, crime victims' compensation cases, claims for time unjustly served in prison. These cases are not appealable to judiciary branch courts. The court sits in Springfield and Chicago. It consists of a chief justice and 6 judges appointed by the governor, with the advice and consent of the senate; 6-year terms.

INDIANA

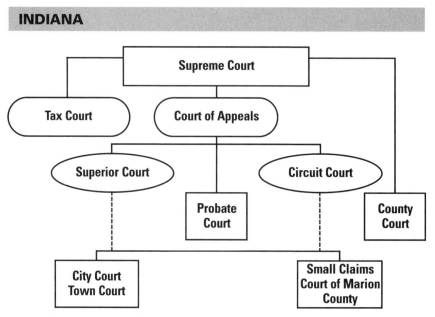

Court Homepage: *www.in.gov/judiciary/courts*

Constitution: Art. VII.
Statutes: West's Annotated Indiana Code (2004), Title 33 (Courts and Court Officers).

SUPREME COURT

Jurisdiction: Appellate jurisdiction in all criminal cases; original jurisdiction in appeals from a judgment imposing a sentence of death, life imprisonment, or imprisonment for a term greater than 50 years for a single offense. Appeals declaring a state or federal statute unconstitutional are taken directly to the Supreme Court. Original jurisdiction over admission to the bar, practice of law, attorney discipline and disbarment, and judicial discipline, removal and retirement. Upon petition, cases involving substantial questions of law, great public importance or emergencies may also be heard by the court. *Judges:* 5; the present court is served by a chief justice and 4 associate justices. However, the Constitution provides that the number of associate justices may be increased to as many as 8 by action of the legislature. The governor appoints justices from the Judicial Nominating Commission's list, and that person serves as a Supreme Court justice for a minimum of 2 years before becoming subject to a retention vote at a General Election. The incumbent justices are subject to statewide yes-or-no votes on the question of their retention in office; if approved, he or she begins a 10-year term.

COURT OF APPEALS

Jurisdiction: Appeals not reserved for Supreme Court review; appeals from some administrative agencies. 5 districts. *Judges:* 15; selection, retention same as for Supreme Court; 10-year terms.

SUPERIOR COURT

Jurisdiction: The Superior Courts are individually created and regulated, therefore, jurisdiction varies from court to court. Generally, the Superior Courts have concurrent civil, criminal and appellate jurisdiction with the Circuit Court and have varying degrees of jurisdiction in probate, juvenile and small claims matters. Jury trials permitted. 74 counties. *Judges:* 193; selection, retention by partisan election (except in Allen, Lake, St. Joseph and Vanderburgh counties, which have their own selection and retention policies); 6-year terms.

CIRCUIT COURT

Jurisdiction: Original jurisdiction in all civil and criminal matters except where exclusive jurisdiction is conferred upon one of the lower courts. In the absence of lower courts in any county, the Circuit Court assumes the jurisdiction reserved for that lower court. Retries appeals from city, town courts. Jury trials permitted. 90 circuits. *Judges:* 102; selection, retention by partisan election (except Vanderburgh County, where nonpartisan elections are held); 6-year terms.

COUNTY COURT

Jurisdiction: Contract and tort cases under $10,000; certain landlord-tenant actions; possession of property cases under $10,000; small claims. Misdemeanors, criminal cases with less than $1,000 fine or 1-year sentence. Jury trials permitted. 3 counties. *Judges:* 4; selection, retention by partisan election; 6-year terms.

PROBATE COURT
Jurisdiction: Probate, guardianship, adoption, cases involving minors. Jury trials permitted. St. Joseph County only. *Judges:* 1; selection, retention same as for County Courts.

SMALL CLAIMS COURT OF MARION COUNTY
Jurisdiction: Small claims (under $6,000). 9 divisions in Marion County. *Judges:* 9; selection, retention by partisan election; 4-year terms.

CITY, TOWN COURTS
Jurisdiction: Jurisdiction varies by county and town. Generally, civil cases under certain amounts, from $500 to $3,000. Misdemeanors with less than $1,000 fine and 1-year sentence; city violations. Jury trials permitted. 48 city, 27 town courts. *Judges:* 48 city, 27 town; selection, retention by partisan election; 4-year terms.

TAX COURT
Jurisdiction: Appeals from Dept. of State Revenue and State Board of Tax Commissioners. In Indianapolis, statewide jurisdiction. *Judges:* 1; selection, retention same as for Supreme Court.

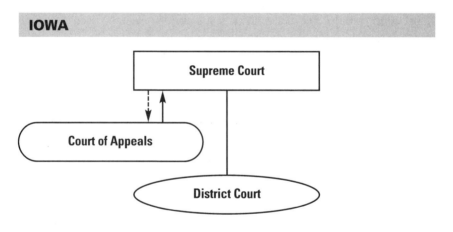

IOWA

Court Homepage: www.judicial.state.ia.us

Constitution: Art. V.
Statutes: Iowa Code (2003), Title 15 (Judicial Branch and Judicial Procedures).

SUPREME COURT
Jurisdiction: Extraordinary writs. Tries legislative redistricting cases. General appellate jurisdiction in civil and criminal cases including questions concerning the constitutionality of legislative or executive acts. May review or transfer to Court of Appeals real-estate cases over $3,000 and civil cases over $4,000. *Judges:* 7; governor appoints from nominating commission's list for at least 1 year; retention by nonpartisan election; 8-year terms.

COURT OF APPEALS
Jurisdiction: Writs. Reviews civil, criminal cases transferred from Supreme Court. *Judges:* 9; governor appoints from nominating commission's list for at least 1 year, retention by nonpartisan election; 6-year terms.

DISTRICT COURT
Jurisdiction: General trial jurisdiction for civil, criminal, probate and juvenile cases. Jury trials permitted. *Judges:* 3 levels of judicial officers: District Court judges, District associate judges and magistrates. District Court judges have general jurisdiction, while District associate judges and magistrates have limited jurisdiction. Currently, there are 116 District Court judges, 67 District associate judges and 133 magistrates; selection, retention for District Court judges same as for the judges in the Court of Appeals; 6-year terms for District Court judges, 4-year terms for associates and magistrates. For magistrates, law degree not required but preferred.

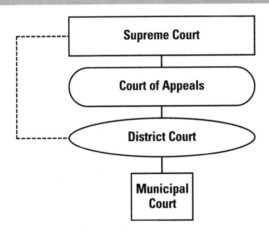

Court Homepage: www.kscourts.org

Constitution: Art. III.
Statutes: Kansas Statutes Annotated (2003), Chapter 12, Articles 41-47 (Code for Municipal Court) & Chapter 20, Articles 1-31 (Courts).

SUPREME COURT
Jurisdiction: Extraordinary writs, legislative redistricting. Reviews life-sentence cases, some constitutional, felony cases. May review other cases from Court of Appeals. *Judges:* 7; governor appoints for 1 year from nominating commission's list, retention by nonpartisan election; 6-year terms.

COURT OF APPEALS
Jurisdiction: Appeals from District Court not reserved for Supreme Court

review. Also original actions in habeas corpus. *Judges:* 11; selection, retention same as for Supreme Court; 4-year terms.

DISTRICT COURT
Jurisdiction: General original jurisdiction over all civil and criminal cases, including divorce and domestic relations, damage suits, probate and administration of estates, guardianships, conservatorships, care of the mentally ill, juvenile matters and small claims. Appeals from Municipal Court, administrative agencies. Jury trials permitted. 31 districts. *Judges:* 160 District judges (plus an additional 74 magistrates); selection, retention by gubernatorial appointment (1 year) from nominating commission in 17 districts and by partisan election (4 year) in the 14 other districts, retention by nonpartisan election; 4-year terms. Law degree not required for magistrates.

MUNICIPAL COURT
Jurisdiction: Violations of city ordinances, such as traffic and other minor offenses. A person charged with an offense in Municipal Court may be represented by a lawyer. Jury trials not allowed. Appeals from Municipal Court are to the District Court. 387 Municipal Courts. *Judges:* 258; selection by appointment by district nominating commission, retention by reappointment; terms vary.

KENTUCKY

Court Homepage: www.kycourts.net

Constitution: Sections 109 to 144
Statutes: Kentucky Revised Statutes (2004), Title 4, Chapters 21 to 34 (Judicial Branch).

SUPREME COURT
Jurisdiction: Necessary writs. Reviews cases in which death penalty or more than 20-year sentence imposed; cases from Court of Appeals involving issues

of "great and immediate public importance." May review all other cases.
Judges: 7; selection, retention by nonpartisan election; 8-year terms.

COURT OF APPEALS
Jurisdiction: Necessary writs. Reviews cases tried in Circuit Court, from some administrative agencies. May review cases from Circuit Court tried in District Court. *Judges:* 14; selection, retention same as for Supreme Court.

CIRCUIT COURT
Jurisdiction: Civil cases over $4,000, contested probate, equity, land title. Felonies. Reviews cases from District Court, some administrative agencies, boards, commissions. Jury trials permitted. 56 circuits. *Judges:* 11; selection, retention same as for Supreme Court.

DISTRICT COURT
Jurisdiction: Juvenile matters, city and county ordinances, misdemeanors, traffic offenses, probate of wills, felony preliminary hearings, civil cases involving $4,000 or less, guardianship and conservatorship for disabled persons, commitment of mentally ill, cases relating to domestic violence and abuse and small claims under $1,500. Retries appeals from local administrative agencies, boards. Jury trials permitted. 59 circuits. *Judges:* 125; selection, retention same as for Supreme Court; 4-year terms.

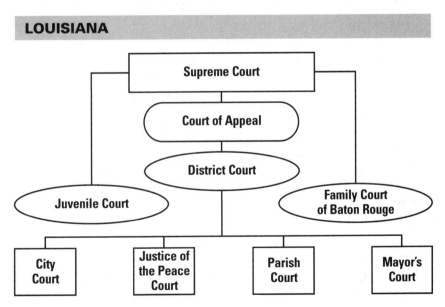

Court Homepage: www.state.la.us/gov_judicial.htm

Constitution: Art. V.
Statutes: Louisiana Revised Statutes (2004), Title 13(Courts and Judicial Procedure).

SUPREME COURT

Jurisdiction: Exclusive original jurisdiction in cases involving disciplinary actions against lawyers and judges. Appellate jurisdiction in cases in which a law or ordinance has been declared unconstitutional and in capital cases where the death penalty has been imposed. These cases originate at the trial court level, but bypass review by the intermediate courts of appeal in order to be heard directly by the Supreme Court. Supervisory jurisdiction over all courts. Discretionary review of Court of Appeal decisions. May issue necessary writs. *Judges:* 7; judges are selected through a partisan election. Louisiana uses a blanket primary, in which all candidates appear with party labels on the primary ballot; then the 2 candidates with the most votes compete in the general election. 10-year terms.

COURT OF APPEAL

Jurisdiction: Extraordinary writs. Appellate jurisdiction over all civil cases, matters from Family Court and Juvenile Court and criminal cases triable by a jury (except death-penalty cases as noted above). 5 circuits. *Judges:* 54; selection, retention same as for Supreme Court.

DISTRICT COURT

Jurisdiction: Civil cases, real property, probate, domestic relations, juvenile matters (in parishes without a separate juvenile court). Criminal appeals and civil trial court appeals. Jury trials permitted in most cases. 41 locations. *Judges:* 214; selection, retention same as for Supreme Court; 6-year terms.

CITY COURT

Jurisdiction: In Louisiana, the primary courts of limited jurisdiction are the City Courts. Civil cases in which the amount in dispute does not exceed an amount between $10,000 and $25,000, depending on the court; ordinance violations; misdemeanors; traffic cases. 49 City Courts. *Judges:* 68; selection, retention by partisan election; 6-year terms.

JUSTICE OF THE PEACE COURT

Jurisdiction: Justice of the Peace Courts are located in cities without City Courts. Civil jurisdiction under $3,000 (with some exceptions), property cases under $2,000, landlord-tenant cases under $2,000, eviction cases. 390 locations. *Judges:* 390; selection, retention same as for City Court; 6-year terms. Law degree not required.

JUVENILE COURT

Jurisdiction: Cases involving minors, adoptions. 4 parishes (Caddo, East Baton Rouge, Jefferson and Orleans). *Judges:* 15; selection, retention same as for City Court; 6-year terms (8-year terms in Orleans).

PARISH COURT

Jurisdiction: Civil cases under $20,000, criminal cases punishable by fines less than $1,000 or imprisonment less than 6 months. One Parish Court in

Ascension; two Parish Courts in Jefferson. *Judges:* 5; selection, retention same as for City Court.

FAMILY COURT OF BATON ROUGE
Jurisdiction: Domestic relations. East Baton Rouge Parish has the only Family Court. *Judges:* 4; selection, retention same as for City Court.

MAYOR'S COURT
Jurisdiction: City, traffic violations. 250 cities. *Judges:* 250; selection, retention varies.

MAINE

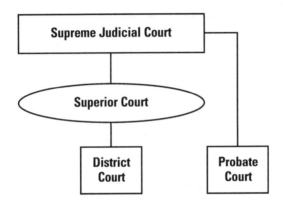

Court Homepage: *www.courts.state.me.us*

Constitution: Art. VI.
Statutes: Maine Revised Statutes (2004), Title 4 (Judiciary).

SUPREME JUDICIAL COURT
Jurisdiction: Necessary writs. Reviews cases from Superior Court, Probate Court, Public Utilities Commission, Worker Compensation Commission's Appellate Division. Reviews some cases from District Court. Conducts appellate review of criminal sentences of 1 year or more. Advisory opinions concerning important questions of law when requested by the governor. *Judges:* 7; Judicial Selection Committee recommends candidates, governor appoints with legislature's consent; 7-year terms.

SUPERIOR COURT
Jurisdiction: Adult criminal cases (including murder and class A, B, C, D and E offenses), post-conviction reviews, civil cases, cases in which equitable relief is requested and appeals from decisions of state and local administrative agencies. Jury trials permitted. 16 counties. *Judges:* 16; selection, retention same as for Supreme Judicial Court.

DISTRICT COURT
Jurisdiction: Civil cases including monetary damages claims, domestic relations cases, involuntary commitments, Class D and E criminal offenses. No jury trials. 13 districts. *Judges:* 33; selection, retention same as for Supreme Judicial Court.

PROBATE COURT
Jurisdiction: Estates and trusts, adoptions and name changes, guardianship and protective proceedings. No jury trials. In all counties. *Judges:* 16; selection, retention by partisan election; 4-year terms.

MARYLAND

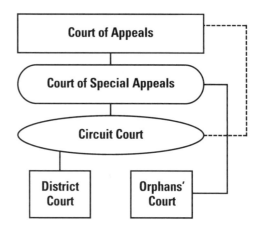

Court Homepage: www.courts.state.md.us

Constitution: Art. IV.
Statutes: Annotated Code of Maryland (2005), Courts and Judicial Proceedings.

COURT OF APPEALS
Jurisdiction: Appeals of legislative redistricting, death-penalty cases and certified questions. May review other appeals. *Judges:* 7; governor appoints, senate confirms; retention by nonpartisan election after at least 1 year; thereafter, 10-year terms.

COURT OF SPECIAL APPEALS
Jurisdiction: Appeals from Circuit and Orphans' courts. *Judges:* 13; selection, retention same as for Court of Appeals.

CIRCUIT COURT
Jurisdiction: Civil cases involving $5,000 or more, tort, contract, real property, estate, mental health, domestic relations. Felonies with more than $2,500 fine

or 3-year sentence, misdemeanors and miscellaneous criminal. Cases involving minors (except Montgomery County). Exclusive appellate jurisdiction over District Court, Orphans' Court and certain administrative agencies. Jury trials permitted. In all counties and Baltimore City; 8 circuits and 24 Circuit Court locations. *Judges:* 146; selection by governor; appointment, retention by nonpartisan election after at least 1 year; thereafter, 15-year terms.

DISTRICT COURT
Jurisdiction: Landlord-tenant cases, replevin actions, motor vehicle violations, misdemeanors and certain felonies. In civil cases the District Court has exclusive jurisdiction in claims for amounts up to $5,000, and concurrent jurisdiction with the Circuit Court in claims for amounts above $5,000 but less than $25,000. The jurisdiction of the court in criminal cases is concurrent with the Circuit Court for offenses in which the penalty may be confinement for 3 years or more, a fine of $2,500 or more or offenses that are felonies. Preliminary felony hearings. In Montgomery County, cases involving minors. No jury trials. 12 districts. *Judges:* 111; governor appoints, senate confirms; 10-year terms.

ORPHANS' COURT
Jurisdiction: Probate, guardianship. In Baltimore City and all counties (except Montgomery and Harford). *Judges:* 66; selection, retention by partisan election; 4-year terms.

MASSACHUSETTS

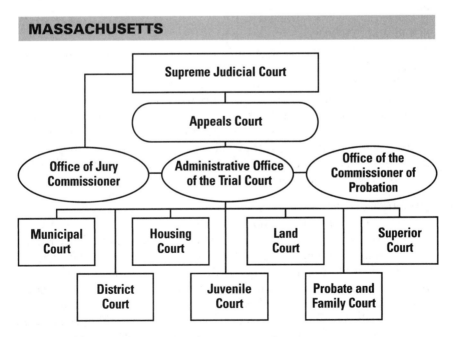

Court Homepage: www.mass.gov/courts

Constitution: Pt. 2, Ch. 3.
Statutes: Massachusetts General Laws (2005), Chapters 185, 211-222.

SUPREME JUDICIAL COURT

Jurisdiction: Concurrent appellate jurisdiction with the Appeals Court over civil and criminal matters in all lower courts; reviews appeals of first-degree murder convictions, cases certified for direct review, cases transferred from Appeals Court if novel legal question or if in the public interest, appeals from single justice sessions, and disciplinary actions against court clerks, judges, or attorneys. Provides advisory opinions, upon request, to the governor and legislature on various legal issues. *Judges:* 7; governor appoints with Executive Counsel's consent; term to age 70. Law degree not required.

APPEALS COURT

Jurisdiction: Most appeals from the several Departments of the Trial Court are entered initially in the Appeals Court; some are then transferred to the Supreme Judicial Court, but a majority will be decided by the Appeals Court. The Appeals Court also has jurisdiction over appeals from final decisions of the Appellate Tax Board, the Labor Relations Commission and the Department of Industrial Accidents. *Judges:* 25; selection, retention same as for Supreme Judicial Court.

TRIAL COURT OF THE COMMONWEALTH OF MASSACHUSETTS

The Trial Court of Massachusetts consists of the seven departments listed below:

SUPERIOR COURT

Jurisdiction: Original jurisdiction in civil actions over $25,000, matters where equitable relief is sought, actions involving labor disputes where injunctive relief is sought. Exclusive authority to convene medical malpractice tribunals. Exclusive original jurisdiction in first degree murder cases and original jurisdiction for all other crimes. Jurisdiction over all felony matters, although it shares jurisdiction over crimes where other Trial Court Departments have concurrent jurisdiction. Appellate jurisdiction over certain administrative proceedings. Jury trials permitted. 14 counties. *Judges:* 82; selection, retention same as for Supreme Judicial Court.

DISTRICT COURT

Jurisdiction: Criminal jurisdiction in all felonies punishable by a sentence of up to 5 years and many other specific felonies with greater potential penalties. Misdemeanors, violations of city and town ordinances and bylaws. In civil matters, District Court judges sitting in Berkshire, Essex, Middlesex and Norfolk counties conduct both jury and jury-waived trials and determine with finality any matter in which the likelihood of recovery does not exceed $25,000. In the Commonwealth's other counties, District Court judges exercise jury-waived trial jurisdiction in civil cases in matters involving $25,000 or less.

In all counties, the District Court tries small claims involving up to $2,000. 62 divisions. *Judges:* 158; selection, retention same as for Supreme Judicial Court.

BOSTON MUNICIPAL COURT
Jurisdiction: Most criminal offenses which do not require the imposition of a state prison sentence; original jurisdiction over a number of serious felonies (concurrent with the Superior Court). Civil jurisdiction in contract and tort actions, cases remanded from the Superior Court, small claims, mental health commitments, summary process, supplementary proceedings, unemployment compensation appeals, paternity and support actions and domestic abuse actions. Jury trials permitted. Boston only. *Judges:* 11; selection, retention same as for Supreme Judicial Court.

JUVENILE COURT
Jurisdiction: Delinquency, children in need of services (CHINS), care and protection petitions, adult contributing to a delinquency of a minor cases, adoption, guardianship, termination of parental rights proceedings, youthful offender cases. Jury trials permitted. 9 established juvenile courts divisions. (Middlesex and Norfolk counties are still operating as District Courts.) *Judges:* 33; selection, retention same as for Supreme Judicial Court.

HOUSING COURT
Jurisdiction: Civil, criminal cases involving health, safety, welfare of housing occupants. Jury trials permitted. 5 divisions. *Judges:* 10; selection, retention same as for Supreme Judicial Court.

LAND COURT
Jurisdiction: Cases involving real property rights, such as land title, boundary disputes, validity and scope of zoning regulations, and foreclosures. In Boston, statewide jurisdiction. *Judges:* 5; selection, retention same as for Supreme Judicial Court.

PROBATE AND FAMILY COURT
Jurisdiction: Family matters such as divorce, paternity, child support, custody, visitation, adoption, termination of parental rights and abuse prevention. Probate matters such as wills, administrations, guardianships, conservatorships and change of name. General equity jurisdiction. In all counties. *Judges:* 51; selection, retention same as for Supreme Judicial Court.

MICHIGAN

Court Homepage: www.courts.michigan.gov

Constitution: Art. VI.
Statutes: Michigan Compiled Laws (2004), Chapters 600, 691, 692, 725-730.

SUPREME COURT
Jurisdiction: Writs. May review appeals from lower courts. *Judges:* 7; selection, retention by nonpartisan election; 8-year terms.

COURT OF APPEALS
Jurisdiction: Appeals from Circuit Court (criminal convictions appealed as a matter of right), Probate Court (certain types of cases may be appealed directly) and Court of Claims. 4 districts. *Judges:* 28; selection, retention by nonpartisan election; 6-year terms.

CIRCUIT COURT
Jurisdiction: Circuit Courts are trial courts of general jurisdiction. The Circuit Court has original jurisdiction in all criminal cases where the offense involves a felony or certain serious misdemeanors, civil cases over $25,000, family division cases, appeals from District Court, Probate Court and administrative agencies and drain code condemnation cases. The family division of the Circuit Court has exclusive jurisdiction over all family matters such as divorce, custody, support, paternity and adoptions. The family division also has ancillary jurisdiction over cases involving guardianships, conservatorships and proceedings involving the mentally ill or developmentally disabled. Jury trials permitted. 57 circuits. *Judges:* 210; selection, retention same as for Court of Appeals.

COURT OF CLAIMS
Jurisdiction: Claims over $1,000 against state. In Lansing, statewide jurisdiction. Part of the 30th Circuit Court. *Judges:* 30th Circuit judges serve.

PROBATE COURT

Jurisdiction: Wills, estates and trusts, guardianships, conservatorships, and the treatment of mentally ill and developmentally disabled persons, land condemnation. Jury trials in some cases. 78 locations. *Judges:* 106; selection, retention same as for Court of Appeals.

DISTRICT COURT

Jurisdiction: Civil cases under $25,000, land title, evictions, mortgage foreclosures, small claims (under $3,000). Criminal cases with less than 1-year sentence. Preliminary felony hearings, bail, traffic violations. Jury trials permitted. 104 locations. *Judges:* 258; selection, retention same as for Court of Appeals.

MUNICIPAL COURT

Jurisdiction: Civil and landlord-tenant cases under $1,500 (this can be raised to $3,000 by city legislature). Misdemeanors and city violations if less than 1-year sentence. Jury trials permitted. 5 cities. *Judges:* 6; selection, retention same as for Court of Appeals.

MINNESOTA

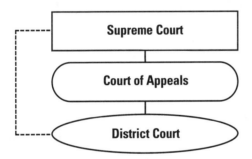

Court Homepage: *www.courts.state.mn.us/home*

Constitution: Art. VI.
Statutes: Minnesota Statutes (2004), Chapter 260 (Juveniles) & Chapters 480-494 (Judiciary).

SUPREME COURT

Jurisdiction: Extraordinary writs. Reviews cases from Court of Appeals involving conflict with Supreme Court precedent, constitutional or other important questions. Reviews first-degree murder, election-contest cases. May review other cases from lower courts. *Justices:* 7; selection, retention by nonpartisan election; 6-year terms.

COURT OF APPEALS

Jurisdiction: Writs. Reviews all final decisions of the District Courts, state agencies and local governments (except those reserved for Supreme Court review and opinions from the Conciliation Division). *Judges:* 16; selection, retention same as for Supreme Court.

DISTRICT COURT

Jurisdiction: The court of general jurisdiction; there are 6 divisions (conciliation, juvenile, probate, criminal, civil and family court). Conciliation Court is a small claims court; no attorneys, no juries, monetary settlements less than $7,500. Juvenile Court hears cases involving minors, delinquency, truancy and minor traffic offenses (closed to the public for the privacy of the juveniles). Probate Court is involved in the disposition of estates. Criminal Court hears traffic violations and murder trials. Civil Court has jurisdiction over cases brought between private parties for a settlement of a grievance. Family Court is involved with dissolution, child support, adoption and some juvenile matters. Jury trials permitted. 10 districts. *Judges:* 272; selection, retention same as for Supreme Court.

MISSISSIPPI

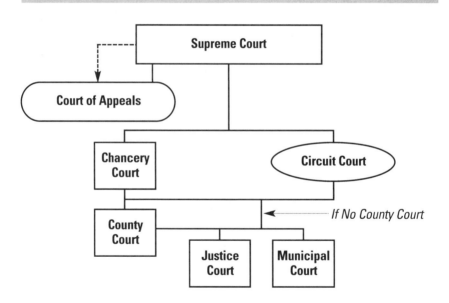

Court Homepage: www.mssc.state.ms.us

Constitution: Art. VI.
Statutes: Mississippi Code (2004), Title 9 (Courts).

SUPREME COURT

Jurisdiction: Extraordinary writs. May review cases from lower courts and administrative-agency cases involving public utility rates. *Judges:* 9; selection, retention by nonpartisan election; 8-year terms.

COURT OF APPEALS
Jurisdiction: Limited appellate jurisdiction; cases assigned to it by the Supreme Court; extraordinary writs. *Judges:* 10; selection, retention same as for Supreme Court.

CIRCUIT COURT
Jurisdiction: Extraordinary writs. Original jurisdiction in civil cases over $2,500 and all criminal cases. Concurrent jurisdiction with Chancery and County courts in other matters. Appellate jurisdiction over cases from County Court, some administrative agencies, Justice Court and Municipal Court. Jury trials permitted. 22 districts. *Judges:* 49; selection, retention by nonpartisan election; 4-year terms.

CHANCERY COURT
Jurisdiction: Extraordinary writs. Equity, probate, guardianship, commitment of mentally ill, domestic relations, land-title cases. Cases involving minors in locations without County Court. Appellate jurisdiction over equity cases and cases involving minors from County Court and some state agency decisions. Jury trials permitted. 20 districts. *Judges:* 45; selection, retention same as for Circuit Court.

COUNTY COURT
Jurisdiction: Concurrent jurisdiction with Circuit and Chancery courts in law and equity cases under $75,000. Concurrent jurisdiction with Circuit Court in all misdemeanor cases. Concurrent jurisdiction with Justice Courts in civil and criminal cases. Exclusive jurisdiction in eminent domain, partition of property and forcible entry and detainer. Youth Court Division—cases involving minors. Retries cases from Justice and Municipal courts. Jury trials permitted. 19 county seats. *Judges:* 24; selection, retention same as for Circuit Court.

JUSTICE COURT
Jurisdiction: Debt, damage, personal property cases under $2,500. Misdemeanors, preliminary felony hearings. Jury trials permitted. 92 courts. *Judges:* 191; selection, retention same as for Circuit Court.

MUNICIPAL COURT
Jurisdiction: City violations, preliminary felony hearings. 223 courts. *Judges:* 224; City governing board appoints lawyer in cities with more than 10,000 population. In other cities, a Justice Court judge of the county may serve. Law degree not required.

MISSOURI

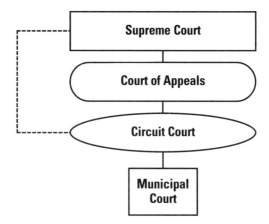

Court Homepage: *www.courts.mo.gov*

Constitution: Art. V.
Statutes: Missouri Revised Statutes (2004), Title 32 (Courts).

SUPREME COURT
Jurisdiction: May review cases from Court of Appeals. Exclusive appellate jurisdiction in cases involving constitutional law, federal treaties or statutes, revenue laws and death penalty or life sentence. *Judges:* 7; governor appoints for 1 year from nominating commission's list, retention by nonpartisan election; 12-year terms.

COURT OF APPEALS
Jurisdiction: Appeals not reserved for Supreme Court review. 3 districts. *Judges:* 32; selection, retention same as for Supreme Court.

CIRCUIT COURT
Jurisdiction: Courts of original civil and criminal jurisdiction. The Circuit Court consists of 6 divisions: Circuit (civil & criminal jurisdiction), Associate (civil cases less than $25,000, small claims, felony preliminary hearings and misdemeanors), Probate (estates and mental health proceedings), Municipal (traffic and ordinance violations), Juvenile (cases involving minors) and Family (dissolution of marriage, separation, custody and adoptions). Jury trials permitted. 45 circuits. *Judges:* Circuit Division has 135 Circuit judges. The other divisions are served by Circuit judges in conjunction with 175 Associate Circuit judges, 331 Municipal judges, and various commissioners. Circuit judges are elected by partisan elections or appointed by the governor (then subject to retention vote); 6-year terms. Associate Circuit judges are appointed in the same manner as Circuit judges; 4-year terms. Municipal judges are elected or appointed according to city ordinance or charter; terms of at least

2 years. Commissioners are appointed by Circuit judges in courts with heavy caseloads; 4-year terms usually.

MONTANA

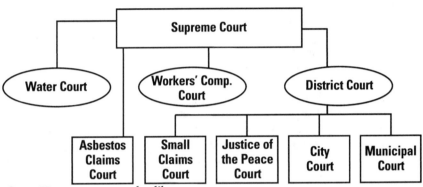

Court Homepage: *www.lawlibrary.state.mt.us*

Constitution: Art. VII.
Statutes: Montana Code Annotated (2003), Title 3 (Judiciary, Courts).

SUPREME COURT
Jurisdiction: Extraordinary writs. Appeals from lower courts. *Judges:* 7; governor appoints from nominating commission's list and senate confirms, retention by nonpartisan election; 8-year terms.

DISTRICT COURT
Jurisdiction: Civil cases, small claims, probate, cases involving minors. Felonies. Appeals from lower courts. Jury trials permitted. 22 districts. *Judges:* 42; selection, retention same as for Supreme Court; 6-year terms.

ASBESTOS CLAIMS COURT
Jurisdiction: Asbestos-related claims. Jury trials permitted. Appeals to Supreme Court. *Judges:* Appointed by the Supreme Court.

WATER COURT
Jurisdiction: Water rights. No jury trials. 4 divisions. *Judges:* 5; designated by committee vote; 4-year terms.

WORKERS' COMPENSATION COURT
Jurisdiction: Workers' compensation disputes. No jury trials. *Judges:* 1; governor appoints from nominating commission's list; 6-year terms.

JUSTICE OF THE PEACE COURT

Jurisdiction: Contracts, torts, real property rights less than $7,000.
Misdemeanors with fines less than $500 or sentences less than 6-months,
fish-and-game violations with less than $1,000 fine or 6-month sentence.
Preliminary hearings. Jury trials permitted except in small claims. In all
counties. *Judges:* 64; selection, retention by nonpartisan election; 4-year terms.

CITY COURT
Jurisdiction: Civil cases by city to recover taxes, debts if less than $5,000 and
small claims if less than $3,000. Ordinance violations, search warrants.
Preliminary hearings. Jury trials in some cases. 83 court locations. *Judges:* 45
(plus 33 who also serve as justices of the peace); elected by general elections;
4-year terms. Law degree not required.

MUNICIPAL COURT
Jurisdiction: Contract, property-damage cases under $300, forcible entry and
detainer. Criminal assault, property theft under $150, misdemeanors with less
than $500 fine or 6-month sentence. Jury trials permitted. 5 courts. *Judges:* 5;
elected by nonpartisan elections; 4-year terms.

SMALL CLAIMS COURT
Jurisdiction: Original jurisdiction, amounts less than $3,000. Appeals to
District Court. *Judges:* Appointed by District Court judges of the district in
which the Small Claims Court is located.

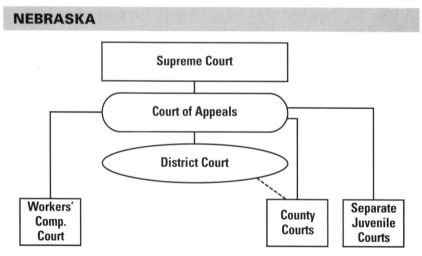

Court Homepage: court.nol.org

Constitution: Art. V.
Statutes: Revised Statutes of Nebraska (2004), Chapters 24-27 (Courts).

SUPREME COURT
Jurisdiction: Discretionary review of cases from Court of Appeals. Cases involving constitutionality of statutes. May review appeals from District, Juvenile, Workmen's Compensation courts, some administrative agencies. *Judges:* 7; governor appoints from nominating commission's list, retention by nonpartisan election after at least 3 years; thereafter, 6-year terms.

COURT OF APPEALS
Jurisdiction: All appeals from the District Court except those regarding constitutional issues and death penalty or life imprisonment. Intermediate appellate court for Workers' Compensation and Juvenile courts. *Judges:* 6; selection, retention same as for Supreme Court.

DISTRICT COURT
Jurisdiction: Civil appeals, miscellaneous civil. Exclusive domestic relations (except adoption). Criminal cases, felonies. Appellate jurisdiction over some cases from County Courts and several administrative agencies; retries appeals of small claims. Jury trials permitted except in appeals. 12 districts. *Judges:* 55; selection, retention same as for Supreme Court.

SEPARATE JUVENILE COURT
Jurisdiction: Cases involving minors. Divorce, alimony suits involving child care, support, custody. No jury trials. Douglas, Lancaster, Sarpy counties only. *Judges:* 10; appointed by the governor, retention same as for Supreme Court.

COUNTY COURT
Jurisdiction: Civil cases under $45,000; small claims under $2,100. Probate, guardianship, adoptions, conservatorship, eminent domain. Cases involving minors in counties without Juvenile Court. Contracts, torts, real property rights less than $15,000. Misdemeanor, DWI/DUI, traffic offenses and violations of municipal ordinances. Jury trials permitted except in small claims and juvenile. 12 districts. *Judges:* 59; selection, retention same as for Supreme Court.

WORKERS' COMPENSATION COURT
Jurisdiction: Workers' compensation disputes. 3-judge panel reviews appeals. No jury trials. *Judges:* 7; selection, retention same as for Supreme Court.

NEVADA

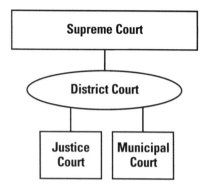

Court Homepage: www.nvsupremecourt.us

Constitution: Art. VI.
Statutes: Nevada Revised Statutes Annotated (2004), Titles 1-6.

SUPREME COURT
Jurisdiction: Writs. Appellate jurisdiction for cases over $300, equity, all civil matters not given to a lower court. Questions of law in criminal cases of District Court. *Judges:* 7; selection, retention by nonpartisan election; 6-year terms.

DISTRICT COURT
Jurisdiction: Civil cases over $7,500, equity, probate, guardianship, mentally ill, forcible entry and detainer, contested elections, real property, mining claims, legality of any tax. Cases involving minors. Criminal cases. Gross misdemeanors with fines greater than $1,000 or sentences greater than 6 months. Retries cases from Justice, Municipal courts. Jury trials permitted. 9 districts. *Judges:* 56; selection, retention same as for Supreme Court.

JUSTICE COURT
Jurisdiction: Civil cases under $7,500 involving personal injury, property damage if no title dispute, contracts, evictions. Misdemeanors with fines under $1,000 and/or sentences under 6 months. Small claims under $5,000. Jury trials except in small claims and parking cases. 53 townships. *Judges:* 67; selection, retention same as for Supreme Court. Some justices of the peace also serve as Municipal Court judges.

MUNICIPAL COURT
Jurisdiction: Civil cases under $2,500, municipal ordinance violations. Misdemeanors with less than $2,500 fines and/or sentences of less than 6 months. 19 incorporated cities and towns. *Judges:* 29; selection, retention by annual nonpartisan election unless city acts/states otherwise. Some judges also serve as justices of the peace.

NEW HAMPSHIRE

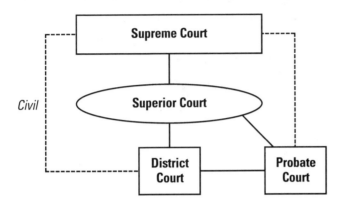

Court Homepage: *www.courts.state.nh.us*

Constitution: Part I, Art. 15, 20; Part II, Art. 76, 80.
Statutes: New Hampshire Revised Statutes Annotated (2004), Titles 51-58.

SUPREME COURT
Jurisdiction: Necessary writs. May review appeals from lower courts. *Judges:* 5; appointed by the governor and the Executive Council; term to age 70.

SUPERIOR COURT
Jurisdiction: Civil cases over $25,000, land title, domestic relations. Felonies. Retries cases from lower courts. Jury trials permitted. 11 courts. *Judges:* 28; selection, retention same as for Supreme Court.

DISTRICT COURT
Jurisdiction: Families, juveniles, small claims, landlord-tenant matters, minor crimes and violations and civil cases in which the disputed amount does not exceed $25,000. 36 courts. *Judges:* 51, of which 33 are special judges; selection, retention same as for Supreme Court.

PROBATE COURT
Jurisdiction: Wills, estates, trusts, probate, guardianship, adoption. In all counties. No jury trials permitted. *Judges:* 10, 5 of which are part-time; selection, retention same as for Supreme Court.

NEW JERSEY

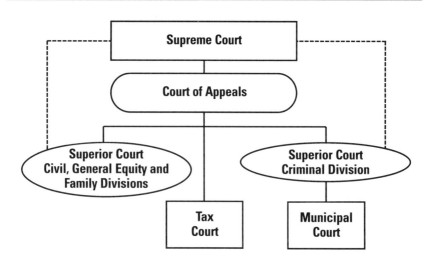

Court Homepage: *www.judiciary.state.nj.us*

Constitution: Art. VI.
Statutes: New Jersey Statutes Annotated (2004), Titles 2A, 2B and 40.

SUPREME COURT
Jurisdiction: Reviews cases in which Appellate Division judges dissent, a substantial constitutional issue is involved or the death penalty is imposed. May review other appeals. *Judges:* 7; governor appoints for 7 years; thereafter, reappointment until age 70.

APPELLATE DIVISION OF SUPERIOR COURT
Jurisdiction: Appeals from decisions of the Trial Courts, Tax Court and state administrative agencies. *Judges:* 32; assigned by the Chief Justice of the Supreme Court from among the Law and Chancery Division judges.

SUPERIOR COURT
Jurisdiction: Family Division—cases involving children, spouses or domestic partners. Criminal Division—criminal cases, drug courts in some counties, appeals from Municipal Court. Civil Division—landlord-tenant disputes, breaches of contract, auto accidents. General Equity Division—non-monetary cases. 15 vicinages (districts). *Judges:* 415; selection, retention same as for Supreme Court.

TAX COURT
Jurisdiction: Retries cases from County Tax Boards, hears appeals on decisions from the Division of Taxation. *Judges:* 12; governor appoints; 7-year terms.

MUNICIPAL COURT
Jurisdiction: Traffic, ordinance, fish-and-game, navigation violations. Minor criminal offenses. 536 courts. *Judges:* 380, many are part-time; mayor or council appoints; in 13 multi-city courts, governor appoints; 3-year terms.

NEW MEXICO

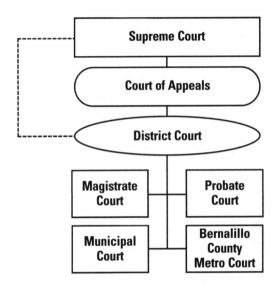

Court Homepage: www.nmcourts.com

Constitution: Art. VI.
Statutes: New Mexico Statutes Annotated (2004), Chapters 34 (Court Structure and Administration) & 35 (Magistrates and Municpal Courts).

SUPREME COURT
Jurisdiction: Necessary writs. Reviews death-penalty, life-sentence cases; may review cases certified by a federal court or cases from the Court of Appeals. *Judges:* 5; selection, retention by partisan election; 8-year terms.

COURT OF APPEALS
Jurisdiction: Reviews cases not reserved for Supreme Court review; discretionary jurisdiction over administrative appeals and in interlocutory decision cases. *Judges:* 10; selection, retention same as for Supreme Court.

DISTRICT COURT
Jurisdiction: Civil cases more than $5,000, equity cases, contested probate cases, domestic relations, mental health cases and cases involving minors.

Criminal cases. Retries appeals from lower courts. Jury trials permitted. 13 districts. *Judges:* 75; selection, retention by partisan election; 6-year terms.

MAGISTRATE COURT
Jurisdiction: Civil cases under $10,000. Misdemeanors, DWI and other traffic violations. Preliminary felony hearings. Jury trials permitted. 54 courts in counties with populations of less than 200,000. *Judges:* 61; selection, retention by partisan election; 4-year terms. Law degree not required (except Bernalillo County).

PROBATE COURT
Jurisdiction: Uncontested cases only. Probate, wills, guardianship. No jury trials. In all counties. *Judges:* 33; selection, retention by partisan election; 2-year terms.

MUNICIPAL COURT
Jurisdiction: Petty misdemeanors, DWI/DUI, traffic violations and other ordinance violations. No jury trials. 83 courts. *Judges:* 85; selection, retention same as for Magistrate Court.

BERNALILLO COUNTY METROPOLITAN COURT
Jurisdiction: Civil cases under $10,000. Misdemeanors, city and traffic violations, preliminary hearings. Jury trials permitted except in traffic. In Albuquerque. *Judges:* 16; selection, retention same as for Magistrate Court.

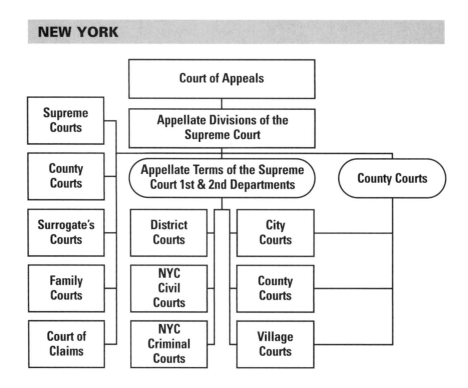

Court Homepage: www.nycourts.gov/home.htm

Constitution: Art. VI.
Statutes: McKinney's Consolidated Laws of New York Annotated (2004), Chapters 8 (Civil Practice Law and Rules), 30 (Judiciary) & 59a (Surrogate's Court Procedure Act).

COURT OF APPEALS

Jurisdiction: Almost exclusively appellate; reviews cases from Supreme Court Appellate Division that originated in lower courts and in which there is a conflict on a question of law. Reviews cases involving death penalty or constitutionality of statute. *Judges:* 7; governor appoints from nominating commission's list, senate confirms; 14-year terms.

APPELLATE DIVISION, SUPREME COURT

Jurisdiction: Reviews civil cases from Appellate Terms, cases from Supreme, County (except non-felonies from 2nd Dept.), Family, Surrogate's courts, Court of Claims. 4 departments. *Judges:* 55; governor appoints Supreme Court justices to Appellate Division; 4 presiding justices' terms concurrent with their Supreme Court terms; other justices' terms concurrent with their Supreme Court terms or 5 years, whichever is shorter.

APPELLATE TERMS, SUPREME COURT

Jurisdiction: Hears appeals from civil and criminal cases originating in the Civil and Criminal courts of the City of New York. In the 2nd Department, the Appellate Terms also have jurisdiction over appeals from civil and criminal cases originating in District, City, Town and Village courts. 3 terms (divisions). *Judges:* 15.

SUPREME COURT

Jurisdiction: Extraordinary writs. Civil, criminal, equity cases. Jury trials permitted. In each of the 62 counties and divided into 12 districts. *Judges:* 416; selection, retention by partisan election; 14-year terms.

COUNTY COURT

Jurisdiction: Tort, contract, real property under $25,000. Felony, DWI/DUI, and criminal cases and appeals. Reviews cases in 3rd and 4th Departments from City Court, Town and Village Justice Court. Jury trials permitted. 57 courts outside New York City. *Judges:* 128; selection, retention same as for Supreme Court; 10-year terms.

FAMILY COURT

Jurisdiction: Child protection, support of dependents, foster care, family offenses, adoptions, other cases involving minors. Jury trials not permitted. 58 courts. *Judges:* 126 (some County Court judges serve); selection, retention by partisan election (mayor appoints in New York City); 10-year terms.

SURROGATE'S COURT
Jurisdiction: Probate, guardianship. Concurrent jurisdiction with Family Court in adoption cases. 62 courts (in all counties). *Surrogates:* 62 (some County Court judges serve); selection, retention by partisan election; 10-year terms (14 years in New York City).

COURT OF CLAIMS
Jurisdiction: Claims against state. Statewide jurisdiction. Sits at Albany with branches throughout the state. No jury trials. *Judges:* 20 (plus 45 Supreme Court justices); governor appoints, senate confirms; 9-year terms.

DISTRICT COURT
Jurisdiction: Tort, contracts, real property under $15,000. Small claims (under $3,000), evictions. Criminal cases with less than $1,000 fine or 1-year sentence, preliminary felony hearings. Traffic and ordinance violation. Jury trials permitted except in traffic. Nassau, Suffolk counties only. *Judges:* 50; selection, retention same as for Surrogate's Court; 6-year terms.

CIVIL COURT OF THE CITY OF NEW YORK
Jurisdiction: Civil cases under $25,000. Small claims (under $3,000), housing partition. Jury trials permitted. In Bronx, Kings, New York, Queens and Richmond counties. *Judges:* 120; selection, retention same as for Surrogate's Court; 10-year terms. Special Housing Part judges are appointed by the administrative judges for 5-year terms (not constitutional judges).

CRIMINAL COURT OF THE CITY OF NEW YORK
Jurisdiction: Misdemeanors, city violations, preliminary felony hearings. Jury trials permitted. In Bronx, Kings, New York, Queens and Richmond counties. *Judges:* 107; appointed by the mayor; 10-year terms.

CITY COURT
Jurisdiction: Civil cases to $15,000; small claims to $3,000; misdemeanors, preliminary felony hearings. Jury trials permitted. 79 courts in 61 cities outside New York City. *Judges:* 158; part-time judges are elected for 6-year terms; full-time judges are elected for 10-year terms.

TOWN AND VILLAGE JUSTICE COURTS
Jurisdiction: Not courts of record. Varies; usually civil cases and small claims (under $3,000). Jury trials permitted. 1,487 courts. *Judges:* more than 2,100; selection, retention determined by local law.

NORTH CAROLINA

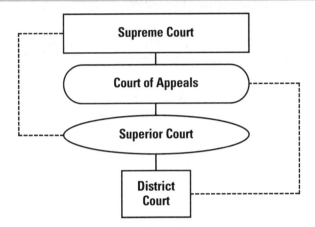

Court Homepage: *www.nccourts.org*

Constitution: Art. IV.
Statutes: General Statutes of North Carolina (2004), Chapter 7A (Judicial Department).

SUPREME COURT
Jurisdiction: Extraordinary writs. Reviews death-penalty, life-sentence cases from Superior Court unless based on guilty plea, cases from Court of Appeals involving constitutional questions, dissent by Court of Appeals judges, Utilities Commission rates. May review other cases from Court of Appeals. *Judges:* 7; selection, retention by nonpartisan election; 8-year terms.

COURT OF APPEALS
Jurisdiction: Reviews civil cases from District Court, cases from Superior Court not reserved for Supreme Court review, appeals from some administrative agencies. *Judges:* 15; selection, retention same as for Supreme Court.

SUPERIOR COURT
Jurisdiction: All felony criminal cases, civil cases involving more than $10,000 and misdemeanor and infraction appeals from District Court. Jury trials in criminal cases. In civil cases, juries are often waived. 46 districts. *Judges:* 93 (plus 13 special judges); selection, retention same as for Supreme Court.

DISTRICT COURT
Jurisdiction: Preliminary "probable cause" hearings in felony cases, misdemeanor and infraction cases. Juvenile proceedings, mental health hospital commitments and domestic relations cases. General civil cases where the amount in controversy is $10,000 or less. Jury trials permitted in civil cases. 39 districts. *Judges:* 235; selection, retention by nonpartisan election; 4-year

terms. ***Magistrates:*** 721 authorized, one or more in each county; Senior Superior Court judge appoints; 2-year terms.

NORTH DAKOTA

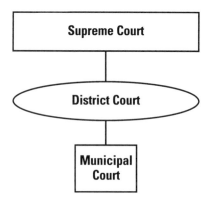

Court Homepage: *www.ndcourts.com*

Constitution: Art. VI.
Statutes: North Dakota Century Code (2003), Titles 27-33 & 40.

SUPREME COURT
Jurisdiction: Extraordinary writs. Tries habeas corpus, certain states' rights cases. Final appellate jurisdiction over cases from District Court. ***Judges:*** 5; selection, retention by nonpartisan election; 10-year terms.

DISTRICT COURT
Jurisdiction: Civil cases, domestic relations, cases involving minors. Criminal cases. Retries cases from Municipal Court, reviews decisions of administrative agencies. Jury trials permitted. 7 districts. ***Judges:*** 42; selection, retention by nonpartisan election; 6-year terms.

MUNICIPAL COURT
Jurisdiction: City violations. 80 municipalities. ***Judges:*** 76; selection, retention by nonpartisan election; 4-year terms. Law degree not required in cities with less than 5,000 population; in other cities, not required if attorney unavailable.

OHIO

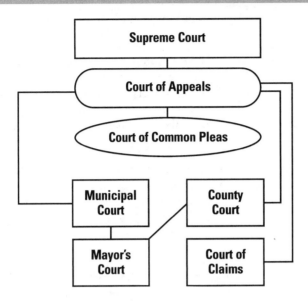

Court Homepage: *www.sconet.state.oh.us*

Constitution: Art. IV.
Statutes: Page's Ohio Revised Code Annotated (2004), Titles 19, 21, 23, 25 & 27.

SUPREME COURT
Jurisdiction: Extraordinary writs. Reviews cases in which Court of Appeals dissent, an issue of great public interest or a constitutional question is raised or death penalty imposed; reviews cases from Public Utilities Commission. May review cases from Board of Tax Appeals. *Judges:* 7; nominated in partisan primaries, retention by nonpartisan election; 6-year terms.

COURT OF APPEALS
Jurisdiction: Extraordinary writs. Appeals from lower courts. May review Board of Tax Appeals cases. 12 courts. *Judges:* 66; selection, retention same as for Supreme Court.

COURT OF COMMON PLEAS
Jurisdiction: Civil cases over $500, domestic relations, probate, cases involving minors. Felonies. Liquor Control Commission cases in Franklin County. Appeals from most administrative agencies. Jury trials permitted. In all counties. *Judges:* 375; selection, retention same as for Supreme Court.

MUNICIPAL COURT
Jurisdiction: Civil cases under $15,000. Misdemeanors, other criminal cases if

less than 1-year sentence, traffic violations, preliminary felony hearings. Retries Mayor's Court appeals. Jury trials permitted. 118 courts. *Judges:* 203; selection, retention same as for Supreme Court unless municipal charter states otherwise.

COUNTY COURT

Jurisdiction: Exclusive original jurisdiction in civil cases under $500, original jurisdiction under $15,000. Forcible entry and detainer, small claims. Misdemeanors, traffic violations, preliminary felony hearings. In counties without Municipal Courts. 47 courts. *Judges:* 55; nominated by nominating petition, retention by nonpartisan ballots at general elections; 6-year terms.

COURT OF CLAIMS

Jurisdiction: Cases against the state for personal injury, property damage, contract and wrongful death. Compensation for victims of crime. Jury trials permitted. In Columbus, statewide jurisdiction. *Judges:* Supreme Court, Court of Appeals and Court of Common Pleas judges as assigned by the Supreme Court Chief Justice.

MAYOR'S COURT

Jurisdiction: Traffic, misdemeanor offenses. No jury trials. In municipalities that do not have a Municipal Court. *Mayors:* Approximately 428; mayors serve by virtue of office.

OKLAHOMA

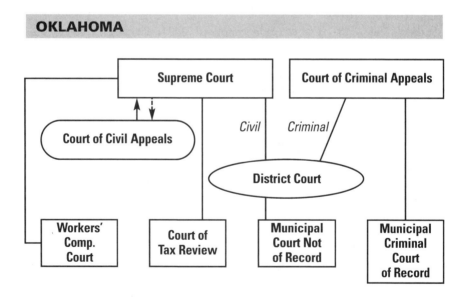

Court Homepage: www.oscn.net

Constitution: Art. VII.
Statutes: Oklahoma Statutes Annotated (2004), Titles 11, 12, 20, 68 & 85.

SUPREME COURT
Jurisdiction: Extraordinary writs. Supreme Court makes final decision in conflicts over jurisdiction between Supreme Court and Court of Criminal Appeals. Appeals of civil, equity cases. *Judges:* 9; appointed by the governor from nominating commission's list, retention by nonpartisan election; 6-year terms.

COURT OF CRIMINAL APPEALS
Jurisdiction: Extraordinary writs. Final review of criminal appeals. *Judges:* 5; selection, retention same as for Supreme Court.

COURT OF CIVIL APPEALS
Jurisdiction: Extraordinary writs. Final review of civil, administrative agency appeals assigned by Supreme Court. *Judges:* 12; selection, retention same as for Supreme Court.

DISTRICT COURT
Jurisdiction: Original jurisdiction over all justiciable matters: civil, probate, domestic relations, felonies, misdemeanors, juvenile. Retries cases from Municipal Court Not of Record. Jury trials permitted. 77 courts in 26 districts. *Judges:* 71 District judges, 77 Associate judges, 73 Special judges; selection, retention by nonpartisan election; 4-year terms.

MUNICIPAL CRIMINAL COURT OF RECORD
Jurisdiction: City ordinance violations with less than $500 fine or 90-day sentence. Jury trials permitted. Oklahoma City, Tulsa only. *Judges:* 8 full-time and 18 part-time; mayor appoints; 2-year terms.

MUNICIPAL COURT NOT OF RECORD
Jurisdiction: City ordinance violations. Jury trials permitted. Supervision of minors. 340 courts. *Judges:* Approximately 350 full/part-time; selection, retention same as for Municipal Criminal Court of Record but with consent of municipal governing body.

WORKERS' COMPENSATION COURT
Jurisdiction: Work-related accident-compensation claims. In Oklahoma City and Tulsa, statewide jurisdiction. *Judges:* 10; governor appoints; 6-year terms.

COURT OF TAX REVIEW
Jurisdiction: Protests against tax levies. In Oklahoma City, statewide jurisdiction. *Judges:* 3; governor appoints.

OREGON

Court Homepage: www.ojd.state.or.us

Constitution: Art. VI.
Statutes: Oregon Revised Statutes (2003), Titles 1-6.

SUPREME COURT
Jurisdiction: Extraordinary writs. Reviews death-penalty cases, cases from Tax Court. May review cases from Court of Appeals, Circuit Court. *Judges:* 7; selection, retention by nonpartisan statewide election; 6-year terms.

COURT OF APPEALS
Jurisdiction: Reviews cases from Circuit Courts (except death-penalty cases). *Judges:* 10; selection, retention same as for Supreme Court.

TAX COURT
Jurisdiction: Cases involving Oregon's tax laws, including income taxes, corporate excise taxes, property taxes, timber taxes, cigarette taxes, local budget laws, property tax limitations, tax refunds not exceeding $5,000. Magistrate decisions in small claims procedures are final. No jury trials. In Salem, statewide jurisdiction. *Judges:* 1; selection, retention of judge same as for Supreme Court. *Magistrates:* 6; appointed by Tax Court judge.

CIRCUIT COURT
Jurisdiction: All civil and criminal matters; cases involving minors, probate in some locations. Retries cases from Justice, County, Municipal courts. Jury trials permitted for most case types. 27 districts. *Judges:* 166; selection, retention by nonpartisan judicial district election; 6-year terms.

JUSTICE COURT
Jurisdiction: Small claims/civil jurisdiction nonexclusive where the money or

damages claimed does not exceed $2,500, except in actions involving title to real property, false imprisonment, libel, slander or malicious prosecution. All criminal prosecutions except felony trials; traffic, boating, wildlife and other violations occurring in their county. Jury trials permitted in some cases. 30 courts in 19 counties. *Judges:* 28; selection, retention by nonpartisan election for terms of varying lengths. Law degree not required.

COUNTY COURT
Jurisdiction: Juvenile and probate matters: probate in Gilliam, Grant, Harney, Malheur, Sherman and Wheeler counties; juvenile in Gilliam, Morrow, Sherman and Wheeler counties. No jury trials. In 7 counties. *Commissioners:* 9; selection, retention by voters of their respective districts. Law degree not required.

MUNICIPAL COURT
Jurisdiction: City, traffic violations. Criminal misdemeanors, including misdemeanor traffic crimes where the maximum penalty does not exceed a $2,500 fine or 1 year in jail or both; other minor traffic infractions; certain minor liquor and drug violations; parking violations; and municipal code violations, such as animal and fire violations. 112 courts. Jury trials for some case types. *Judges:* 94; appointed by city council or elected by voters of the respective city; terms vary. Law degree not required.

PENNSYLVANIA

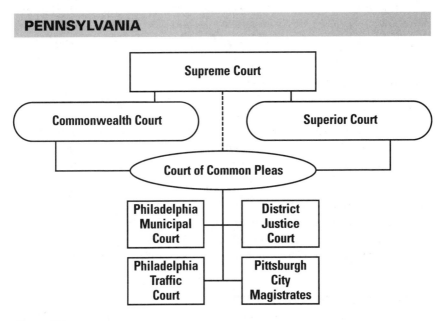

Court Homepage: www.courts.state.pa.us or www.aopc.org

Constitution: Art. V.
Statutes: Purdon's Pennsylvania Consolidated Statutes Annotated (2003), Title 42 (Judiciary and Judicial Procedure).

SUPREME COURT

Jurisdiction: Extraordinary writs. May try cases of immediate public importance filed in lower court. Reviews cases from Court of Common Pleas involving the death penalty. Original jurisdiction of right to hold a public office. Reviews cases tried in Commonwealth Court and appeals of certain final orders issued by either the Court of Common Pleas or specific constitutional and judicial agencies. May review other cases from Superior Court, and certain boards/commissions. *Judges:* 7; selection by partisan election, retention by nonpartisan election; 10-year terms.

SUPERIOR COURT

Jurisdiction: Reviews civil and criminal cases from Court of Common Pleas including child custody, armed robbery, breach of contract. 3 districts. *Judges:* 15; selection, retention and terms same as for Supreme Court.

COMMONWEALTH COURT

Jurisdiction: Cases involving state and state officials. Reviews some cases from Court of Common Pleas; appeals from most state administrative agencies; appeals of eminent domain; non-profit corporation cases. *Judges:* 9; selection, retention and terms same as for Supreme Court.

COURT OF COMMON PLEAS

Jurisdiction: Civil, cases involving minors. Criminal cases. Retries appeals from lower courts. Reviews cases from certain state and most local government agencies. Jury trials permitted. 60 districts. *Judges:* 394; selection, retention and terms same as for Supreme Court.

PHILADELPHIA MUNICIPAL COURT

Jurisdiction: Civil cases less than $10,000. All criminal cases except summary traffic offenses that are punishable by a term of imprisonment of less than 5 years, preliminary felony hearings (except rape, homicide cases). No jury trials permitted. In Philadelphia County only. *Judges:* 25; selection, retention same as for Supreme Court; 6-year terms. Judges need not be lawyers but must complete course and pass examination.

DISTRICT JUSTICE COURTS

Jurisdiction: Landlord-tenant, some civil claims under $8,000, trespass, government-fine cases. Some misdemeanors. 549 courts in all counties but Philadelphia. *Judges:* 549: selection, retention same as for Supreme Court; 6-year terms.

PHILADELPHIA TRAFFIC COURT

Jurisdiction: Traffic violations under the Motor Vehicle Code. In Philadelphia county only. *Judges:* 7; selection, retention by partisan election; 6-year terms. Judges need not be lawyers but must complete course and pass examination.

PITTSBURGH CITY MAGISTRATES
Jurisdiction: Criminal cases involving city ordinance violations, traffic violations.
Magistrates: 6; mayor appoints with City Council consent; 4-year terms.

PUERTO RICO

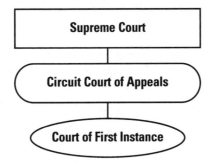

Court Homepage: www.tribunalpr.org

Constitution: Art. V.
Statutes: Laws of Puerto Rico Annotated (2004), Title, 4, 4A & 32.

SUPREME COURT
Jurisdiction: Extraordinary writs. Reviews constitutional questions from Circuit Court of Appeals. May review appeals from some administrative agencies. *Judges:* 7; governor appoints with senate consent; terms to age 70.

CIRCUIT COURT OF APPEALS
Jurisdiction: Reviews sentences and opinions of the Court of First Instance, reviews the final decisions of the administrative agencies. The seat of the court in San Juan. *Judges:* 33; governor appoints with senate consent; 16-year terms.

COURT OF FIRST INSTANCE
Superior Division
Jurisdiction: General jurisdiction over all civil, criminal and juvenile cases. *Judges:* 223; selection, retention same as for Supreme Court; 12-year terms.

Municipal Division
Jurisdiction: Holds preliminary hearings, issues protective orders, reviews administrative traffic decisions, small claims under $3,000. *Judges:* 105; selection, retention same as for Supreme Court; 8-year terms.

RHODE ISLAND

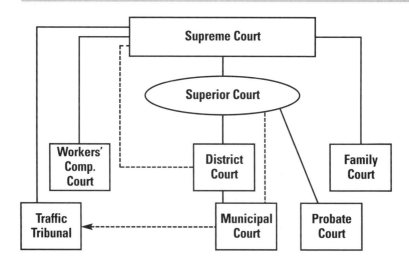

Court Homepage: www.courts.state.ri.us

Constitution: Art. X.
Statutes: General Laws of Rhode Island (2004), Titles 8-10.

SUPREME COURT
Jurisdiction: Extraordinary writs. May review civil, criminal cases. *Judges:* 5; governor appoints, legislature confirms for life term during good behavior.

SUPERIOR COURT
Jurisdiction: Extraordinary writs. Civil cases over $5,000; equity, land-title, condemnation cases. Felonies. Appeals from administrative agencies. Retries cases from District, Municipal, Probate courts. Jury trials permitted. 4 locations.
Judges: 22; governor appoints, senate confirms for life term during good behavior.

WORKERS' COMPENSATION COURT
Jurisdiction: Appeals from administrative agencies (workers' compensation);
Judges: 10; selection, retention same as for Superior Court.

FAMILY COURT
Jurisdiction: Domestic relations. Cases involving minors. Reviews administrative agency decisions that affect minors. 4 locations. *Judges:* 12 (6 magistrates); selection, retention same as for Superior Court.

DISTRICT COURT
Jurisdiction: Civil cases under $10,000, small claims (under $1,500), housing code violations, landlord-tenant actions. Misdemeanors, felony arraignments. Reviews appeals from Traffic Tribunal and reviews decisions of various

regulatory boards and agencies. 8 locations. *Judges:* 13 (2 magistrates); selection, retention same as for Superior Court.

TRAFFIC TRIBUNAL
Jurisdiction: Traffic cases. *Judges:* 4 (3 magistrates); selection, retention same as for Superior Court.

PROBATE COURT
Jurisdiction: Probate, guardianship, adoption. 39 locations. *Judges:* 39; mayor or local council appoints (except New Shoreham, where council members serve); in most locations, 2-year terms.

MUNICIPAL COURT
Jurisdiction: Minor traffic violations and municipal ordinances. In Providence, Warwick, Pawtucket. *Judges:* 21 (2 magistrates); city council appoints; 2-year terms.

SOUTH CAROLINA

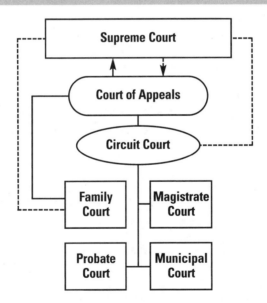

Court Homepage: www.sccourts.org

Constitution: Art. V.
Statutes: Code of Laws of South Carolina (2004) Titles 14, 15, 18 & 22.

SUPREME COURT
Jurisdiction: Extraordinary writs. Appeals from Circuit Court involving death penalty, significant constitutional issues, public-utility rates, public bonds,

elections. May review cases from Court of Appeals and civil cases from other courts not tried by jury. *Judges:* 5; General Assembly appoints from nominating commission's list; 10-year terms.

COURT OF APPEALS

Jurisdiction: Appeals from Circuit, Family courts not reserved for Supreme Court review. Cases assigned by Supreme Court. *Judges:* 9; General Assembly appoints from nominating commission's list; 6-year terms.

CIRCUIT COURT

Jurisdiction: Civil, criminal cases. Equity cases referred to Master-in-Equity at parties' or court's request. Appeals from Probate, Magistrate, Municipal courts. Jury trials permitted. 16 circuits. *Judges:* 51; selection, retention same as for Court of Appeals. *Masters-in-Equity:* 21; governor appoints, General Assembly confirms; 6-year terms.

FAMILY COURT

Jurisdiction: Domestic relations, cases involving minors. 45 locations. *Judges:* 60; General Assembly elects; 6-year terms.

MAGISTRATE COURT

Jurisdiction: Civil cases under $7,500. Criminal cases with less than $500 fine or 30-day sentence. *Magistrates:* 311; governor appoints, senate confirms; 4-year terms.

MUNICIPAL COURT

Jurisdiction: Criminal cases with less than $500 fine or 30-day sentence; city violations. Jury trials permitted. *Judges:* 378; mayor serves or city council appoints 'municipal recorder'; 4-year terms. Law degree not required.

PROBATE COURT

Jurisdiction: Probate, commitment of mentally ill. In all counties. *Judges:* 46; selection, retention by partisan election; 4-year terms. Law degree not required.

SOUTH DAKOTA

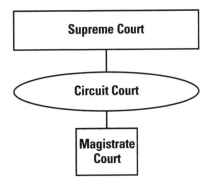

Court Homepage: *www.sdjudicial.com*

Constitution: Art. V.
Statutes: South Dakota Codified Laws (2004), Title 16 (Courts and Judiciary).

SUPREME COURT
Jurisdiction: Extraordinary writs. Reviews civil, criminal cases, appeals from the Circuit Court and most administrative agencies, supervisory boards.
Judges: 5; governor appoints from nominating commission; initial term for 3 years; retention by nonpartisan election; subsequent 8-year terms; mandatory retirement at age 70.

CIRCUIT COURT
Jurisdiction: Extraordinary writs. Civil, equity cases including domestic relations, disputes over $8,000, land disputes, probate, cases involving minors. Reviews cases from Magistrate Court, some administrative agencies. Jury trials permitted. 7 circuits. **Judges:** 38; selection, retention by nonpartisan election; 8-year terms.

MAGISTRATE COURT
Jurisdiction: Assists the Circuit Court in processing minor criminal cases and less serious civil actions. Lawyer Division—civil cases under $10,000, small claims under $8,000, commitment of mentally ill, misdemeanors, city violations, preliminary felony hearings, warrants. Jury trials permitted. Lay Division—some civil cases under $8,000, small claims. Guilty pleas for misdemeanors, city violations, preliminary hearings, warrants. 64 locations.
Magistrates: Lawyer—11 full-time, 3 part-time; presiding Circuit Court judge appoints with Supreme Court's approval; 4-year terms. Lay—87 (61 also serve as clerks of court); presiding Circuit Court judge appoints to serve at judge's pleasure. Law degree not required.

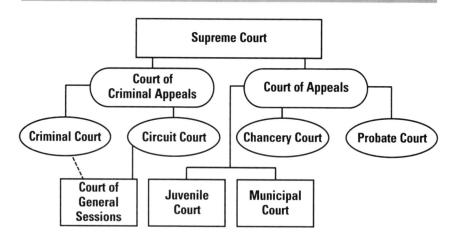

TENNESSEE

Court Homepage: *www.tsc.state.tn.us*

Constitution: Art. VI; Tennessee Code Annotated (2003).
Statutes: Tennessee Code Annotated (2004), Titles 16 (Courts) & 37 (Juveniles).

SUPREME COURT
Jurisdiction: Reviews cases involving constitutional questions, right to hold public office, workers' compensation, state revenues, death penalty. Reviews other appellate court decisions. *Judges:* 5; governor appoints from nominating commission's list until next biennial election, retention by partisan election; 8-year terms.

COURT OF APPEALS
Jurisdiction: Reviews cases from Chancery, Circuit courts, paternity cases from Juvenile Court, all civil cases not reserved for Supreme Court review. 3 divisions. *Judges:* 12; selection, retention same as for Supreme Court.

COURT OF CRIMINAL APPEALS
Jurisdiction: Reviews criminal cases. 3 divisions. *Judges:* 12; selection, retention same as for Supreme Court.

CHANCERY COURT
Jurisdiction: Civil cases (except damage cases), equity cases over $50, domestic relations, probate, boundary disputes, workers' compensation. Appeals from administrative agencies, boards, commissions. Jury trials permitted. 27 districts. *Chancellors:* 33; selection and retention by partisan election (however, each local government has the discretion to require nonpartisan elections); 8-year terms.

CIRCUIT COURT
Jurisdiction: Civil cases, equity cases if parties agree, contested probate, land title, eminent domain, breach of duty by public treasurers. Criminal cases where no Criminal Court. Retries cases from lower courts. Jury trials permitted. 31 districts. *Judges:* 85; selection, retention same as for Chancery Court.

CRIMINAL COURT
Jurisdiction: Criminal cases. Jury trials permitted. 13 districts. *Judges:* 29; selection, retention same as for Chancery Court.

JUVENILE COURT
Jurisdiction: Cases involving minors. 15 counties. *Judges:* 17; selection, retention determined by local law.

PROBATE COURT
Jurisdiction: Probate, wills, guardianship. In Memphis only. *Judges:* 2; selection, retention by nonpartisan election; 8-year terms.

COURT OF GENERAL SESSIONS
Jurisdiction: Civil cases under $15,000 ($25,000 in counties with over 700,000 population), landlord-tenant, forcible entry and detainer, workers' compensation. Misdemeanors with less than $50 fine or 1-year sentence, preliminary felony hearings. In some counties, probate, domestic relations, cases involving minors. 92 counties. *Judges:* 154; selection, retention same as for Chancery Court.

MUNICIPAL COURT
Jurisdiction: Varies; usually city violations, criminal cases with less than $500 fine or 30-day sentence; sometimes traffic violations. 300 cities. *Judges:* 170; selection, retention set by local law.

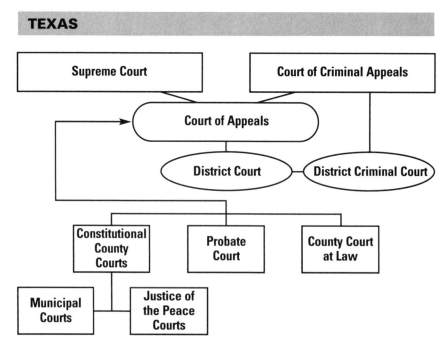

TEXAS

Court Homepage: www.courts.state.tx.us

Constitution: Art. V.
Statutes: Vernon's Texas Codes Annotated (2003), Government Code, Title 2 (Judicial Branch).

SUPREME COURT
Jurisdiction: Extraordinary writs. Final appellate jurisdiction over all civil and juvenile cases. *Judges:* 9; selection, retention by partisan election; 6-year terms.

COURT OF CRIMINAL APPEALS
Jurisdiction: Extraordinary writs. Mandatory final review of death-penalty cases, discretionary final review of other criminal cases. *Judges:* 9; selection, retention same as for Supreme Court.

COURT OF APPEALS
Jurisdiction: Extraordinary writs. Reviews civil and noncapital criminal cases (except probate). May review election contest, divorce, slander. 14 courts. *Judges:* 80; selection, retention same as for Supreme Court.

DISTRICT COURTS
Jurisdiction: Extraordinary writs. Miscellaneous criminal cases, civil cases over $200. Land title, mortgage foreclosure, liens, divorce, cases involving minors, election contests. Contested probate cases if no other court has jurisdiction. Appeals from administrative agencies. Jury trials permitted. In all counties. *Judges:* 418; selection, retention by partisan election; 4-year terms.

CONSTITUTIONAL COUNTY COURT
Jurisdiction: Civil cases between $200 and $5,000, uncontested probate. Misdemeanors with more than $500 fine. Retries appeals from Justice of the Peace, Municipal courts. Jury trials permitted. 254 courts. *Judges:* 254; selection, retention same as for District Court. Law degree not required.

COUNTY COURT AT LAW
Jurisdiction: Varies. Civil cases and criminal cases. Jury trials permitted. 192 courts. *Judges:* 202; selection, retention often same as for District Court. Law degree not required in some counties.

PROBATE COURT
Jurisdiction: Probate. Jury trials permitted. 16 courts. *Judges:* 16; selection, retention same as for District Court. Law degree required.

JUSTICE OF THE PEACE COURT
Jurisdiction: Criminal cases under $500 fine, civil cases under $5,000, small claims (under $5,000), traffic, preliminary hearings, misdemeanors. 834 courts. *Judges:* 834; selection, retention same as for District Court.

MUNICIPAL COURT
Jurisdiction: City violations with less than $500 fine, preliminary hearings, ordinance violation. Jury trials permitted. 877 courts. *Judges:* 1,310; elected or appointed by local governing board; on average, 2-year terms.

UTAH

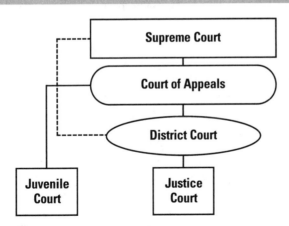

Court Homepage: www.ut.courts.gov

Constitution: Art. VIII.
Statutes: Utah Annotated Code (2004), Title 78 (Judicial Code).

SUPREME COURT

Jurisdiction: Extraordinary writs. Appeals involving death penalty, interpretation of state constitution or statute, election contests, removal of public officers, tax and revenue, water allocations. May review cases from some state agencies and Court of Appeals. *Judges:* 5; governor appoints from nominating commission's list and senate confirms, retention by nonpartisan election after at least 3 years; thereafter, 10-year terms.

COURT OF APPEALS

Jurisdiction: Extraordinary writs. Reviews cases from Circuit, Juvenile courts (except first-degree, death-penalty cases), domestic relations cases from District Court. Reviews agency decisions not reserved for Supreme Court review, cases transferred from Supreme Court. *Judges:* 7; selection, retention same as for Supreme Court; 6-year terms.

DISTRICT COURT

Jurisdiction: Extraordinary writs. Civil cases, probate, domestic relations. Criminal cases. Jury trials permitted. 40 courts. *Judges:* 70; governor appoints, retention by nonpartisan election after at least 3 years; thereafter, 6-year terms.

JUVENILE COURT

Jurisdiction: Cases involving minors. 20 courts. *Judges:* 25 judges and one commissioner; selection by local commission appointment, retention by election. Must be admitted to practice law in Utah.

JUSTICE COURT

Jurisdiction: Misdemeanors, ordinance violations, small claims less than $5,000, infractions. 139 courts. *Judges:* 123; selection by local commission appointment, retention varies.

VERMONT

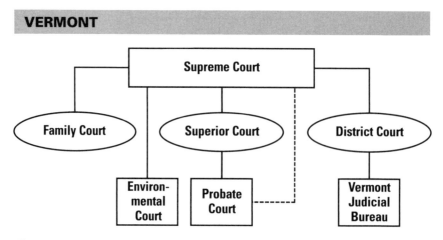

Court Homepage: www.vermontjudiciary.org

Constitution: Ch. II.
Statutes: Vermont Statutes Annotated (2004), Titles 4 (Judiciary) and 12 (Court Procedure).

SUPREME COURT

Jurisdiction: Extraordinary writs. Reviews cases from lower courts, administrative agencies, boards and commissions, officials. *Judges:* 5; governor appoints from nominating commission's list and senate confirms, retention by General Assembly election; 6-year terms; mandatory retirement at age 70.

SUPERIOR COURT

Jurisdiction: Civil cases over $200. Equity, domestic relations, land-title cases. Criminal cases. Appeals from Probate Court. Jury trials permitted. *Judges:* 15; selection, retention same as for Supreme Court.

DISTRICT COURT

Jurisdiction: Civil cases under $5,000 (except land title), small claims, commitment of mentally ill, cases involving minors. Criminal cases, traffic, city violations. Jury trials permitted. *Judges:* 17; selection, retention same as for Supreme Court.

FAMILY COURT

Jurisdiction: Divorce, juvenile, domestic abuse and child support cases. Jury trials permitted. *Judges:* assigned from Superior or District courts, 6 child-support magistrates.

ENVIRONMENTAL COURT

Jurisdiction: Appeals of Act 250 (land use and development) enforcement orders, appeals zoning decisions. *Judges:* 1; selection, retention same as for Supreme Court.

PROBATE COURT

Jurisdiction: Wills, probate, guardianship, adoption. *Judges:* 18; selection, retention by partisan election; 4-year terms.

VERMONT JUDICIAL BUREAU

Jurisdiction: Civil violation complaints, violations of municipal ordinances; *Judges:* 4 hearing officers; appointed by administrative judge; must be state bar member.

VIRGIN ISLANDS

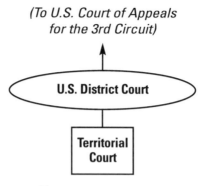

*(To U.S. Court of Appeals
for the 3rd Circuit)*

U.S. District Court

Territorial
Court

Court Homepage: www.vid.uscourts.gov

Constitution: (Revised Organic Act of 1954, Sec. 21-23)
Statutes: Virgin Islands Code (2004), Titles 4 (Judiciary) and 5 (Judicial Procedure).

U.S. DISTRICT COURT

Jurisdiction: Extraordinary writs. Cases arising under U.S. Constitution, laws and treaties. Under territorial law, civil cases over $2,000, criminal cases with more than $100 fine or 6-month sentence, income-tax cases. Cases transferred from Territorial Court. Reviews civil, juvenile, domestic relations and criminal cases (except if guilty plea entered) from Territorial Court. Jury trials permitted. 2 divisions. *Judges:* 2; U.S. President appoints, U.S. Senate confirms; 10-year terms.

TERRITORIAL COURT

Jurisdiction: All civil cases regardless of amount of controversy, probate, guardianship, domestic relations, cases involving minors. Criminal cases with fine or less than 15-year sentence; city violations. Jury trials permitted. 2 courts. *Judges:* no less than 6; governor appoints, territorial senate confirms; 6-year terms.

VIRGINIA

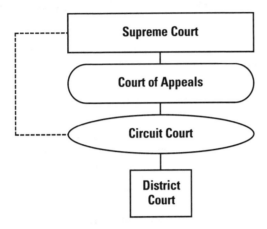

Court Homepage: *www.courts.state.va.us*

Constitution: Art. I, VI.
Statutes: Code of Virginia (2004), Titles 16.1 (Courts not of Record), 17.1 (Courts of Record).

SUPREME COURT
Jurisdiction: Extraordinary writs. Appeals of lower court decisions. Discretionary review of death-penalty cases and cases involving the State Corporation Commission. *Judges:* 7; legislature elects; 12-year terms.

COURT OF APPEALS
Jurisdiction: Extraordinary writs. Appeals from Circuit Court except death-penalty cases; appeals from administrative agencies. May review criminal, domestic relations, traffic and workers' compensation cases. *Judges:* 11; selection, retention same as for Supreme Court; 8-year terms.

CIRCUIT COURT
Jurisdiction: Civil law cases over $4,000, equity cases, property disputes, domestic relations, wills, probate. Felonies and related misdemeanors. Retries cases from lower courts; reviews cases from administrative agencies. Jury trials permitted. 31 circuits. *Judges:* 150; selection, retention same as for Supreme Court; 8-year terms.

DISTRICT COURT
Jurisdiction: General District Courts: civil cases under $15,000; state revenue, election-law violations; misdemeanors with less than $2,500 fine and 1-year sentence; city, county, traffic violations, preliminary felony hearings. Juvenile and Domestic Relations District courts: juvenile traffic offenses, child abuse,

custody disputes, visitation, child support, foster care, rehabilitation services. 204 courts. *Judges:* 124 general district; 110 juvenile and domestic relations; selection, retention same as for Supreme Court; 6-year terms. Mandatory retirement at age 70.

WASHINGTON

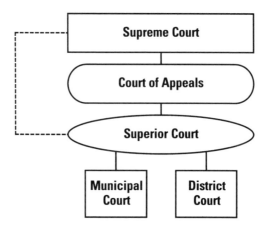

Court Homepage: *www.courts.wa.gov*

Constitution: Art. IV.
Statutes: Revised Code of Washington (2004) Titles 2, 3, 12, & 13.

SUPREME COURT
Jurisdiction: Extraordinary writs. Reviews cases involving death penalty, constitutional questions, conflict among statutes, rules of law, issues of broad public importance, cases against state officials. May review cases from Court of Appeals. *Judges:* 9; selection, retention by nonpartisan election; 6-year terms.

COURT OF APPEALS
Jurisdiction: Reviews Superior Court cases not reserved for Supreme Court review. 3 divisions. *Judges:* 22; selection, retention same as for Supreme Court.

SUPERIOR COURT
Jurisdiction: Civil matters over $50,000, probate, domestic relations, cases involving minors, challenges of taxes. Felonies. Retries appeals from District, Municipal courts. Jury trials permitted. 29 courts. *Judges:* 175; selection, retention by nonpartisan election; 4-year terms.

DISTRICT COURT
Jurisdiction: Civil cases under $50,000, small claims. Criminal cases with less

than $5,000 fine or 1-year sentence, traffic violations, preliminary felony hearings. Jury trials permitted. In each county seat and in cities without a Municipal Court. *Judges:* 113; selection, retention same as for Superior Court.

MUNICIPAL COURT
Jurisdiction: City violations, preliminary hearings. Jury trials permitted. In 136 cities. *Judges:* 108; may be elected or appointed depending on local statutory provision.

WEST VIRGINIA

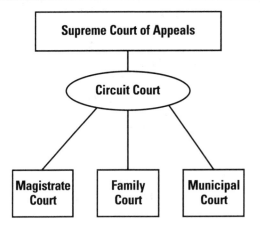

Court Homepage: www.state.wv.us/wvsca

Constitution: Art. VIII.
Statutes: West Virginia Code (2004) Chapters 50-58.

SUPREME COURT OF APPEALS
Jurisdiction: Extraordinary writs. Reviews constitutional questions, felonies, misdemeanors from Circuit Court, some family court decisions. May review civil cases over $300, equity, land title. *Judges:* 5; selection, retention by partisan election; 12-year terms.

CIRCUIT COURT
Jurisdiction: Civil cases over $300. Criminal cases. Reviews cases from Magistrate, Family and Municipal courts, state administrative agencies. Jury trials permitted. 31 circuits. *Judges:* 65; selection, retention same as for Supreme Court; 8-year terms.

FAMILY COURT
Jurisdiction: Divorce, annulment, family support, paternity, visitation, allocation of parental responsibility. 26 circuits. *Judges:* 35; selection, retention by partisan election; initial term of 6 years; subsequent 8-year terms.

MAGISTRATE COURT
Jurisdiction: Civil cases under $5,000. Misdemeanors, traffic violations, preliminary felony hearings, emergency protective orders. Jury trials permitted. 55 counties. *Magistrates:* 158; selection, retention by partisan election; 4-year terms. Law degree not required.

MUNICIPAL COURT
Jurisdiction: City, traffic violations. 234 cities. *Judges:* 175; selection, retention set by local law. Mayor serves as judge in some small towns.

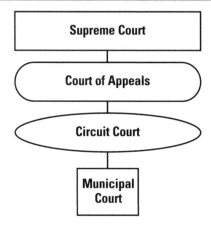

WISCONSIN

Court Homepage: www.wicourts.gov

Constitution: Art. VII.
Statutes: Wisconsin Statutes Annotated (2004) Sec. 750-758.

SUPREME COURT
Jurisdiction: Extraordinary writs. May review cases from Court of Appeals. *Judges:* 7; selection, retention by nonpartisan election; 10-year terms. Mandatory retirement at age 70.

COURT OF APPEALS
Jurisdiction: Extraordinary writs. Appeals from Circuit Court. 4 districts. *Judges:* 16; selection, retention by nonpartisan election; 6-year terms. Mandatory retirement at age 70.

CIRCUIT COURT
Jurisdiction: Civil, equity, probate, juvenile. Criminal cases. Appeals from Municipal Court, reviews administrative decisions. Jury trials permitted. 69 circuits. *Judges:* 241; selection, retention same as for Court of Appeals. Mandatory retirement at age 70.

MUNICIPAL COURT
Jurisdiction: Most city violations. In 224 cities, towns, villages. *Judges:* 226; selection, retention by nonpartisan election; 2- to 4-year terms.

WYOMING

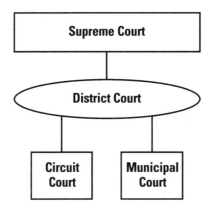

Court Homepage: *www.courts.state.wy.us*

Constitution: Art. V.
Statutes: Wyoming Statutes Annotated (2004) Title 5 (Courts).

SUPREME COURT
Jurisdiction: Extraordinary writs. Appeals from District Court. *Judges:* 5; governor appoints for 1 year from nominating commission's list, retention by nonpartisan election; 8-year terms. Mandatory retirement at age 70.

DISTRICT COURT
Jurisdiction: Civil, probate, guardianship, domestic relations, cases involving minors (except ordinance violations). Criminal cases. Reviews cases of record from Municipal Court and administrative agencies. Jury trials permitted. 9 districts. *Judges:* 19; selection, retention same as for Supreme Court; 6-year terms. Mandatory retirement at age 70.

CIRCUIT COURT
Jurisdiction: Civil cases under $7,000; misdemeanors, small claims, some city violations. Jury trials permitted. *Judges:* 24; selection, retention by nonpartisan election; 4-year terms.

MUNICIPAL COURT
Jurisdiction: City violations with less than $750 fine or 6-month sentence. Jury trials in some courts. *Judges:* 2 full-time, 73 part-time; mayor appoints with council's consent; terms set by local law. Law degree is not required.

APPENDIX II

STAGES OF A LAWSUIT

STAGES OF A LAWSUIT: PLEADING

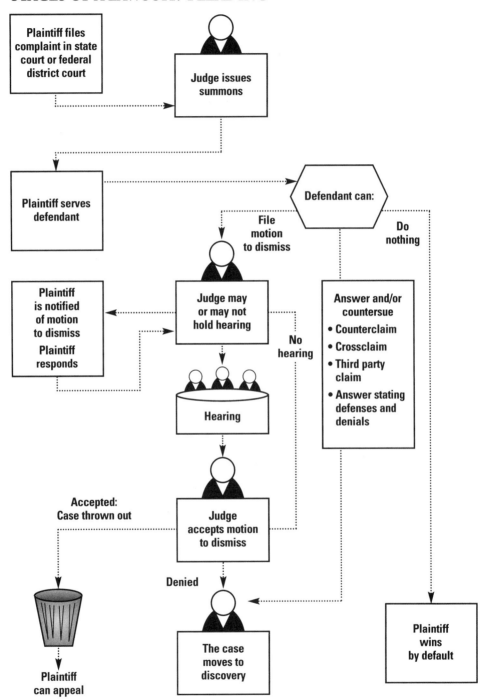

STAGES OF A LAWSUIT: DISCOVERY

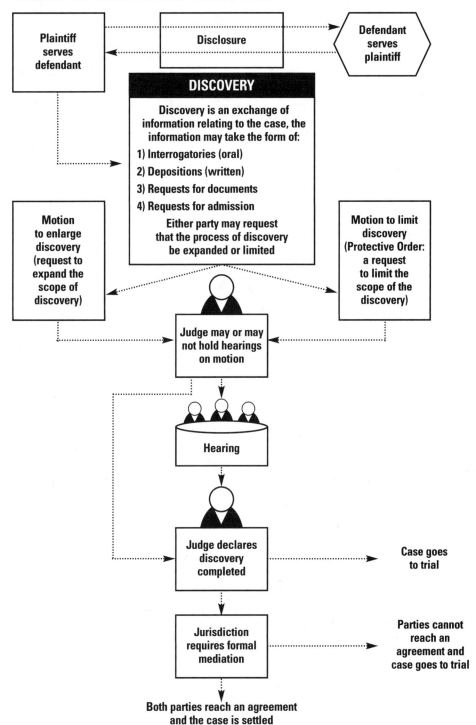

STAGES OF A LAWSUIT: PRE-TRIAL

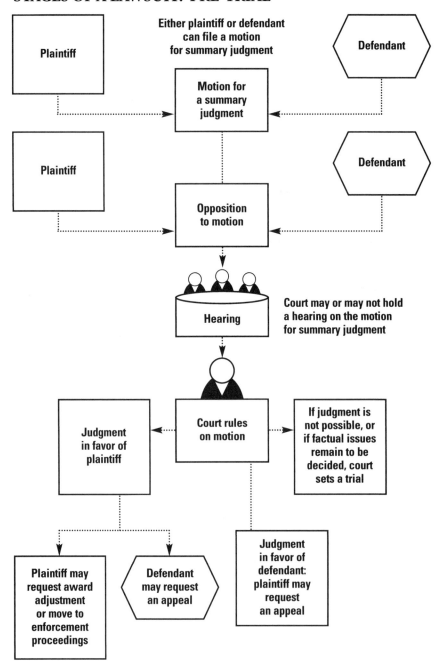

STAGES OF A LAWSUIT: TRIAL

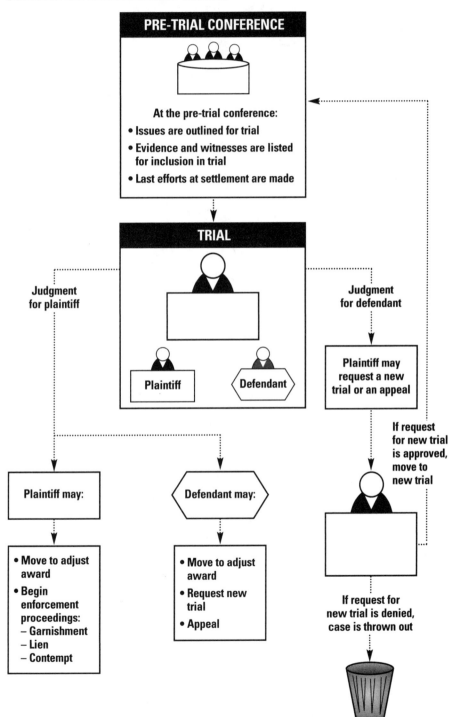

PRE-TRIAL CONFERENCE

At the pre-trial conference:
- Issues are outlined for trial
- Evidence and witnesses are listed for inclusion in trial
- Last efforts at settlement are made

TRIAL

Plaintiff

Defendant

Judgment for plaintiff

Judgment for defendant

Plaintiff may request a new trial or an appeal

If request for new trial is approved, move to new trial

Plaintiff may:

- Move to adjust award
- Begin enforcement proceedings:
  - Garnishment
  - Lien
  - Contempt

Defendant may:

- Move to adjust award
- Request new trial
- Appeal

If request for new trial is denied, case is thrown out

APPENDIX III

Judicial Conduct Organizations

Judicial conduct organizations have been created in each state to address consumer complaints concerning the integrity of judges and the court system. Possible issues may include willful misconduct, ethical violations or other breaches of the state code. If it is found that a violation has occurred, the commission's course of action may consist of privately or publicly reprimanding the judge, recommending that he or she be removed or another similar decision.

ALABAMA
Judicial Inquiry Commission
P.O. Box 303400
Montgomery, AL 36130-3400
Phone: (334) 242-4089
Fax: (334) 353-4043
E-mail: *jic@alaline.net*
Web site: *www.alalinc.net/jic*

ALASKA
Commission on Judicial Conduct
1029 W. 3rd Ave., Ste. 550
Anchorage, AK 99501
Phone: (907) 272-1033
Toll free: (888) 790-2526
Fax: (907) 272-9309
E-mail: *mgreenstein@acjc.state.ak.us*
Web site: *www.ajc.state.ak.us/
    CONDUCT.htm*

ARIZONA
Commission on Judicial Conduct
1501 W. Washington St., Ste. 229
Phoenix, AZ 85007
Phone: (602) 542-5200
Fax: (602) 542-5201
E-mail: *cjc@supreme.sp.state.az.us*
Web site: *www.supreme.state.az.us/ethics*

ARKANSAS
Judicial Discipline & Disability
    Commission
323 Center St., Ste. 1060
Little Rock, AR 72201
Phone: (501) 682-1050
Fax: (501) 682-1049
E-mail: *jddc@mail.state.ar.us*
Web site: *www.state.ar.us/jddc*

CALIFORNIA
Commission on Judicial Performance
455 Golden Gate Ave., Ste. 14400
San Francisco, CA 94102
Phone: (415) 557-1200
Fax: (415) 557-1266
Web site: *http://cjp.ca.gov*

COLORADO
Commission on Judicial Discipline
899 Logan St., Ste. 307
Denver, CO 80203
Phone: (303) 894-2110
Fax: (303) 894-2112
Web site: *www.courts.state.co.us/supct/
    committees/judicialdiscipline.htm*

CONNECTICUT
Judicial Review Council
505 Hudson St., Rm. 116
P.O. Box 260099
Hartford, CT 06126-0099
Phone: (860) 566-5424
Fax: (860) 566-6617

DELAWARE
Court on the Judiciary
P.O. Box 369
Georgetown, DE 19947
Phone: (302) 855-7454
Fax: (302) 854-6991

DISTRICT OF COLUMBIA
Commission on Judicial Disabilities
    and Tenure
515 5th St., NW, Bldg. A, Rm. 312
Washington, DC 20001
Phone: (202) 727-1363
Fax: (202) 727-9718

FLORIDA
Judicial Qualifications Commission
1110 Thomasville Rd.
Tallahassee, FL 32303-6224
Phone: (850) 488-1581
Fax: (850) 922-6781
Web site: *www.flabar.org/DIVCOM/PI/
    BIPS2001.nsf*

GEORGIA
Judicial Qualifications Commission
8206 Hazelbrand Rd., Ste. C
Covington, GA 30014
Phone: (770) 784-3189
Fax: (770) 784-2454
Web site: *www.georgiacourts.org/
    agencies/jqc*

HAWAII
Commission on Judicial Conduct
426 Queen St., Rm. 106
Honolulu, HI 96813-1924
Phone: (808) 539-4790
Fax: (808) 539-4756
Web site: *www.courts.state.hi.us/*

IDAHO
Judicial Council
P.O. Box 9495
Boise, ID 83707
Phone: (208) 334-5213
Fax: (208) 383-9516
E-mail: *ijc@ijc.state.id.us*
Web site: *www.state.id.us/ijc*

ILLINOIS
Judicial Inquiry Board
100 W. Randolph St., Ste. 14-500
Chicago, IL 60601
Phone: (312) 814-5554
Fax: (312) 814-5719
Web site: *www.state.il.us/jib*

INDIANA
Commission on Judicial Qualifications
115 W. Washington St., Ste. 1080
Indianapolis, IN 46204-3417
Phone: (317) 232-4706
Fax: (317) 233-6586
Web site: *www.in.gov/judiciary/admin/
judqual*

IOWA
Commission on Judicial Qualifications
State Capitol
Des Moines, IA 50319
Phone: (515) 281-5241
Fax: (515) 242-6164
Web site: *www.judicial.state.ia.us*

KANSAS
Commission on Judicial Qualifications
Kansas Judicial Center, Rm. 374
301 S.W. 10th Ave.
Topeka, KS 66612-1507
Phone: (785) 296-3229
Fax: (785) 296-1028
Web site: *www.kscourts.org/ctruls/
judruls.htm*

KENTUCKY
Judicial Conduct Commission
P.O. Box 21868
Lexington, KY 40522-1868
Phone and Fax: (859) 233-4128
Web site: *www.kyfamilysafety.org/
JudicialConductInfo.pdf*

LOUISIANA
Judiciary Commission of Louisiana
400 Royal St., Ste. 1190
New Orleans, LA 70130
Phone: (504) 310-2605
Fax: (504) 310-2596
Web site: *www.lasc.org/lajao/jcomm.html*

MAINE
Committee on Judicial Responsibility
and Disability
P.O. Box 8058
Portland, ME 04104-8058
Phone: (207) 780-4375
Fax: (207) 780-4239
Web site: *www.courts.state.me.us/
index.html*

MARYLAND
Commission on Judicial Disabilities
100 Community Pl., Rm. 1.210
Crownsville, MD 21032
Phone: (410) 514-7044
Fax: (410) 514-7098
Web site: *www.courts.state.md.us/
juddisable.html*

MASSACHUSETTS
Commission on Judicial Conduct
14 Beacon St., Ste. 102
Boston, MA 02108-3704
Phone: (617) 725-8050
Fax: (617) 248-9938
Web site: *www.mass.gov/cjc*

MICHIGAN
Judicial Tenure Commission
3034 W. Grand Blvd., Ste. 8-450
Detroit, MI 48202
Phone: (313) 875-5110
Fax: (313) 875-5154
Web site: *www.jtc.courts.mi.gov*

MINNESOTA
Board on Judicial Standards
2025 Centre Pointe Blvd., Ste. 180
Mendota Heights, MN 55120
Phone: (651) 296-3999
Fax: (651) 688-1865
E-mail: *judicial.standard@state.mn.us*
Web site: *www.bjs.state.mn.us*

MISSISSIPPI
Commission on Judicial Performance
P.O. Box 22527
Jackson, MS 39225-2527
Phone: (601) 359-1273
Fax: (601) 354-6277
E-mail: *brantley@judperf.state.ms.us*
Web site: *www.judperf.state.ms.us*

MISSOURI
Commission on Retirement, Removal
and Discipline
2190 S. Mason Rd., Ste. 201
St. Louis, MO 63131
Phone: (314) 966-1007
Fax: (314) 966-0076
E-mail: *jsmith@ocsa.state.mo.us*
Web site: *www.osca.state.mo.us*

MONTANA
Judicial Standards Commission
215 N. Sanders, Justice Bldg., Rm. 315
Helena, MT 59620-3002
Phone: (406) 444-2608
Fax: (406) 444-0834

NEBRASKA
Commission on Judicial Qualifications
1220 State Capitol
P.O. Box 98910
Lincoln, NE 68509
Phone: (402) 471-3730
Fax: (402) 471-2197
Web site: *http://court.nol.org/comm/ jqc.htm*

NEVADA
Commission on Judicial Discipline
P.O. Box 48
Carson City, NV 89702
Phone: (775) 687-4017
Fax: (775) 687-3607
E-mail: *ncdinfo@judicial.state.nv.us*
Web site: *www.judicial.state.nv.us*

NEW HAMPSHIRE
Supreme Court Committee
  on Judicial Conduct
100 Main St., Rm. 303
Dover, NH 03820
Phone: (603) 749-3635
Fax: (603) 749-5780
Web site: *www.courts.state.nh.us/*
  committees/judconductcomm/index.htm

NEW JERSEY
Advisory Committee
  on Judicial Conduct
Hughes Justice Complex
7th Fl., North Wing, C.N. 037
Trenton, NJ 08625
Phone: (609) 292-2552
Fax: (609) 292-6848
Web site: *www.facenj.org/aboutface/*
  00q3/complain.html

NEW MEXICO
Judicial Standards Commission
P.O. Box 27248
Albuquerque, NM 87125-7248
Phone: (505) 222-9353
Web site: *www.fscll.org/JSC/Main.htm*

ROCHESTER, NEW YORK
Commission on Judicial Conduct
400 Andrews St., Ste. 700
Rochester, NY 14604
Phone: (585) 232-5756
Fax: (585) 232-7834

NEW YORK STATE
Commission on Judicial Conduct
61 Broadway
New York, NY 10006
Phone: (212) 809-0566
Fax: (212) 809-3664
E-mail: *scjc@scjc.state.ny.us*
Web site: *www.scjc.state.ny.us*

NORTH CAROLINA
Judicial Standards Commission
P.O. Box 1122
Raleigh, NC 27602
Phone: (919) 733-2690
Fax: (919) 715-4703
Web site: *www.nccourts.org/Courts/CRS/*
  Councils/Standards.asp

NORTH DAKOTA
Judicial Conduct Commission
512 1/2 E. Broadway, Ste. 101
P.O. Box 2297
Bismarck, ND 58502
Phone: (701) 328-3926
Fax: (701) 328-3924
Web site: *www.ndcourts.com*

OHIO
Board of Commissioners
  on Grievances and Discipline
65 S. Front St., 5th floor
Columbus, OH 43215-3431
Phone: (614) 387-9370
Toll free: (888) 664-8354
Fax: (614) 387-9397
Web site: *www.sconet.state.oh.us/BOC*

OKLAHOMA
Council on Judicial Complaints
1901 N. Lincoln Blvd.
Oklahoma City, OK 73105
Phone: (405) 522-4800
Fax: (405) 522-4752
E-mail: *emits@mhs.oklaosf.state.ok.us*
Web site: *www.okbar.org/judges/ council.htm*

OREGON
Commission on Judicial Fitness
and Disability
P.O. Box 1130
Beaverton, OR 97075
Phone: (503) 626-6776
Fax: (503) 626-6787
E-mail: *judfit@worldstar.com*
Web site: *www.ojd.state.or.us/aboutus/ cjfd*

PENNSYLVANIA
Judicial Conduct Board
301 Chestnut St.
Pennsylvania Place, Ste. 403
Harrisburg, PA 17101
Phone: (717) 234-7911
Fax: (717) 234-9307
Web site: *www.judicialconductboard ofpa.org*

RHODE ISLAND
Commission on Judicial Tenure
and Disability
Licht Judicial Complex
250 Benefit St., Rm. 604
Providence, RI 02903
Phone: (401) 222-1188
Fax: (401) 222-1493
Web site: *www.courts.state.ri.us/ supreme/jtd/defaultjtd.htm*

SOUTH CAROLINA
Commission on Judicial Conduct
1015 Sumter St., Ste. 111
Columbia, SC 29201
Phone: (803) 734-1965
Fax: (803) 734-0369
Web site: *www.judicial.state.sc.us/disc Counsel/commjudcon.cfm*

SOUTH DAKOTA
Judicial Qualifications Commission
200 E. 4th Ave.
Mitchell, SD 57301-2962
Phone: (605) 995-8100
Fax: (605) 995-8469

TENNESSEE
Court on the Judiciary
100 Supreme Court Bldg., Rm. 211
Nashville, TN 37243-0606
Phone: (615) 741-2681
Fax: (615) 532-8757

TEXAS
State Commission on Judicial Conduct
P.O. Box 12265, Capitol Station
Austin, TX 78711
Phone: (512) 463-5533
Toll free: (877) 228-5750
Fax: (512) 463-0511
Web site: *www.scjc.state.tx.us*

UTAH
Judicial Conduct Commission
645 S. 200, East, Ste. 104
Salt Lake City, UT 84111
Phone: (801) 533-3200
Fax: (801) 533-3208
E-mail: *colin.winchester@utahbar.org*
Web site: *www.utahbar.org/uljc/ judicial_conduct_commission.html*

VERMONT
Judicial Conduct Board
P.O. Box 721
Burlington, VT 05402-0721
Phone: (802) 864-0217
Web site: *www.vermontjudiciary.org/*
Committes/boards/jcb.htm

VIRGINIA
Judicial Inquiry and Review
Commission
P.O. Box 367
Richmond, VA 23218-0367
Phone: (804) 786-6636
Fax: (804) 371-0650
Web site: *www.courts.state.va.us/*
pamphlets/inquiry.htm

WASHINGTON
Commission on Judicial Conduct
P.O. Box 1817
Olympia, WA 98507
Phone: (360) 753-4585
Fax: (360) 586-2918
E-mail: *balthoff@cjc.state.wa.us*
Web site: *www.cjc.state.wa.us*

WEST VIRGINIA
Judicial Investigation Commission
910 Quarrier St., Ste. 212
P.O. Box 1629
Charleston, WV 25326-1629
Phone: (304) 558-0169
Fax: (304) 558-0831
Web site: *www.state.wv.us/wvsca/JIC/*
cover.htm

WISCONSIN
Judicial Commission
110 E. Main St., Ste. 606
Madison, WI 53703-3328
Phone: (608) 266-7637
Fax: (608) 266-8647
E-mail: *judcom@courts.state.wi.us*
Web site: *www.courts.state.wi.us*

WYOMING
Commission on Judicial Conduct
and Ethics
P.O. Box 1585
Cheyenne, WY 82003
Phone: (307) 778-7792
E-mail: *wyjsc@worldnet.att.net*

*(This list was compiled in October, 2004
by HALT — An Organization of
Americans for Legal Reform)*

Court Reform Organizations

The following organizations are engaged in a variety of activities—research, education, policy analysis, publishing, lobbying—aimed at improving the operation of the judicial system. Most of them are national groups. Be aware, however, that many state and local groups not included in this list are also active. Those that are listed are included because of their unique or significant contributions.

The organizations are grouped in three categories: those that seek to improve court administration, those that advocate alternatives to courtroom litigation; and those that work to improve or influence judicial selection or discipline. Note that the work of some organizations overlaps these distinctions and that a few aren't exclusively engaged in court reform.

I. COURT ADMINISTRATION

COSCA – Conference of State Court Administrators
National Center for State Courts
300 Newport Ave.
Williamsburg, VA 23185
Toll free: (800) 877-1233
Web site: *www.cosca.ncsc.dni.us/index.html*

The Conference of State Court Administrators identifies and studies issues and then develops policies, principles and standards relating to the administration of judicial systems. It has created an effective network for the exchange of information, ideas and methods to improve state courts, facilitate cooperation, consultation and the exchange of information by and among organizations directly concerned with court administration.

Council for Court Excellence
1717 K St., NW, Ste. 510
Washington, DC 20036
Phone: (202) 785-5917
Fax: (202) 785-5922
E-mail: *office@courtexcellence.org*
Web site: *www.courtexcellence.org*

> The Council works to improve the administration of justice in the local and federal courts, related agencies in the Washington metropolitan area and in the nation by identifying and promoting specific court reforms, improving public access to justice and increasing public understanding and support of our justice system.

Federal Judicial Center
Thurgood Marshall Federal Judiciary Building
One Columbus Cir., NE
Washington, DC 20002-8003
Phone: (202) 502-4160
Fax: (202) 502-4099
Web site: *www.fjc.gov*

> The Federal Judicial Center is the research, development and training arm of the federal judiciary. It develops recommendations for improving the administration of U.S. courts, conducts continuing education and training for court personnel and provides assistance to the U.S. Judicial Conference.

Fund for Modern Courts
351 W. 44th St.
New York, NY 10019
Phone: (212) 541-6741
Fax: (212) 541-7301
E-mail: *justice@moderncourts.org*
Web site: *www.moderncourts.org*

> The Fund for Modern Courts addresses the quality and administration of justice in New York. It researches problems confronting state courts and sponsors public education programs and monitors trial courts in 16 counties across New York. Published the *Citizens Jury Project Special Report: Access to Information in the Courts* in 2002.

Institute of Judicial Administration
IJA Program Coordinator
110 W. 3rd St., Rm. 218
New York, NY 10012
Phone: (212) 998-6149 or (212) 998-6196
Fax: (212) 995-4036
E-mail: *alison.kinney@nyu.edu*
Web site: *www.law.nyu.edu/institutes/judicial*

The Institute of Judicial Administration conducts research and publishes studies on the administration of justice. It educates judges, court administrators, legislators and attorneys who have an interest in improving the courts. Among its projects: appellate judges' seminars, workshops on special topics in the law, the Brennan Lecture series honoring the state judiciary and a biennial research conference.

National Center for State Courts
300 Newport Ave.
Williamsburg, VA 23185-4147
Toll free: (800) 450-0391
Fax: (757) 564-2022
Web site: *www.ncsconline.org*

The National Center for State Courts offers direct services to individual courts, such as designing an automated case-flow system or preparing a staff-orientation manual; conducts research on court management; serves as a clearinghouse of information on court administration. Also operates an education and training division (Institute for Court Management) for court officials.

RAND Institute for Civil Justice
1700 Main St.
P.O. Box 2138
Santa Monica, CA 90407-2138
Phone: (310) 393-0411 x7356
Fax: (310) 451-6979
E-mail: *zakaras@rand.org*
Web site: *www.rand.org/icj*

RAND does independent policy analysis and research on the American civil justice system but it does not make policy recommendations. Its principal purpose is to give policymakers empirical, analytic research on court costs, efficiency and the results of reforms such as mediation, arbitration, no-fault auto insurance and other alternatives for compensating accident victims.

Street Law, Inc.
1010 Wayne Ave., Ste. 870
Silver Spring, MD 20910
Phone: (301) 589-1130
Fax: (301) 589-1131
E-mail: *clearinghouse@streetlaw.org*
Web site: *www.streetlaw.org*

> Street Law uses techniques that promote cooperative learning, critical thinking
> and the ability to participate in a democratic society. For 30 years, Street Law,
> Inc.'s programs have promoted knowledge of and engagement in the demo-
> cratic process, and belief in the rule of law, among both youth and adults.

II. ALTERNATIVES TO THE COURTROOM

American Bar Association Section of Dispute Resolution
740 15th St., NW
Washington, DC 20005-1009
Phone: (202) 662-1680
Fax: (202) 662-1683
E-mail: *dispute@abanet.org*
Web site: *www.abanet.org/dispute*

> The American Bar Association Section of Dispute Resolution is dedicated to
> providing leadership in the dispute resolution field by fostering diversity, pro-
> ducing and presenting educational programs, providing technical assistance
> and publishing works that promote problem-solving and excellence in the pro-
> vision of dispute resolution services.

Association for Conflict Resolution
1015 18th St., NW, Ste. 1150
Washington, DC 20036
Phone: (202) 464-9700
Fax: (202) 464-9720
E-mail: *acr@acrnet.org*
Web site: *www.acrnet.org*

The Association for Conflict Resolution is an alternative dispute resolution organization that seeks to enhance the practice and public understanding of conflict resolution. It has more than 6,000 mediators, arbitrators, facilitators and educators. The Association has quality assurance initiatives for mediators, including the Advanced Practitioner Workgroup and the Certification Task Force. It is also actively working on a Uniform Mediation Act and is involved in initiatives regarding the unauthorized practice of law, access to neutrals and the United States Consensus Council.

Center for Restorative Justice & Peacemaking
School of Social Work
University of Minnesota
1404 Gortner Ave., 105 Peters Hall
St. Paul, MN 55108-6160
Phone: (612) 624-4923
Fax: (612) 624-3744
E-mail: *rjp@che.umn.edu*
Web site: *http://2ssw.che.umn.edu/rjp*

The University of Minnesota's School of Social Work hosts this clearinghouse for online publications, training and information about community-based restorative responses to crime and violence.

Community Dispute Resolution Centers Program
New York Unified Court
25 Beaver St., 8th Fl.
New York, NY 10004
For a list of centers by county see:
Web site: *www.courts.state.ny.us/ip/adr/ProgramList.shtml*

The Community Dispute Resolution Centers Program funds and establishes guidelines for dispute-resolution projects throughout the state, conducts workshops, coordinates mediation-training sessions, hosts a statewide conference and serves as a clearinghouse of information on alternative dispute resolution. This program is funded and regulated by the state and monitored by the New York Unified Court.

Program on Negotiation at Harvard Law School
513 Pound Hall
Cambridge, MA 02138
Phone: (617) 495-1684
Fax: (617) 495-7818
E-mail: *pon@law.harvard.edu*
Web site: *www.pon.harvard.edu/main/home/index.php3*

The Program on Negotiation is a collaborative effort of faculty, students and staff from several disciplines and professional schools at Harvard, M.I.T. and other schools. It helps design, implement and evaluate improved dispute resolution practices; promotes communication among dispute-resolution practitioners and academics; develops educational materials; promotes public awareness of successful conflict-resolution efforts.

III. JUDICIAL SELECTION OR DISCIPLINE

Alliance for Justice
11 Dupont Cir., NW, 2nd Fl.
Washington, DC 20036
Phone: (202) 822-6070
Fax: (202) 822-6068
E-mail: *Alliance@afj.org*
Web site: *www.afj.org*

The Alliance for Justice is a national coalition of public-interest advocacy organizations and lawyers that monitors and reports to its members on federal legislation and court developments that affect their funding; provides technical assistance and suggestions for pooling resources; speaks for the public-interest community on issues that affect equal access to justice and the legal process. Its Judicial Selection Project monitors federal judicial selection and coordinates opposition to nominees it finds objectionable. You can also track the path of individual judicial nominees on their Web site which provides current information and the latest news on nominations to the federal bench at: *www.independentjudiciary.com*

American Bar Association Standing Committee on Federal Judicial Improvements

321 N. Clark St.
Chicago, IL 60610
Phone: (312) 988-5105
Fax: (312) 988-6100
E-mail: *gallaghe@staff.abanet.org*
Web site: *www.abanet.org/scfji/home.html*

The Standing Committee develops policy on issues relating to the federal judiciary and monitors Congressional activity that impacts the judicial branch. The committee studies and makes recommendations for improving the federal judicial system, works to maintain effective liaison with the federal judiciary and other appropriate governmental and non-governmental entities involved in judicial reform and works to help coordinate activities within the ABA relating to improvements in the federal judicial system.

American Judicature Society

The Opperman Center at Drake University
2700 University Ave.
Des Moines, IA 50311
Phone: (515) 271-2281
Fax: (515) 279-3090
Web site: *www.ajs.org/ajs/home.asp*

The American Judicature Society maintains a site with information on judicial ethics, judicial independence and judicial selection. It is a nonpartisan organization with a national membership of judges, lawyers and citizens. It promotes the effective administration of justice through research, conferences, seminars and information and consultation services. The Society's Center for Judicial Conduct Organizations is a national clearinghouse for information on these conduct boards and on resources about judicial conduct and ethics. It promotes merit-based selection and judicial accountability while protecting judicial independence.

Center for Judicial Accountability, Inc.
Box 69, Gedney Station
White Plains, NY 10605-0069
Phone: (914) 421-1200
Fax: (914) 428-4994
E-mail: *judgewatch@aol.com*
Web site: *www.judgewatch.org*

> The Center for Judicial Accountability is a national nonprofit citizens' group that works to improve the quality of the judiciary by removing political considerations from the judicial selection process and by ensuring that the process of disciplining and removing judges is effective and meaningful.

Fair Courts Project at Brennan Center for Justice
  at New York University School of Law
161 Avenue of the Americas, 12th Fl.
New York, NY 10013
Phone: (212) 998-6730
Fax: (212) 995-4550
E-mail: *brennan.center@nyu.edu*
Web site: *www.brennancenter.org*

> The Fair Courts Project focuses on improving judicial selection processes (including elections), increasing diversity on the bench, preserving judicial independence and accountability and keeping courts in balance with other governmental branches.

Justice at Stake Campaign
717 D St., NW, Ste. 203
Washington, DC 20004
Phone: (202) 588-9700
Fax: (202) 588-9485
E-mail: *info@justiceatstake.org*
Web site: *www.justiceatstake.org*

> The Justice at Stake Campaign is a nationwide, nonpartisan partnership of more than 30 judicial, legal and citizen organizations concerned about the growing impact of money and politics on fair and impartial courts. The organization strives to educate the public and work for reforms to keep politics and special interests out of the courtroom.

National Center for State Courts
300 Newport Ave.
Williamsburg, VA 23185-4147
Toll free: (800) 616-6164
Fax: (757) 564-2022
Web site: *www.ncsconline.org*

The National Center for State Courts is a national clearinghouse for court information and provides links to court Web sites and information on court statistics, best practices, jury studies, family violence, civil justice reform and public access to the courts.

Washington Legal Foundation
2009 Massachusetts Ave., NW
Washington, DC 20036
Phone: (202) 588-0302
E-mail: *info@wlf.org*
Web site: *www.wlf.org*

The Washington Legal Foundation is a nonpartisan, public-interest research and litigation center that promotes principles of limited government and a free-market economy. It publishes reports analyzing significant issues facing the courts and regulatory agencies and has challenged the confidentiality of the American Bar Association's review process in the selection of federal judges.

Pro Se Resources

If you are interested in representing yourself (going *pro se*) take some time to familiarize yourself with the variety of legal resources available. This appendix catalogs only a selection of the growing number of resources available to people who want to handle their own legal matters. In this appendix, you will find resources such as *pro se* guides, government and commercial Web sites, *pro se* centers and online legal research sites.

BOOKS

Whether you're a *pro se* litigant or someone who wants to learn how to write a will, there's a wealth of self-help legal information available. For a complete listing of do-it-yourself legal resources on topics like family law, bankruptcy, property, estate planning and small business, see HALT's book, *Do-It-Yourself Law: HALT's Guide to Self-Help Books, Kits & Software.*

The titles below are primarily for the *pro se* litigant in a general civil court or small claims court. Some offer step-by-step instructions, but usually only for a certain court or type of case. Many will focus on the plaintiff's case but are also useful for those defending against a lawsuit. A few resources listed below are not "do-it-yourself" guides but are, nevertheless, helpful to the *pro se* litigant.

The Anatomy of a Lawsuit, revised ed., Simon, Peter, N. The Michie Co.,
Charlottesville, VA, 1996.
Overview of the procedure and strategy of a lawsuit, but not a "how-to" guide.
Follows a Colorado lawsuit from the time of an auto collision through jury trial
and appeals.

The Easy Way to Probate: A Step-by-Step Guide to Settling an Estate, HALT, Washington DC, 1994.
This plain-language guide tells you how to handle probate with ease. It includes a list of the most important probate rules and death-tax rates for each state as well as a checklist of tasks that need to be done.

Fundamentals of Trial Techniques, 4th ed., Mauet, Thomas A. Little, Brown and Co., Boston, MA, 1996.
Detailed look at courtroom procedures and strategy, including *voir dire,* opening statements, cross-examination, introducing evidence and closing arguments. Won't help with filing your lawsuit or pre-trial strategies. Written for lawyers but in plain language that non-lawyers can understand.

Represent Yourself in Court: How to Prepare and Try a Winning Case, 4th Ed., Bergman, Paul & Sara J. Berman-Barrett. Nolo, Berkeley, CA. 2003.
A step-by-step guide to preparing for a civil court case. Takes you through all of the preparation and steps in a lawsuit. Includes information on divorce, personal injury, breach of contract, malpractice, fraud and business dispute cases. Some general sample forms are included.

Small Claims Court: Making Your Way Through the System, HALT, Washington DC, 2001.
This step-by-step guide explains how to handle your case in small claims court whether you are suing someone or being sued. It includes the rules governing small claims courts in every state.

LEGAL SELF-HELP CENTERS

There has been an explosion of legal self-help Web sites that offer consumers free information on a variety of topics. Often, these Web sites have information specific to the type of problem you have. For example, several Web sites have information about filing for divorce *pro se,* gaining custody of your child and modifying child support. The following is just a sampling of the centers that exist. Many more state courts are in the process of creating self-help centers to help the ever-increasing number of people doing their own legal work. To see if a center has been created in your state, visit the American Bar Association Web site *www.abanet.org/legalservices/findlegal help/selfhelp.html.*

NATIONAL

LawHelp.Org
Web site: *www.lawhelp.org/*
Type in your Zip Code to find *pro se* resources for your area. Not every state is a
  part of LawHelp.Org yet, but the Web site is adding new resources frequently.
  Check back to see if anything has been added in your area.

Arizona
Self-Service Center
Web site: *www.superiorcourt.maricopa.gov/ssc/sschome.html*
The Web site for the Self-Service Center (program of Supreme Court of Arizona
  in Maricopa County), which was designed to help people help themselves in
  court. The site features general information on a variety of topics, court forms
  and instructions and lists of lawyers and mediators who will help by providing
  expert advice.

California
California Courts Self-Help Center
Web site: *www.courtinfo.ca.gov/selfhelp*
This Web site has a huge self-help directory with information on going *pro se* for a
  variety of everyday disputes. Information also available in Chinese, Vietnamese,
  Korean and Spanish.

Colorado
Judicial Branch Self-Help Center
Web site: *www.courts.state.co.us/chs/court/forms/selfhelpcenter.htm*
This Web site has forms and information to guide you through just about any type
  of case. It also has case and statute information for Colorado as well as general
  information about the courts.

Connecticut
Judicial Branch Self-Help Center
Web site: *www.jud.state.ct.us/selfhelp.htm*
This Web site has publications, answers to frequently asked questions, forms and
  other helpful information. It also has general information about the court system.

Delaware

Family Court Self-Help Center

Web site: *http://courts.state.de.us/family*

This Web site has a variety of resources for the *pro se* litigant trying to navigate the family court system. From divorce to custody, you can find detailed information here that can help you solve your own legal issues.

Florida

State Court Self-Help Center

Web site: *www.flcourts.org/*

(Click on "Self-Help" Center)

This site has forms and information dealing with a variety of everyday law problems, mostly family law issues. It also links you to self-help centers all over the state.

Hawaii

State Judiciary

Web site: *www.state.hi.us/jud*

(Click on "Self Help")

The Hawaii Self-Help Center's Web site offers general information on Hawaii's judiciary, downloadable court forms, links to legal references, services and attorneys. The site also links people to LawLine, a community service of the Hawaii State Bar and State Judiciary. People are given a number to call to receive free-recorded messages on various legal topics.

Idaho

Court Assistance Offices Project

Web site: *www2.state.id.us/cao*

This Web site is a clearinghouse for all *pro se* resources in Idaho—from court forms to bar brochures to directories of lawyers who are willing to look at your completed *pro se* pleadings. The site also has a general explanation of the court system.

Illinois

Self-Help Law Legal Center

Web site: *www.law.siu.edu/selfhelp/index.htm*

The Self-Help Legal Center provides assistance to the institutions that come into contact with *pro se* litigants. It also helps *pro se* litigants directly by helping them find the information they need, and it acts as a clearinghouse for self-help legal information. The site is sponsored by the Southern Illinois University School of Law.

Maine

Help ME Law

Web site: *www.helpmelaw.org*

Help ME Law provide legal information for low-income people in the State of
Maine. This includes easy-to-read self-help information on topics such as
divorce and tenants rights, Medicaid and food stamps, as well as information
about free and low-cost legal services in Maine. Links to other Maine legal service providers also included.

Maryland

People's Law Library

Web site: *www.peoples-law.org*

The People's Law Library provides explanations of legal subjects, step-by-step procedures, legal forms and other legal information resources for the citizens of
Maryland. The Web site is sponsored by the Maryland Legal Assistance Network.

Massachusetts

Court System Self-Help Center

Web site: *www.state.ma.us/courts/selfhelp/*

This self-help center has information on proceeding with your case *pro se*—from
filing your documents correctly to preparing to appear in court and researching
legal topics.

New Jersey

Representing Yourself in Court

Web site: *www.judiciary.state.nj.us/prose/index.htm*

This Web site has forms and instructions that can guide the *pro se* litigant through
civil, criminal, family and appeals courts. This great resource has step-by-step
instructions that inform you of the court process every step of the way.

Oregon

Judicial Department

Web site: *www.ojd.state.or.us/*

(Click on "Forms")

The court's Web site has forms for *pro se* litigants trying a case in civil and family
courts, including drug, traffic and tax court. However, there is little information
about the court process itself, and the site seems to be aimed at lawyers.

Utah

State Court Web Site

Web site: *http://courtlink.utcourts.gov*

This great Web site has information for *pro se* litigants on the court process, forms
and legal research materials. There is also a special section called "Representing
Yourself in Court" that deals with the pitfalls of acting as your own lawyer.

Washington

Court Forms

Web site: *www.courts.wa.gov/forms*

The court's Web site has forms on a variety of legal issues. From bankruptcy to
small claims to family court, this Web site has court forms for almost every situation you could imagine. However, there are no instructions or guides to go with
them, so you are on your own—the site is designed more for lawyers.

Northwest Justice Project

Web site: *www.nwjustice.org*

The Northwest Justice Project's (NJP) Web site serves as a clearinghouse of legal
self-help materials and tools that provide information about non-criminal legal
problems affecting low-income people in Washington state. To learn whether
you qualify for free assistance, contact the CLEAR hotline at 1-888-201-1014 or
in King County, call (206) 464-1519; TTY 1-888-201-9737. NJP is a not-for-
profit statewide organization that provides free civil legal services to low-income
people from nine offices throughout the state of Washington.

COMMERCIAL WEB SITES

You can buy a lot of good (and not so good) things over the Internet. The
same is true for legal services—be it advice, legal forms or legal products.
The following is a sample list of commercial providers who have created Web
sites to sell you something—typically their "legal" advice, books, software,
kits or specific forms. New and similar Web sites are appearing all the time.
Most include a fair amount of "free" legal information and simple free legal
forms to go along with their sale items. Most of the information offered is for
people handling out-of-court legal work (such as writing a will or filing for
bankruptcy). But you can find court forms and help on most of these sites.

Before using any Web site, it's a good idea to browse around and see what
each one has to offer. You can get a feel for how detailed oriented the Web
sites are by visiting more than one and comparing notes.

All About Law.com

Web site: *www.selfhelplaw.com*

This Web site offers more than 2,000 free legal forms that a *pro se* litigant can use in the courtroom. However, the site doesn't tell consumers how to file the documents and urges you to have a lawyer check your work. You can join for 90 days ($24.95 in 2004) to gain access to their attorneys, who will check the documents, and get a free downloaded copy of Quicken Lawyer (Year) Personal Deluxe.

American *Pro Se* Association

Web site: *www.legalhelp.org*

American *Pro Se* Association is a non-profit, volunteer organization whose mission is to help people with financial and legal problems or questions. Basic information is free to the public and members who pay have access to Approved Legal Advisors and additional information on various financial and legal subjects.

Divorcelawinfo.com

Web site: *www.divorcelawinfo.com*

The Divorce Law Information Center is owned by licensed attorney Richard Granat who has hands-on experience in helping *pro se* litigants in family law matters. Since 1997, the center has helped thousands of couples do their own divorce. Links on the Web site send you to state specific information on divorce, child support calculators, custody and visitation information and divorce and marital separation agreements.

Law Made Easy Press

Web site: *www.laweasy.com*

Law Made Easy Press is hosted by New Jersey lawyer and author Martin Shenkman. The Web site provides information on tax, estate, divorce, real estate and financial planning. Also included are links to audio clips from the Law Made Easy radio show, free legal forms and other features to help keep you informed.

LegalAdviceLine.com

Web site: *www.legaladviceline.com*

Legal Advice Line is a law firm online that helps you represent yourself in routine matters, reviews executed legal documents, prepares legal documents for you and helps you through a variety of situations including court hearings, negotiations or mediation with a unique brand of unbundled legal services. The site includes a toll free number (1-888-367-5252).

Nolo.com

Web site: *www.nolo.com*

From the premiere publisher of do-it-yourself legal materials, Nolo's Web site
offers a huge selection of law-related articles in plain language. If you don't get
your answers from the free stuff, you can order more comprehensive books and
software to do your own legal work. You can also, for a fee, download electronic
form kits or fill out a single legal form online.

USlegalforms.com

Web site: *www.uslegalforms.com*

U.S. Legal Forms offers thousands of legal forms. Many are related to business or litigating in Federal court. Others cover the typical range of legal topics including real
estate, name change, wills, premarital agreements and promissory notes. Forms are
available to attorneys, the public and businesses directly over the Internet.

ONLINE LEGAL RESEARCH

If you're looking for legal information, a particular case or state statute,
you don't have to visit a bricks and mortar law library anymore. You can get
a wealth of legal information right at your fingertips if you have access to the
Internet—everything from breaking legal news to the definition of a particular legal word. We've identified some of the better-known legal portals and
research Web sites in the list below.

American Law Sources Online

Web site: *www.lawsource.com/also*

American Law Sources Online is a Web site that links to all on-line sources of
American law that are available without charge. A well-organized access point to
legal material for all states and the federal government.

FindLaw

Web site: *www.findlaw.com*

Findlaw offers a fully searchable guide to legal information and Web sites on the
net. The site includes a legal subject index and access to cases and codes, law
school information, law reviews and legal organizations. If your research
requires access to judicial opinions, case law, law journals, law reviews, international resources, U.S. government resources, state government resources, library
information, legal associations, experts/consultants, law firms, legal news or law
course outlines, you can start by searching this frequently updated site.

Hieros Gamos

Web site: *www.hg.org/index.html*

Hieros Gamos is informative to lawyers, law students and consumers. The site offers information on legal organizations, government Web sites, practice areas, discussion groups, business guides and online seminars. The Web site also includes searchable databases for lawyers, experts and court reporters.

Internet Legal Research Group

Web site: *www.ilrg.com*

The Internet Legal Research Group is a categorized index of 4,000 Web sites in 238 nations, islands and territories as well as more than 850 locally stored web pages and downloadable files. It is designed for use by legal scholars and lay persons alike. Searchable categories include: law school rankings, law school course archives, law journals and reviews, news sources, law-related news groups, U.S. federal case law, legal associations, legal experts and legal forms archives.

JURIST

Web site: *www.jurist.law.pitt.edu*

Offered through the University of Pittsburgh School of Law, this Web site has won awards for its coverage of U.S. legal news and current events. JURIST also offers links to case law and statutes, law review articles, law schools, academic papers and foreign legal news coverage.

Law Library Catalogs

Web site: *www.washlaw.edu/lawcat*

Law Library Catalogs is a list of links to law school law libraries across the country. The Web site offers instructions for tele-netting into law school libraries in order to search collections such as those of Cornell and Washburn University.

Legal Information Institute

Web site: *www.law.cornell.edu*

The Legal Information Institute is a premiere legal portal offered through Cornell Law School. The Web site receives over 7 million hits a week and according to Alta Vista, there are over 180,000 links to the Legal Information Institute materials from other Web sites. The site offers expansive listings of legal references including court opinions, statutes, legal organizations, bar journals and U.S. legal news.

Washburn University Law Library

Web site: *http://lawlib.wuacc.edu*

The Washburn University Law Library's Web site competes with Cornell's as one of
the best online law libraries. The site includes its own navigation system which
permits access to U.S. Supreme Court opinions through Cornell Law School, all
Federal Case law, all Circuit Court of Appeals opinions, U.S. tax code, legislation,
Congressional Record and Code of Federal Regulations.

Bibilography

The following sources contain information about federal and state courts and judges. These sources provide in-depth treatment of the subjects covered in this book.

The American Bench—Judges of the Nation 2003-2004, Foster-Long, Inc., Sacramento, CA.
> This book contains brief biographies of federal and state judges and summaries of federal and state court systems. You can also consult your local law library to help you find more in-depth biographical information on judges.

American Judicial Politics, 2nd ed., Stumpf, Harry P. with Kevin C. Paul. Upper Saddle River, Prentice Hall, NJ. 1998.
> This book thoroughly covers the influence of politics on the judicial selection and decision-making processes.

Court-Annexed Mediation: Critical Perspectives on Selected State and Federal Programs, Bergman, Edward J. and John G. Bickerman. American Bar Association, Bethesda, MD. 1998.
> A detailed discussion of mediation programs in selected courtrooms.

Directory of Minority Judges in the United States, 3rd ed., American Bar Association, Judicial Division, Standing Committee on Minorities in the Judiciary. Chicago, IL. 2001.
> This edition includes a total of 4,045 judges who are African American, Asian, Pacific Islanders, Hispanic, Native American and Tribal Court judges.

Facts About the American Judicial System, American Bar Association, Division for Media Relation and Public Affairs. 1999. Available online at *www.abanet.org/media/factbooks/judifact.pdf.*
   This publication provides an easy-to-use overview of the American judicial system.

Federal Judicial Caseload Statistics, 2004. Available online at *www.uscourts.gov/caseload2004/contents.html.*
   Produced by the statistics division of the Administrative Division of the U.S. Courts.

Judicial Disqualification: Recusal and Disqualification of Judges, Flamm, Richard E. Little, Brown & Company, Boston, MA. 1996.
   This book is a great resource for information on the disqualification of judges for the federal courts and all 50 states.

Judicial Selection in the States, American Judicature Society. Available online at *www.ajs.org/js.*
   An excellent Web site of current and comprehensive information on the judicial selection process for all state court jurisdictions in the 50 states and the District of Columbia.

Judicial Selection in the United States: A Special Report, Berkson, Larry, updated by Seth Anderson. American Judicature Society. 1999. Available online at *www.ajs.org/selection/berkson.pdf.*
   A short, historical overview of judicial selection in the United States.

Mediation: Mandatory or Discretionary; a State-by-State Summary, National Center for State Courts. Available online at *www.ncsc.dni.us/KMO/Topics/ADR/FAQs/Mandatory.htm.*
   The National Center for State Courts' 2000 table on mediation practices, state by state.

State Court Organization, 1998. U.S. Department of Justice, Office of Justice Programs, Bureau of Justice Statistics, Washington, DC. Available online at *www.ojp.usdoj.gov/bjs/abstract/sco98.htm.*

Your Appeal Rights and How to Prepare a Protest If You Don't Agree,
U.S. Department of the Treasury, Internal Revenue Service. Publication 5.
Available online at *www.irs.gov/pub/irs-pdf/p5.pdf*
> This publication tells you how to appeal your tax case if you don't agree
> with the Internal Revenue Service (IRS) findings.

Want's Federal-State Court Directory, 2005, Want Publishing Co., 2004.
Washington, DC.
> An up-to-date directory of state and federal judges, court structures and
> jurisdictions.

Glossary

Italicized terms are defined in other entries in this glossary.

ADJUDICATION
Process of hearing and deciding a case.

APPELLATE COURT
Court that hears appeals of cases in which a party has challenged the decision of the lower court, usually a *trial court*. Some appellate courts hear cases appealed from a lower appellate court.

APPELLATE JURISDICTION
Authority to review cases appealed from lower courts or administrative agencies.

ARBITRATION
Out-of-court method of resolving disputes in which an arbitrator (a neutral third party) listens to each side's arguments in an informal hearing, then makes a decision.

CERTIORARI (also WRIT OF CERTIORARI)
Latin for "to be informed." A *prerogative writ* that asks the lower court for the record of a case so the higher court may review it.

CHALLENGE FOR CAUSE
Way in which a lawyer may excuse a juror, if there is reason to question the juror's impartiality or qualifications for that case (compare with *peremptory challenge*).

CONCURRENT JURISDICTION
Power to hear cases that a court shares with other courts. For instance, federal and state courts may hear disputes between residents of different states. Within a state, two courts may have concurrent jurisdiction, for example, over contract cases.

COURT OF LAST RESORT
Court with the final say in each state's court system and in the federal court system. Usually called "Supreme Court."

COURT OF RECORD
Court in which, an official record is made of the proceedings by court stenographer or tape recorder.

DE NOVO
Completely new, as if it hadn't happened before; again.

DISCOVERY
Formal and informal exchange of information between sides in a lawsuit before going to trial.

DISCRETIONARY POWER
Power of an *appellate court* to decide whether or not it will hear a case appealed to it.

DIVERSITY JURISDICTION
Power of federal courts to hear cases between citizens of different states.

EN BANC
French for "on the bench." Hearing at which all judges of an *appellate court* hear a case. Usually requested after a smaller panel of judges of that court has heard the case. Rarely granted.

EQUITY
Principles of fairness and justice, used in those rare instances when a court determines that strict application of the law produces unjust results or offers inadequate redress.

EXCLUSIVE JURISDICTION
Power of a court to hear cases no other courts may hear. For instance, only federal courts may hear bankruptcy cases: they have *exclusive jurisdiction* over them.

EXTRAORDINARY WRITS
Prerogative and other *writs* used by *appellate courts* in exercising their *discretionary powers.*

FEDERAL QUESTION JURISDICTION
Authority granted by the U.S. Constitution to federal courts to hear cases involving federal law.

FORCIBLE ENTRY AND DETAINER
Court proceeding to restore possession of land or property to a person who was wrongfully deprived of possession.

GENERAL JURISDICTION
Trial court's power to hear many kinds of civil and criminal cases, regardless of subject matter, amount of money involved or severity of crime.

GEOGRAPHIC JURISDICTION
Court's power to hear only those cases that involve parties or disputes that arise within a specified geographic area.

GRAND JURY
Type of jury that decides what cases should be brought to trial (compare with *petit jury*).

HABEAS CORPUS
Latin for "you have the body." A *prerogative writ* used to challenge the legality of a person's custody. For example, in criminal cases, used by prisoners to challenge their imprisonment; in civil cases, used to challenge child custody.

INJUNCTION
Order to do or refrain from doing a specified thing. For example, a court might issue an injunction that orders a manufacturing company to stop dumping toxic wastes into a river.

INTERMEDIATE APPELLATE COURT
Court with mostly *appellate jurisdiction* that is not the highest court in its court system.

JUDICIAL IMMUNITY
Rule that protects judges in lawsuits against them for rulings, decisions, orders or other actions they take as judges.

JURISDICTION
Court's power to hear and decide cases. Power to hear the kind of controversy being decided or power over the parties to the lawsuit is called "subject matter" jurisdiction; power over the cases in a specified location is called "geographic" jurisdiction. (See also, *concurrent* and *exclusive jurisdiction.*)

LIEN
A legal claim to hold or sell property as security for a debt.

LIMITED JURISDICTION
Trial court's power to hear only cases of a certain subject matter (for instance, only traffic violations) or only cases involving less than a certain dollar amount.

MANDATORY REVIEW
Review that must be undertaken by the *appellate court.* In such cases the court may not exercise its *discretionary power* and refuse to hear a case.

MECHANIC'S LIEN
A lien, usually created by statute, that establishes who should be paid first for work done or materials supplied in building or repairing a structure; also applies to automobiles and other goods. For example, a car mechanic has a right to hold the car until the repairs done on it are paid for.

MEDIATION
Out-of-court dispute-settlement process in which a mediator (neutral third party) helps the two sides fashion their own solution.

OF RIGHT or AS OF RIGHT
Must; a matter of right or a matter of course.

ORIGINAL JURISDICTION
Power of a court to first hear a case. All *trial courts* have original jurisdiction; some *appellate courts* do.

PEREMPTORY CHALLENGE
Way in which a lawyer can exclude a juror without having to state a reason (compare with *challenge for cause*); may be exercised only a specified number of times.

PETIT JURY
Jury that hears cases and renders a verdict at a trial (compare with *grand jury*).

PRECEDENT
A binding pronouncement of how the law is to be interpreted and applied in the future.

PREROGATIVE WRIT
Court order based on its *discretionary powers. Certiorari* and *habeas corpus* are prerogative writs.

REVIEW 'AS OF RIGHT'
See *mandatory review.*

STANDING
Legal right to bring a lawsuit; based on the notion that the one who sues must have suffered a wrong or injury.

TORT
A wrong or injury resulting from a breach of legal duty.

TRIAL COURT
Court that first hears a lawsuit. The trial court is where you first enter the court system.

TRIAL 'DE NOVO'
Latin for "from the start." A completely new trial over the facts. For most appeals, the *appellate court* only reviews the *trial court* record, but in some instances, it can conduct a new trial.

VENIREMEN
Group of prospective jurors.

VOIR DIRE
From the old French for "to speak the truth." Questioning by which the judge and lawyers determine potential jurors' suitability for a case.

WRIT
A written court order to compel someone to take specified action. For instance, the U.S. Supreme Court may issue a *writ of certiorari* directing a Court of Appeals to send its record of a case for Supreme Court review.

About HALT

HALT – An Organization of Americans for Legal Reform is a national, non-profit, non-partisan public interest group of more than 50,000 members. Through its advocacy and education programs, HALT empowers ordinary Americans to take charge of their own legal affairs while pressing a reform agenda that improves access, increases accountability and reduces costs in our civil justice system at both the state and federal levels.

Founded in 1978 by two Rhodes scholars, HALT has distributed more than one million self-help manuals to its members and the general public and has provided legal information and referrals to more than 100,000 individuals.

HALT's selection of publications ranges from brief introductions (tri-fold brochures and articles from HALT's *Everyday Law Series*) to full-length books, such as this *Citizens Legal Manual*. For the legal consumer whose needs are not extensive enough to require a book, HALT also produces free *Citizens Legal Guides*, 8-page pamphlets that offer a broad overview of a legal subject.

HALT also publishes *The Legal Reformer*, a quarterly newsletter that covers legal reform news and opinion, and the HALT *eJournal*, a bi-weekly online newsletter to keep readers informed about major legal reform developments as they happen.

Our Web site (*www.halt.org*) offers a wealth of legal information, news, and opinion to members and the general public.

In addition to our education efforts, HALT pursues a set of complementary reform projects to help make the civil justice system more accessible and accountable to all Americans:

- The twin goals of the **Lawyer Accountability Project** are to make lawyers more responsive to the needs of legal consumers and to empower legal consumers to protect themselves from negligent, unscrupulous and incompetent attorneys. HALT has been on the forefront of fights to improve systems that weed out unethical lawyers and provide recourse to victimized legal consumers.

- The **Judicial Integrity Project** promotes higher ethical standards for federal and local judges and empowers litigants to ensure that judges are presiding over their cases with fairness and impartiality. To achieve these goals, HALT directs its advocacy efforts on convenient access to judges' full financial records and strict limitations on judicial junkets.

- The **Freedom of Legal Information Project** aims to widen access to the legal system by both educating legal consumers about and protecting their right to a variety of legal services provided by lawyers and nonlawyers.

- HALT's **Small Claims Reform Project** publicizes the advantages of small claims courts and educates consumers about how to take advantage of these user-friendly courts. At the same time, the project advocates for systemic reforms that increase access to these courts, which are a valuable option for people who want to take control of their own routine legal needs.

HALT's activities are funded through member contributions and foundation support.

Join HALT

HALT accomplishes its mission through the generous support of its 50,000 members. We invite your participation.

❏ *Yes!*

I want to help reform America's civil justice system.
Enclosed is a check for my membership dues of:

❏ $25 *(minimum)*　　❏ $100
❏ $35　　　　　　　　❏ $250
❏ $50　　　　　　　　❏ $500

Or, please charge my contribution to:

❏ Visa　　❏ Mastercard　　❏ American Express

Credit Card No. _____

Expiration date _____

Signature _____

Name _____

Address _____

City/State/Zip _____

Phone _____

E-mail _____

Benefits of HALT Membership

- A free copy of **Using a Lawyer: And What To Do If Things Go Wrong**
- Action Alerts reporting on legal reform developments in your state
- HALT's quarterly newsletter *The Legal Reformer*
- Free subscription to HALT's online newsletter *e-Journal*
- A voice for your concerns about the lack of accessibility and affordability of America's civil justice system

1612 K Street, NW, Suite 510 • Washington, DC 20006
(202) 887-8255 • (202) 887-9699 fax
E-mail: *halt@halt.org* • *www.halt.org*